Cynthia Cockburn is a researcher in the Department of
Social Science and Humanities at the City University,
London. She was born in 1934, has two teenage daughters
and lives in London. She is a member of the National
Union of Journalists.

Her previous publications include *The Local State*
(Pluto 1977) and *Brothers – Male Dominance and Technological Change* (Pluto 1983). She also co-authored *In
and Against the State* (Pluto 1981).

Cynthia Cockburn

Machinery of Dominance

Women, Men and Technical Know-how

Pluto Press

London   Sydney   Dover New Hampshire

First published in 1985 by Pluto Press Limited,
The Works, 105a Torriano Avenue, London NW5 2RX
and Pluto Press Australia Limited, PO Box 199, Leichhardt,
New South Wales 2040, Australia. Also Pluto Press,
51 Washington Street, Dover, New Hampshire 03820 USA

Copyright © Cynthia Cockburn

7 6 5 4 3 2 1

90 89 88 87 86

Phototypeset by AKM Associates (UK) Ltd
Ajmal House, Hayes Road, Southall, Greater London
Printed in Great Britain by Guernsey Press Co. Limited,
Guernsey, C.I.

British Library Cataloguing in Publication Data
Cockburn, Cynthia
   Machinery of dominance: women, men and
   technical knowhow
   1. Women technicians   2. Sex discrimination
   in employment
   I. Title
   331.4'133   HD6060

ISBN 0 7453 0065 0

Contents

Preface

Electronic technology is changing many workplaces. It is affecting the kind of work people do and the skills they need to do it. The research on which this book is based looks at the way these changes affect the relations between employer and worker and the relative position of female and male workers. Key questions were: what are the types and levels of skill or knowledge called for in the new jobs? What prospects do they offer? And who has them, men or women? The research found evidence of women mainly filling relatively routine occupations, operating the new kinds of equipment. It found very few women indeed in the genuinely technical jobs, from first-line maintenance through to the loftier reaches of design and development engineering.

This is an appropriate time to be considering the issue of women and technological competence. The year 1984 was designated 'Women Into Science and Engineering Year' by the Engineering Council and the Equal Opportunities Commission. 'From all the information available,' they announced in a pamphlet launching WISE Year, 'it is clear that in the present economic climate the sciences, engineering and technology offer better prospects for employment than many areas which have previously attracted girls and women . . . Women can no longer afford to ignore the opportunities which the engineering and science-related professions open up for them and, at the same time, the engineering industry can no longer afford to neglect the talent and ability which women have to offer.' The policy-makers for the industry took up the cue and adopted the public relations line 'engineering needs a woman's touch'. It was a matter, it seemed, simply of getting women to *want* technical competence and getting employers to *want* women within their technical cadres. The main impediments were seen as a lack of will-power, combined with a misunderstanding about technology. The Engineering Industry Training Board, for instance, in its WISE Year publication *Women and Engineering*, suggested that 'the very low proportions of women in the technological and technical jobs are a result primarily of certain myths surrounding these occupations which make them seem unattractive careers for women. Probably the most prevalent is the view that the work of skilled engineers is . . . dirty, greasy and heavy and therefore deemed unsuitable for women.' They went on to emphasize that many engineering jobs today are office jobs and require intellectual rather than manual skills.

It was widely believed that the advent of the computer and electronics, involving a lighter, cleaner and more sedentary set of occupations than the technologies of iron, oil and steam, could, assisted by a brief campaign, break the segregation barrier for women so that they would come into technical work in much greater numbers. The research reported here, however, suggests that the problem is more complicated than this. Women do not appear to be acquiring technical work in 'electronic' workplaces in notably greater numbers than in the older 'electro-mechanical' processes. The research exposes a flaw in the good-natured concept of 'equal opportunity' that underlay not only WISE Year but also the Equal Pay Act of 1970 and the Sex Discrimination Act of 1975. Equal opportunity implies a pushing open of doors. There are still, of course, many prejudiced attitudes, discriminatory practices and myopic training policies to be done away with. But the problem for women does not end here.

As we shall see, there are historical processes of tremendous power and longevity sustaining the sexual division of labour in society and at work. Those pioneering women who do step into fields of work that are non-traditional for their sex pay dearly for the privilege. It is not legitimate simply to urge women forward without considering what waits for them in the workplaces on the other side of the notionally open door of equal opportunity. Helping women to gain technological competence requires a more radical perspective on change than the Equal Opportunities Commission or the Engineering Council have yet dreamed of.

The research reported here was a two-year project. It involved setting up what was in effect a 'panel' of three technologies for questioning about the effects of technological change. One was in the clothing industry where the computer was transforming pattern and cutting processes. The second was in mail order firms, computerizing and mechanizing certain goods-handling processes in the warehouse. The third technology was computed tomography scanning, which has been rapidly gaining importance in the radiography departments of hospitals. In each of these a case study was made of one workplace with traditional techniques and one with new technology. In the case of the warehouse technology, I also include, in addition to one conventional and one modernized warehouse, information on two additional 'high technology' warehouses that I call Alpha Catalogues Ltd. and Beta Warehouses PLC. The account of Alpha is based on first-hand observation and interviews with management and trade union shop stewards. My request for access to workers was refused. Likewise, Beta Warehouses would not grant access to the warehouse or to workers and neither would management see me. The account is based on published material, interviews with consultants, former personnel of Beta and trade unionists.

I also followed the three computer-based technologies 'upstream' to their point of origin, or as near to this as it is possible to get in a country whose engineering base has so precipitately declined. At this level five enterprises are included. Two are import agencies representing overseas engineering firms selling the computer-aided pattern systems to the British clothing industry. One is the consultancy group, specializing in warehouse reorganization and automation, that specified the new system described in the principal mail order case study. In addition I looked at the small engineering firm that actually manufactured the physical components of this new warehouse system. Finally, I include the very large US electronic engineering firm, one of whose British factories was part-producing scanners and other diagnostic equipment and which was selling imaging equipment in Britain and other European countries.

A series of visits was made to each of the 11 firms (or hospitals) involved. I observed people at work and gained familiarity with the technologies in use. In addition to informal contacts during these periods of observation, I carried out formal interviews with relevant managers, trade union representatives and employees in a range of occupations clustered about the technology in question. On average, 20 people were interviewed in each of the six institutions applying the technology, 35 in total in the supplying firms. The total number of interviews involved in the research was 196, of which 113 were with men and 83 with women. These people varied very widely by occupation, status, age and training and include some informants in the industries, professions or trade unions concerned but outside the immediate case study settings.

Basic checklists of questions were devised for each occupational or situational group of informants and working schedules constructed by reference to these for each interview or group of interviews. The interviews were thus formal and structured, but they were open-ended and discursive. Some were as short as 20 minutes, others as long as three hours. Most were carried out in a private room within the work situation, by agreement with employers. Most were tape recorded and transcribed.

Surveys of other known users of the new technologies in question were also carried out by postal questionnaire. Usable responses were obtained from 18 clothing firms and 60 hospitals, and included data on 15 mail order warehouses.

My approach to analysis was to map out a field of 'issues' emerging in the interview transcripts and then to determine the range of responses to them. The issues of course were partly introduced by my questions, partly by the interests contributed by the subjects themselves. As should be expected, individuals seldom expressed unequivocal views on any issue. Nonetheless, certain sets of meanings emerged as 'hegemonic', dominating and ordering the general field of ideas, throwing others into the stance of opposition or rebellion. In reporting, I tried not to simplify or conceal contradictions but to give a fair rendering of the spectrum of attitudes, while making clear where I found the emphasis to rest.

The research was jointly funded by the Equal Opportunities Commission and the Economic and Social Research Council. It was carried out during 1983–4 in the Department of Social Science and Humanities, The City University, London, where I am a research fellow. I would like to thank these organizations for their invaluable support and help.

Penguin Books and Little, Brown and Co. kindly gave permission to reproduce passages from Tracy Kidder's book, *The Soul of a New Machine*.

I owe a substantial debt to the workers, trade union representatives and managers of the 11 workplaces in which I was able to make case studies, and to the many other people I visited in connection with the research. People were generous with their time, patient in explaining work processes and techniques and in describing their feelings about technical competence and change. Many of them also read and commented on drafts to help me clarify the facts. I would very much like to acknowledge them by name but cannot do so without breaching anonymity.

I can and do, however, thank the following for patiently reading and commenting on particular chapters: Angela Coyle, Michael Gordon, Barbara Lee, Annie Phizaklea, Barny Schuster and Colin Thorne. I am specially grateful to Anne Phillips and Joy Schaverien for their friendship in helping my tussle with the final manuscript – and likewise to Richard Kuper of Pluto. It was essential to me to know that his enthusiasm for the subject and his editorial skill were waiting at the end of the line. Finally, my loving appreciation to my daughters Jess and Claudi for their understanding company.

Thanks, then, to all these people. If there is anything worthwhile in the book it owes much to them. Its many shortcomings are entirely my own responsibility.

Introduction

Popular sayings are often close to the mark. None less so, however, than the one that goes: 'the hand that rocks the cradle rules the world'. The world is really ruled by people who left the cradle to others and instead invested their time and energy in amassing and deploying wealth and skills 'out there' in the economic world. Since long before the industrial revolution, a good deal of wealth has taken the form of tools, equipment and machinery, and a good many of the abilities needed to make more wealth and to generate more power have been technological skills. This book is about technological competence, who has it, what authority it confers and what connection it has with ruling the world and rocking the cradle.

Technology is a medium of power. At the simplest level the lever or the pulley adds power to the arm. The thumbscrew, the battering ram and the nuclear arsenal amplify the physical strength of the state. Owning tools, equipment and machinery and putting other people to work on them, uniting the two great forces of production, has been the primary source of economic power. The person who possesses special knowledge and competence with technology has always had a valuable asset, whether to put to use autonomously or to place at the service of an employer. 'Know-how' about making or using tools or machines affords a measure of power not only over matter but also over people. Those who do not have it must depend on those who do to achieve their ends: to win a war, keep a factory running or a car on the road. In the context of social production, in the factory for instance, the authority of know-how over the instruments of labour, the machinery, is extended to authority over the worker. The engineer who knows about the mechanisms of the assembly line governs the movements not only of materials but of human beings.

Technology has an inescapable bond with wealth. Even simple tools are no use without the resources to acquire land or materials on which to use them. Larger-scale technologies, such as those of warfare, irrigation or construction, depend on massive economic surpluses to be effective. The engineer has always needed a patron. Once capitalist industrial production developed, the skilled technologist was obliged to turn to the manufacturer if he wanted a chance to exchange his skill for a living. Since the advent of twentieth-century corporate capitalism, the 'technological innovator' has often been a team in the employ of a giant firm, since it takes a multinational to launch a major new product or process onto the market.

As technologies change and displace each other, there is disturbance among the technically skilled strata. Some gain and some lose position; some help push others down. The relationship of the person who has the relatively powerful attribute of technological competence to the person or organization with the absolutely powerful attribute of wealth has always been a negotiated one, highly ambiguous. The place of technology and technological skills in class struggle has been an important theme in economic history.

Technology, however, plays a part in a second set of power relations that is often overlooked. Among the haves and have-nots of technological competence, women and men are unevenly represented. When the United Nations reported in 1980 that 'women constitute half the world's population, perform nearly two-thirds of its work-hours, receive one-tenth of the world's income and own less than one hundredth of the world's property' they might well have added that women possess an all-but-invisible fraction of its technological know-how and technical jobs. (They might also have noted that just such a tiny proportion of the world's cradles are rocked by men.) The technical competence that men as a sex possess and women as a sex lack is an extension of the physical domination of women by men. It also has, as we shall see, extensive effects in differential earnings and social authority.

It is common sense to suppose that technology, as a medium of power, will be developed and used in any system of dominance to further the interests of those who are on top. As women, then, we have to consider technology from, at the very least, the perspectives of both class and sex, two systems of power that bear heavily on us. Only very recently have women begun to aspire to technical training and work. In a sense, this book responds to that aspiration, assessing the scale and nature of our undertaking. Women's project of learning technical skills is clearly fraught with contradiction. If technology is a historical aspect of male power, can women participate in it at all without becoming 'honorary men'? If it is an aspect of class domination, how can women engage in it without lending a hand to exploitation? Can women, however, do without this knowledge?

The particular context within which technology is considered in this book is the *sexual division of labour*, the way work is divided up between women and men. That means we are not immediately concerned with military technology, nor with technologies of contraception, genetics or housework, although these have significant effects on women. The technologies in question here are those used in paid work. They are, broadly speaking, *technologies of production*.

Within this context of production the focus is not a narrow one, on 'the engineer' alone, but includes all those that deal with the technology. It is only in their relationships that we can trace the divisions of class and sex. This supposes an interest in owners, inventors and managers of technology; in professional and academic engineers, technician engineers and craft workers – mechanics, fitters, turners (who also often call themselves 'engineers'). We have to include semi-skilled and unskilled workers assembling machinery and operating it. Drawing on recent instances of technological change in the workplace, we will see how, though occupations themselves may have been transformed, the relations of technology continue. A sexual division of labour in and around technology persists and survives.

Chapter 1 begins with a discussion of the sexual division of labour itself. Segregation of occupation by sex is an enduring feature of economic life and, along with male supremacy, seems to occur to a varying degree in all known contemporary societies. Technological competence is a factor in sex-segregation, women clustering in jobs that require little or none, men spreading across a wider range of occupations which include those that call for technical training. There is nothing 'natural' about this affinity of men to technology. It has, like gender difference itself, been developed in a social process over a long historical period in conjunction with the growth of hierarchical systems of power. Men controlled the technological knowledge that governed the instruments of labour and the work processes of other men and of all women. With the rise of capitalism, an economic system based on continual advances in technology, men were thrown into perennial conflict with capital and with each other over the possession of technological competence and the power to use it. Women were actively excluded from technological knowledge, acted upon by the technology and not interactive with it.

In the ensuing three chapters I examine some contemporary labour processes in detail and trace the effect on them of electronic technology and the way sexual divisions change but survive through a period of economic crisis and technical transformation. In Chapter 2 I look at the clothing industry and in particular at two clothing firms. One is still using conventional methods of producing patterns with pencil and paper, cutting cloth with simple portable electric tools. The second firm has brought the computer to the pattern room, where the grading of patterns and the preparation of lays of pattern parts is now carried out at a video screen. The cloth is cut, with dramatic increases in productivity, by a computer-driven knife. This is a classic story of the dispossession of the traditional male craft producer and the scrapping of the simple tools over which he, not a company engineer, had effective control. In his place have been installed two new kinds of employee: a semi-skilled operator, characteristically female; and a system technologist (male), on whose know-how depends the management of the new equipment and the new labour processes.

Chapter 3 looks at the reorganization of warehouses in mail order firms, those houses that sell their goods to the public by means of a printed catalogue. I look at one warehouse that uses the time-honoured hand method of order filling, and then survey the technological developments sweeping through more advanced firms in the sector, including one particular company that has taken the step of moving goods instead of people. Here again the computer (in this case associated with materials-handling equipment) can be seen bringing about a restructuring of the labour force. Many workers are made redundant while the remainder become more productive and more disciplined. Again, women and men play different parts in the drama: men do the jobs that require technical skill or physical competence and which afford a degree of physical mobility. They are to be found managing, maintaining and repairing the machinery on which the women work. Women are confined to less mobile, unskilled, low-paid and non-technical jobs.

The third technology, described in Chapter 4, lies outside the business world, within the X-ray departments of National Health Service hospitals. One hospital looked at has only conventional X-ray equipment, the other has acquired, additionally, a powerful new diagnostic tool, the computed tomography scanner. In contrast to the two previous studies, situated among skilled and unskilled manual workers, this one is located among professionals and para-professionals in the male-dominated hierarchy of medicine. Here the staff of the X-ray department is mainly female, and this study proves, if such proof were called for, that women are quite capable of gaining technological knowledge and practical technical skills and are keen to do so. There is still, however, a group in the hospital with greater technical authority than they: the scientists and technicians of the medical physics department. The more senior and technology-oriented members of the physics team are male. Like the manufacturers of the new equipment, physicists and doctors fail to share the radiographer's priority of keeping a high level of technical skill in the practice of radiography. They often distinguish technological ability from the quality needed for patient care, linking men with the former, women with the latter.

One industry plays a key part in the cyclical transformation of the forces of production: the engineering industry. This is where the machinery and equipment set to work in other industries actually originate. Though these capital goods firms too are subject to competition and some go to the wall in times of crisis, certain sectors of engineering are bound by their nature to thrive on technological change. So I followed the three computer-based technologies 'upstream' to find out how women are faring in firms involved in producing and disseminating the 'new technology'. Chapter 5 looks at the technical labour processes and the division of labour in a large engineering firm producing X-ray equipment; in two import agencies marketing computer clothing systems; in a consultancy advising on warehouse innovations, and in an engineering workshop making electrically controlled mechanical equipment for warehouses. This is the heartland of technological skills. The firms employ technically qualified managers, professional engineers in design and development, many technician engineers in maintenance, installation and repair, and craft engineers, along with less skilled workers, in production. Here we can see technological segregation by sex painfully spread out to view. The technologists, with few exceptions, are men. Women play the support role of office secretary to the professional engineers and, in production, they are the base-line, least-skilled, lowest-paid assembly hands.

The consistent theme unfolding here is this: women are to be found in great numbers *operating* machinery, and some operating jobs are more skill-demanding than others. But women continue to be rarities in those occupations that involve knowing about what goes on inside the machine. The electronic revolution is making little difference. The flexible, transferable skills of engineering are still the property of males. With few exceptions, the designer and developer of the new systems, the people who market and sell, install, manage and service machinery, are men. Women may push the buttons but they may not meddle with the works.

The advantages to men of this sexual division of labour give them every reason to strive to perpetuate it. What of employers, however? While I encountered some prejudiced attitudes among employers, several managers said their main problem was a shortage of appropriate skills. They would be willing to employ good technologists of either sex. Women, they said, were just not coming forward. Chapter 6 therefore looks behind the notion of 'equal opportunity' to some of the cultural processes that go on in the technological workplace and help to explain women's reluctance to enter it. From men's own words it is possible to see how they ascribe high value to technology and technological work and how they identify their masculinity with their skills and careers. They relate to each other through competing over or sharing their manly competences, meanwhile relegating women to a different, lower, domestic sphere. Technology enters into our sexual identity: femininity is incompatible with technological competence; to feel technically competent is to feel manly. The gendering of men and women into 'masculine' and 'feminine' is a cultural process of immense power. People suffer for disregarding its dictates. It is, besides, not only people who get gendered but also occupations.

In Chapter 7 we hear what women have to say about their jobs, their commitment to work and their appetite for the technical competence that few get a chance to acquire. We also get a sense of their understanding that for a woman to cross into male work is to transgress gender rules and to invite penalties. It involves abandoning women's traditional values and concerns. Unlike women, men relate to the responsibilities of 'home' from a position of relative autonomy. They choose to give priority to earning and to work, leaving domestic responsibility to women. In this way they compete with women for training and in the labour market on unequal terms. In addition, women and men talk here about the way a sexual division of labour in technology exists in the home as well as at work: while women are occupied with cooking, cleaning and child care, it is almost exclusively men who do maintenance work on house or vehicles. At this intimate scale it is possible to see that the grasp men have of technology and tools impedes women from gaining competence.

Finally, in Chapter 8, some conclusions are drawn as to why technologies may change but sex inequalities remain. Two factors emerge as helping men maintain their separation from women and their control of technological occupations. One is the active gendering of jobs and people. The second is the continual creation of sub-divisions in work processes, and levels in workplace hierarchies, into which men can move in order to keep their distance from women.

I discuss practical steps that can be taken to help women get technical skills and in particular the kinds of employment practices trade unions can press for and ways they too could usefully change. But we have to acknowledge women's reluctance to take up technical careers. It does not spring from inadequacy or lack of interest but from a keen perception of the costs involved: isolation, discomfort, harassment and, often, wasted time and energy. To equalize the presence of women with that of men in technological qualification and work we need not a few hundred more but tens of thousands of women at professional level, hundreds of thousands at craft and technician level. If the majority of women are refusing to follow the pioneers, turning their faces the other way, it is not surprising. Technology and the relations of technical work have to change before most women will choose to engage with them.

Some women have found a way forward, meanwhile, in organizing autonomously to get technical training for women in circumstances free of men. If this book has a single urgent message it is a plea for more commitment of support to women-only projects. There is, however, only one way of getting fully above and beyond the contradictions and legitimately encouraging women to abandon their boycott of technology. This is the long-term project of dismantling gender, both of people and of occupations. Gender difference, like apartheid, has always meant separate development for inequality. When women's and men's lives are no longer complementary but similar, then women will share in technical skills and an unaccustomed hand will share in the rocking of the cradle too. What the cradle symbolizes, the human factor in human life, has to replace power as the purpose of production and technology.

1. Technology, production and power

It is a fact known to the youngest school child that women and men 'do different jobs'. A sexual division of labour is one of the most marked and persistent of the patterns that characterize human society everywhere. In Britain, men and women cluster in different industries. For example, while women are only 14.8 per cent of the labour force in the industrial group called the 'mechanical engineering industry', they are 70.3 per cent of the labour force in 'footwear and clothing'.[1] Within any one industry of course there will be people doing many different kinds of job. So a large proportion of that female 14.8 per cent in 'mechanical engineering' is in fact doing traditional women's work in the offices and canteens of engineering firms. The closer we look the more differences we find between what women do and what men do. Using 'occupational' in place of 'industrial' statistics – what we actually work at rather than the type of firm we work in – we find that 76.7 per cent of the clerical labour force is women. On the other hand, only 4.8 per cent of people in processing, making and repairing jobs in connection with metal or electrical products are women.[2]

Women are clustered into relatively few occupations. Of women manual workers, 85 per cent work in three broad occupational groups: catering, cleaning, hairdressing and other personal services; painting, repetitive assembling, product inspecting, packaging and similar occupations; and making and repairing jobs (excluding those in metal and electrical work). Of women non-manual workers, no less than 91 per cent are to be found within three categories: selling; clerical jobs; and professional and related work in education, welfare and health services.[3]

Men, by contrast, are engaged in a far wider range of activities and there are few from which they are entirely absent. More importantly, they monopolize the higher ranks of most. It is useful to distinguish 'horizontal' segregation of occupations, whereby men and women engage in different *kinds* of work, from 'vertical' segregation, whereby the sexes attain different *levels* of seniority in their occupations. The statistics show that men occupy a disproportionate number of higher-grade positions and women are concentrated in the lower grades of the rather limited range of work they do.[4]

Studies of individual industries or firms show that when one gets down to workplace level the divisions between women and men are yet more pronounced. An occupational category such as 'warehouse hand' is likely to conceal a situation in which heavy work like pushing goods around is done by men, sedentary work like checking delivery notes is done by women. In particular, sex divisions nearly always break cleanly along the line of skill. Jobs formally classified as skilled are done by men. Women are found in jobs that are considered unskilled and semi-skilled.[5]

A recent British survey involving over 3,000 women obtained an even closer look at segregation by sex. Working women reported in 63 per cent of cases that they worked in 'women-only' jobs. The occupational segregation was higher still if the professions and office work were weeded out. For instance, of semi-skilled factory workers no less than 73 per cent were working only with women in their particular job. Even more of men's work is exclusively male. Of the smaller number of husbands interviewed in this same survey, 81 per cent of those working with other people worked only with men, and 98 per cent had male supervisors.[6]

Surprisingly, there has been little lessening of occupational segregation by sex during this century. Catherine Hakim used a number of different measures to find out whether a change had occurred between 1901 and 1971. She found that the proportion of occupations without any women workers at all was relatively constant at around 9 per cent between 1901 and 1961, but an improvement had been detectable by 1971, as a few women pioneers penetrated male fields in the forward-looking decade of the 1960s. The proportion of all occupations in which women were at least as well represented as men in the labour force as a whole, however, remained virtually constant over the 70-year period, at the low level of 25 per cent of the total. Typically male occupations remained at a fairly constant high level of 73 per cent of all occupations listed. The proportion of occupations in which women were greatly over-represented (at 70 per cent or more of the workforce) actually *increased* slightly, from 9 per cent to 12 per cent. In addition, Hakim's data indicated a trend towards greater vertical segregation over the period. Men, not women, were climbing. She summarized: 'Occupational concentration and occupational segregation have remained relatively unchanged in Britain over seven decades.'[7]

It seems that the phenomenon of sex segregation is not limited to Britain. Reports from the USA[8] and European countries[9] show a similar situation. In Third World countries, though the actual occupations done by women and by men may vary widely, the existence of a clear sexual division of labour of some kind characterizes them all.[10] Even in the USSR, where the ideology of the 1917 Revolution and the shortage of skilled labour in the period that followed gave a boost to women's entry into non-traditional work, the return of a measure of normalcy was accompanied by an increase in occupational segregation by sex. Though more women than in Britain are scientists, engineers and technicians, they tend to be in the lower-ranking branches and grades of the fields in which they work. The 1970 census in the USSR showed that men were not taking their place alongside women in traditionally female jobs. Ninety-eight per cent of nurses and nursery school personnel, 99 per cent of stenographers and 91 per cent of catering employees were female.[11]

Divided by technology

Technology has an important position in this widespread sexual division of labour. Technological knowledge at the professional level, and technological know-how at the practical level, are sharp differentiators of men and women. Taking occupational categories, for instance: in 1983 in Britain, women were only 8.6 per cent of the professionals in science, engineering and technology, and 4.8 per cent of the labour force who process, make and repair metal and electrical goods.[12] The former figures show a slight gain (of 1.5 per cent) since 1975, the latter a slight fall (1.1 per cent).

More detailed information is obtainable from the statistics of education and training. These, besides, are a better pointer to the future. Again, a difference is observable between the educational levels. Girls and boys start out on their different routes while still at school. If we take maths, physics, computer studies and technical drawing as indicators of future technological career choices, we find females already disadvantaged at 16 years of age. At GCE O-level, for instance, though the percentages have been slowly rising since 1970, girls still had only 43.6 per cent of the passes in maths, 27.9 per cent in physics, 27.3 per cent in the relatively new subject of computer studies, and 4.6 per cent in technical drawing in 1983. The disadvantage is confirmed and deepened by 18 years of age. At A-level these percentages fall to 31.1, 21.0, 19.6 and 2.9 per cent respectively.[13]

If we move up the age range to vocational training, we find in 1982–3 women representing only a negligible 1 per cent of those entering for the craft engineering exams of the City and Guilds of London Institute, the body officially responsible for qualifying craft workers.[14] The situation is hardly better on the courses leading to the somewhat higher level of engineering technician exams, which are certified by the Business and Technical Education Council: a little over 2 per cent of those entering were women in 1982–3.[15] Among students of English polytechnics enrolling on advanced 'engineering and technology' courses in 1983 there were 720 full-time female students to 7,125 male (9.2 per cent). Against 1,172 female 'sandwich' students there were 17,917 males (6.1 per cent), and only 419 young women were getting day release to attend these courses as against 10,798 young men (3.7 per cent).[16] Finally, among full-time university undergraduates in 'engineering and techno-logy', women represented 9.1 per cent in 1983. This proportion had, however, doubled since 1975.[17] The picture is of an overwhelmingly male field of work into which a few women pioneers are making their way. It is a little easier for those who make it over the A-level threshhold and can follow the professional route, unremittingly hard for those young women who must take the manual, vocational route. At all levels, while the pioneers have a little more female company each year, pioneers they remain.

The effect on women as people and as workers of their exclusion from the skills needed to govern the technologies of production will gradually become clear in the course of this book. One point is worth making here, however. It is costing women money. The Equal Pay Act of 1970, operational in 1975, promised to bring women's pay up to the level of men's. Yet while women's average gross hourly earnings as a propor-tion of men's were boosted, partly by the new legislation, from 63 per cent to 75 per cent between 1970 and 1977, they then slipped and stood at 73.5 per cent in 1984.[18] If we consider average gross weekly earnings, which include the fact that men have access to more overtime possibilities than women, we find that women's pay packets look even thinner. They earned 54.5 per cent of what men earned in 1974 and had only crept up to 65.8 per cent of men's weekly earnings by 1984.[19]

It is by now widely accepted that the reason the Equal Pay legislation of the 1970s failed to achieve equal pay for women is that the majority of women are segregated into fields of employment in which they are unable to compare themselves with men for purposes of grading and pay.[20] Skilled manual work pays more than unskilled; professional jobs pay more than office work. In technology, as in other fields, women are not on the career paths that offer pay and prospects. In the engineering industry, for example, of a total of 2.3 million employed in 1982, 22 per cent, or around half a million, were women. Yet their share of the industry's wage bill was certainly not proportional to their numbers, since 45 per cent were in relatively low-paid operator jobs and almost all the remainder in equally ill-rewarded clerical work. Only 2.5 per cent of the women working in the engineering industry were in managerial, scientific, technological or technician occupations.[21] It is the men in the industry who earn the skilled wages and the professional salaries. And the same technological division of labour by sex, with the same pecuniary effects, applies outside as within the engineering industry proper.

Men's appropriation of technology

To understand the different relation the sexes have to technology today we need to recognize the relevance of technology to power and to the emergence of power systems in the past. Despite the stereotype of the stone-age cave man dragging 'his' woman along by the hair and wielding a club (technology?) in his free hand, the evidence of archaeology does not point to any 'natural' distance between women and technology.[22] Today, when explaining the emergence of human societies, the emphasis has shifted from Man The Hunter to Woman The Gatherer.[23] It is suggested that females, not males, were the first technologists. Under pressure of nutritional stress, caring for both self and young, females are the more likely sex to have invented the digging stick, the carrying sling or bag, the reaping knife and sickle, pestles and pounders, methods of winnowing, washing, detoxifying and preserving food.[24] It is well established that women were the first horticulturalists, purposefully growing selected plants in and around their settlements.[25] They may well have invented and used the hoe, spade, shovel and scratch-plough.[26] Whether hunting animals (large or small), or herding, gardening and farming, a simple division of labour may have occurred. We need not suppose, however, that it gave one sex a marked monopoly of technological skills.[27]

As human societies have developed, in different parts of the world at different times, they have tended to pass through broadly similar phases. Often these are designated by archaeologists according to the material of the dominant technology: stone age, bronze age, iron age. Associated with the technologies are successive stages in social organization. Women appear to have been central to the organization of social life until the late neolithic age. As the neolithic ceded to the bronze age, however, in many cultures of which a record exists it is possible to see a shift towards male dominance. A relatively egalitarian and peaceful community of woman-centred kinship clans gave way to an increasingly centralized society divided into hierarchical classes, based on agriculture, warfare and slavery. As this occurred, it seems, women were actively subjugated by men, excluded from many crafts and trades and displaced from their positions of political and religious authority.[29] The rise of class society is associated with a shift to patrilineality (determining descent through the male blood line) and to patrilocality (a wife moving to the domain of her husband's family on marriage).[30] It is also associated with an increasing division of labour, the emergence of specific crafts and trades.

In particular the new occupations surrounding metallurgy were highly significant. The importance of metals and of the skills of smelter, founder and smith to the military and agricultural exploits of rulers and ruling classes can be in no doubt. It seems that in male-dominated societies these occupations are seen as male. Technological skills are a source of power and where men were in possession of all other vehicles of power, from state organizaton to marriage, it would have been surprising to find women in possession of mechanical powers. The 'mighty five' devices – lever, wedge, screw, wheel and inclined plane – that made it possible to move mountains and build pyramids were the technical armoury of men.

It was not in the cradles of 'civilization', however, but in the western extremities of Europe that technology would explode in the eighteenth and nineteenth centuries AD, and it is of interest to trace the technological division of labour by sex as it progressed there. As the use of iron was rapidly expanded in the eighth and ninth centuries,[31] it is clear that women's role in production, though of prime importance then as it has continued to be ever since ('two-thirds of the world's work hours'), was nonetheless confined to particular activities associated with domestic consumption. Apart from food preparation and child care, women were responsible for 'spinning, dyeing, weaving, tending the garden, raising livestock and . . . cultivating land'.[32] It was men who were the goldsmith, weapon-smith and blacksmith, 'making ploughshare and coulter, goad and fish-hook, awl and needle', and the carpenter, 'responsible not only for various tools and utensils but for houses and ships'.[33]

In the later Middle Ages again we find rural women involved with 'dairy work, gardening, food preparation and the textile crafts of carding, slubbing, spinning and weaving', while their male equivalents 'worked the land, reared livestock, repaired hedges, ditches and tools'.[34] Among these tools were more and more made of iron. Iron was rapidly becoming the basis of the dominant technology. 'It is the consensus among historians of agriculture that the mediaeval peasantry used an amount of iron which would have seemed inconceivable to any earlier rural population and that the smithy became integral to every village.'[35] And there were few trades more associated with manliness than that of smith.

The towns, which grew rapidly in importance in the thirteenth and fourteenth centuries, were the centres of specialized handicrafts. Under the authority of the feudal state, the craft and merchant guilds laid down the rules by which apprentices might be recruited and trained and business carried on. The guilds covered certain skilled techniques producing goods for consumption, such as printing. But they also included those that produced tools and implements: carpenter, wright and various kinds of smith. The guilds were male in character.[36] Women engaged extensively in economic life in the towns, but mainly in sex-specific areas that had by long tradition been female. They were domestic servants, washerwomen, bakers, brewers and inn-keepers, roles that were extensions into trade of the concerns of domestic life: food, drink and textiles, goods and services for domestic consumption.

The sexual division of labour was not absolutely total at this period, however. Women appear listed alongside men as engaging in certain kinds of production (shoe making for instance) and in certain fields of commerce (as drapers, chandlers and even ironmongers). The pattern that we have seen to exist today, however, whereby women cluster in a few occupations and men spread across many, is evident in the Middle Ages. Poll tax returns for Oxford in 1380, for instance, mention six trades followed by women, six in which both women and men were employed, and no fewer than 81 that were followed exclusively by men. Alice Clark concluded from her study of mediaeval trades that, though women followed some skilled and semi-skilled occupations, 'no traces can be found of any organisation existing' within them.[37] Certainly women were not considered a threat to male occupational rights. A statute of Edward III expressly exempted women from the ordinance that men should not follow more than a single craft. 'But the intent of the King and his Council,' it reads, 'is that Women, that is to say Brewers, Bakers, Carders and Spinners and Workers as well of Wool as of Linen Cloth and of Silk, Brawdesters and Breakers of Wool and all other that do use and work all Handy Works may freely use and work as they have done before this time . . .'[38]

The role of the guilds extended beyond an immediate trade to social organization within the town. A woman therefore might be a member of a guild without actually plying its trade. A daughter might take up right of patrimony in her father's guild for the civic advantages it afforded. Some are known to have become apprenticed to a master in his guild so as to work as a domestic servant to his wife. Widows frequently inherited their husbands' enterprises. Widows are therefore sometimes named even as farriers and smiths. An exceptional woman might have broken the convention to carry out this work herself, but a commoner practice was for a widow to manage the business while hired journeymen and apprentices carried out the skilled practical aspects of the work.

Tools that make tools

In this account of early divisions of labour we can distinguish certain skills which were of special significance in production and which yielded, as a consequence, greater influence to those who possessed them than was yielded by ordinary productive abilities. They are the skills that were required for making tools, implements and weapons. In other words, *they involved competence in the production or adaptation of other producers' instruments of labour*. Eventually we will see these skills evolve into those that make machinery and later still into those that build computer systems.

Why should these abilities afford greater power than others: than the knowledge needed to nurture children, for instance, or to weave cloth or plough the land? The answer is, first, related to systems of class power. Those who own the means of production, whether slave-owning emperors, land-owning feudal nobles or factory-owning capitalists, depend for the making of their wealth on a yoking in tandem of labour and tools, labour and machinery. They may be expected therefore to pay well, in cash or food, freedom or status, for the skills they need to effect this linkage and continually to improve its productivity. Other talents could, in another world, have been valued more highly. But from the onset of male-dominated class-structured societies, the priority has been supremacy in a struggle for ownership and control of disposable surpluses. That priority has forced the development of technology in a certain direction. The forcing-house has often been warfare.

Secondly, however, those who possessed these skills had a source of power over everyone who did not. Such men rendered other people dependent on them for the maintenance of their own environment and instruments of labour. They were in a position to impede or enhance, direct or redirect other producers' labour processes. They acquired a degree of authority among other men of those classes who worked manually. It will be clear also that the skills enhanced men's power over women. Not only were women firmly subordinated to men in the patriarchal family, but they were also dependent on them for certain important practical processes of everyday life. The technological skills, defined as male property, were therefore both a cause and an effect of male supremacy.

Meanwhile, technological knowledge was evolving. By the early fourteenth century Europe had made considerable progress towards substituting water and wind power for human labour in apparatus of many different kinds. Applications of the new sources of power were advancing in step: the cam in the eleventh and twelfth centuries; the spring and treadle in the thirteenth; complex forms of gearing in the fourteenth. In the fifteenth century the crank, connecting-rod and governor were coming into widespread use, aiding the very significant step of converting reciprocating to continuous rotary motion. By the sixteenth century, 'Europe was equipped not only with sources of power far more diversified than those known to any previous culture, but also with an arsenal of technical means for grasping, guiding and utilizing such energies which was immeasurably more varied and skilful than any people of the past had possessed or than was known to any contemporary society.'[39]

The history of invention represents the inventors of antiquity, the Middle Ages and the Renaissance as invariably male. A hefty and comprehensive 'history of the machine' published in 1979 encompasses technological development from the Cro-Magnon anvil to the space rocket. Among approximately 450 men named in connection with invention in this book there is one woman, Ada Lady Lovelace, mathematician.[40] The question of what part women did or did not play in technological invention is a knotty one. Women have almost always been 'hidden from history' when the historians were men. Autumn Stanley's work reaffirms women's creativeness.[41] She suggests that we should be sceptical of the male historians of technology and look for the hidden women. We should, besides, give greater emphasis to the activities to which women notably *have* contributed their ideas: preparing food, healing, making garments, caring for children. After all, the significance ascribed to any productive practice has been largely a male choice.

Stanley proposes that 'all else being equal' we may assume that those who work in a process invent the tools by which it is carried on.[42] While this is likely to be true for very early periods of human history, it is to miss a crucial characteristic of subsequent patriarchal and class societies. Women were systematically excluded from all sources of power, including the technologies that held sway over their own female areas of production. The development of textile technology, for instance, has been a male not a female project. The following discussion by Lynn White Jr of the technology of the spinning wheel makes clear how differentiated were the considerations of *mechanics* from the consideration of spinning thread:

> The spinning wheel is mechanically interesting not only because it is the first instance of the belt transmission of power and a notably early example of the flywheel principle, but because it focussed attention upon the problem of producing and controlling the various rates of speed in different moving parts of the same machine. One turn of the great wheel sent the spindle twirling many times; but not content with this, by c.1480 crafts*men* (my italics) had developed a U-shaped flyer rotating around the spindle and permitting the operations of both spinning and winding the thread on a bobbin to proceed simultaneously. To accomplish this, spindle and flyer had to rotate at different speeds, each driven by a separate belt from the large wheel, which, of course, revolved at a third speed. Finally, by 1524, the crank, connecting-rod and treadle had been added to the spinning wheel.[43]

Was White being sexist in assuming that these developments originated with men? I think not. Leonardo da Vinci is credited with the invention of the flyer for the spindle in 1490. Johann Jurgen, a woodcarver of Brunswick, invented a partly automatic spinning wheel employing a flyer around 1530.[44] The way of thinking that would have enabled such innovations arose not in the main from the spinning of thread but from a familiarity with other kinds of apparatus and technique. The matter of differential speeds, for instance, was being explored in clock-making at this time; the notion of the flywheel and the transmission belt were used in the developing of grinding mills. Technological knowledge is essentially a *transferable* knowledge, profitably carried from one kind of production to another. It is a field of its own. We will see this in the contemporary studies that follow: computer-aided design and cutting systems built for use with metals are adapted for use with cloth; a robot developed for use in the car industry stimulates developments that will solve management problems in warehousing. Men move from industry to industry carrying know-how across the boundaries of firm and sector. Then, as now, it was men and not women who had mobility (intellectual, occupational and physical mobility) and the overview it afforded. Later of course it would be other men – Hargreave, Arkwright, Crompton, Kay – who would adapt the domestic textile apparatus for factory and mechanized use.

What is at issue here is not women's inventiveness. There is no doubt that women have the ability to be as imaginative and innovative as men. Women have frequently 'had ideas' for the improvement of tools and machinery with which they worked. They have seldom had the craft skills to effect in wood or metal the improvements they conceived. Besides, despite the frequent adulation by historians of male inventors, technological development is not in reality a series of brainwaves. A materialist understanding of history gives the personal less significance than the social. In tracing technological change, therefore, the focus needs to be 'not upon individuals, however heroic, but upon a collective, social process in which the institutional and economic environments play major roles'.[45] The social process of technological development has been overwhelmingly a male process. It is women's lack of social and economic power that holds them 'down' to the role of producer of goods for immediate consumption. Since the bronze age, women have worked *for* men, whether the man was head of household, slave-owner or feudal lord. It is clear that they also produced *by means of* man-made technologies. They were subject to that particular form of material control that comes of men as a sex having appropriated the role of tool-maker to the world.

Machines that make machines

The departure that was about to change the world dramatically for both women and men, however, was not a technical invention. It was capitalism: an entirely new set of social relationships that would find the organizational means to bring science and technology together and harness them for production. During the sixteenth and seventeenth centuries the peasant economy of the countryside and the craft economy of the towns, both essentially home-based domestic forms of production, changed their character. From among the yeoman farmers and the guild masters emerged a new stratum of large-scale producers. The merchant class also grew in number and in influence. Wealth, accumulated through trade in England and overseas, sought new ways of making more wealth. Independent craft production gave way to 'manufacture' as merchants became entrepreneurs, no longer simply buying from but actively employing the producers.

At first the new capitalist class 'put out' the material to scattered producers to work on in their homes, and in this way the domestic system continued for a while within the new mode of production. Much of women's production continued to be carried on under the authority of father or husband. Eventually, however, entrepreneurs saw advantage in gathering producers into workshops and factories where an employer could enjoy economies of scale and supervise production more closely.

As the restraints of the guild system were shrugged off, the new class of employers found it possible and profitable to introduce a sub-division of the work process. Merchandise that had once been produced by a single craftsman undertaking all the varied parts of the process was now the product of a series of manual workers, each of whom repeated a part of the task over and over again with a single tool. Some of the detail tasks were more skill-demanding than others. The workforce could be differentiated: some remained relatively skilled and costly, but others could now be less skilled, and a new cheap category of entirely unskilled 'hands' was called into play. Often these were women or children, many of whom were drawn from the surplus population thrown off the land by the agrarian revolution.

A significant change began to occur in the relationship between producers and 'their' technologies. The craftsman had owned his own tools. This included the tools owned by those men who made the tools that other producers used. The craftsman guarded the 'mystery' of how to use them. As Marx put it, 'the labourer and his means of production remained closely united, like the snail with its shell'.[46] Now the snail had to be prised from its shell if capitalism was to fulfil its potential: in the new factories the employer owned the instruments of labour and put the worker to work on them. For many artisans who had once purchased materials with their own money, worked with their own tools and sold to their own customers, the change was historic. Now what they sold, all they had to sell, was their labour power.

So, as the capitalist initiative (which was also, it must be noted, a masculine initiative) drew into existence this new class of wage workers, unknown in the feudal world, men of the two classes were drawn into endemic conflict. Capital might own the instruments of production but working men alone had the craft know-how to use them. How and by whom, for how long and for what reward, the tools and techniques were to be used became the basis of the struggle that has been the prime mover of history in the intervening 200 or 300 years.

The process, however, had a long way yet to go. Technology would not only set in opposition the interests of the employing class and the working class. It would also be instrumental in forming the new working class as a stratified and divided one. As the general-purpose tools of the craftsmen were put to use in a sub-divided production process, the tools too were altered – simplified and multiplied – to suit the new detail tasks.[47] Simple tools, combined and associated with a power source and a transmitting mechanism, resulted in a machine. The machine was soon associated with others in a factory system that itself had the characteristics of a machine. The groundwork was laid for vast new possibilities of accumulation for the owner of the new mechanical means of production.

Machinery offered men as a sex opportunities that were not open to women. Already certain technologies of which men had exclusive tenure had a special significance in production; now they took on an amplified importance. Those who had traditionally worked the materials from which tools were made would now adapt their skills to the new machine age. What capital needed in place of smiths and wrights were 'mechanics' and 'engineers'. It was only men, inevitably, who had the tradition, the confidence and in many cases also the transferable skills to make the leap. It was therefore exclusively men who became the maintenance mechanics and the production engineers in the new factories, governing capital's new forces of production.

Marx singled out these key employees in the new 'machino-facture'. He noted the essential division between the operators, who are actually employed on the machines, and their unskilled attendants. But, he wrote, in addition a historically new worker appears, a 'class of persons, whose occupation it is to look after the whole of the machinery and repair it from time to time; such as engineers, mechanics, joiners etc. This is a superior class of workmen, some of them scientifically educated, others brought up to a trade; it is distinct from the factory operative class and merely aggregated to it. This division of labour is purely technical.'[48] These technical men were the one category of worker whose earning power was not reduced by the intro-duction of machinery.[49] If one mechanic, together with a handful of unskilled, low-paid machine operators, can put out of work many craftsmen, capital could (and as we shall see later still can) afford to pay the technical newcomer relatively well.

The old-style smith and wright, new-style mechanic and engineer, however, were also to play another part in production history. Machinery was crippled in its complete development so long as machine-building itself remained a handicraft affair. As Marx noted: 'The expansion of industries carried on by means of machinery, and the invasion by machinery of fresh branches of production, were dependent on the growth of a class of workmen who, owing to the almost artistic nature of their employment, could increase their numbers only gradually and not by leaps and bounds.'[50] Besides, because of the increasing size of the prime movers and the use of iron and steel – as Marx put it 'a more refractory material', huge masses of which had now 'to be forged, to be welded, to be cut, to be bored and to be shaped' – it was inevitable that machines had to be invented with which to build machines.[51]

Skills, however, were still needed to design, develop and build these machines that were to make machines to do the work of men and women. While one kind of skilled man, therefore, had become the mechanic and engineer of the 'downstream' processes of what Marx called Department II, where they supervised the machines that produced the means of consumption, his brother now moved 'upstream' to become the mechanic and engineer of Department I, the influential machine-building or capital goods industry producing the means of production for others.[52] We will see men of these two categories in the story ahead, for Chapters 2–4 in a sense deal with Department II, where services and goods are produced for consumption, while Chapter 5 looks at some of the inheritors of the capital goods industries of Department I.

The struggle over technical skills

The Combination Acts, which had outlawed collective organization by workers, were repealed in 1824–5. After this, journeymen from many of the male crafts formed trade unions. At first there existed a variety of societies, local or regional in scope, representing millwrights, machinists and other categories of technical skill. The strongest of these was the Steam Engine Makers, founded in 1826, and later known as the 'Old Mechanics'. In 1851, many of the smaller societies joined together to form a new union, the Amalgamated Society of Engineers, Machinists, Smiths, Millwrights and Pattern-Makers. It was an exclusive, skilled union, characterized by high membership subscriptions and generous benefits, and it became a model for other skilled unions. Not all metal-workers belonged to it: the Old Mechanics among other societies kept apart; later the United Pattern-Makers, a highly elite section, would break away. But the ASE nonetheless quickly became one of the largest unions in the country and had a membership of 72,000 by 1891.[53]

Meanwhile the scope of the industry itself was expanding to

encompass different kinds of metal-work: the heavy sectors of ship and locomotive building, the machine tool industry and eventually lighter sectors producing consumer goods such as bicycles. In the 1870s the employers organized themselves into the Iron Trades Employers' Association, the better to fight back against the unions. The employers, by repeated cycles of technological innovation, attempted to deskill the work of the engineering industry and divest themselves of dependence on the craft engineers. The skilled workers of the ASE and other engineering unions on the contrary struggled to maintain craft regulation of work, including an agreed ratio of apprentices to journeymen, and to prevent the employers fragmenting the labour process and using unskilled handymen on the machines.[54]

> Pattern-making foundry work, blacksmiths' work and boiler-making all saw the appearance of minor labour-saving devices; but the most fundamental and rapid changes were taking place in the machine shop, which with its fitters and turners, was the heart of the Engineers' empire. About 1890 came the capstan and turret lathe, the vertical, horizontal and later the universal milling machine, the external and surface grinder, the vertical borer, and the radial drill. Work on these specialist machines did not require the all-round competence of the craftsman and many of the men put onto them, at wage rates below craft standards, had neither served an apprenticeship nor picked up a broad experience on the shop floor.[55]

Instrumental in bringing about this sub-division of work and the deskilling of craft engineers was a new breed of formally educated professional engineers. Civil engineers – men like Isambard Kingdom Brunel – had already achieved status and acclaim as architects of the era of canal, road and rail. Now, towards the end of the nineteenth century, the new high-status industrial engineer was interposing himself between the mechanic and the employer in science-based manufacture. Entire new industries such as electrical and chemical engineering grew up, which had no craft basis. In these the engineer was not only key employee but also often manager.[56]

The engineering employers were in perpetual struggle with the craft engineering unions and took the offensive in a nationwide lockout in 1897. Bitterness lay in the fact that while the capitalist and the skilled men needed each other, they did not need each other equally. As David Noble points out, technological innovation was often achieved by their combined efforts. The skilled man saw in new scientific knowledge about the nature of the material world the basis for new or refined methods of production; the capitalist recognized the potential for enhancing profitability. Often, 'these two visions took shape as one in a single mind: the capitalist was frequently an inventor of sorts, while the inventive craftsman shared not a little of the entrepreneurial spirit of the capitalist.'[57] The difference was that the capitalist would readily turn the skilled man's own inventions against him, with the help of other brands of engineer.

From this history it will be clear that the technically knowledgeable and skilled fraternity is by no means simply a 'superior class of workman', as Marx put it. It is varied, it is hierarchically stratified and its component parts are continually shifting in relative status. Technological skills are forced by capital to adapt and change. They do not only act on others' skills, they are also acted upon. The skilled men respond by demarcating and defending areas of competence. As a result the unions at one moment join forces, at another split apart. Some categories of technical men are always ahead of 'the state of the art', and consequently in demand. Some are running to keep up, fearful of technological redundancy, the obsolescence of their knowledge, the demise of the process they are accustomed to work at. The challenge for all of them is to keep abreast of technology, maintain marketable skills and retain a governing role over the machinery on which other people produce, at the point both of its manufacture and of its application. Those technologists who succeed, 'do well' by themselves. Their role develops more and more from control of machinery to control of labour processes and so to control of people:

They are entrusted not only with planning the labour process and with keeping production up to pre-established technical standards, but also, and mainly, with maintaining the hierarchical structure of the labour force and with perpetuating capitalist social relations, that is with keeping the producers separated (alienated) from the product of their collective labour and from the production process.[58]

The advent of powered machinery was, then, profoundly contradictory for men as a sex. On the one hand many men could view it only with hatred. It was the enemy. It enabled capital to dispense with the skills of the skilled man and the muscle power of the labourer. On the other hand, mechanical skills were the property of men as a sex, much as machinery itself was the property of the dominant class. Men's power over women could only be enhanced by advances in technology.

The vested interests of men with technical skills led them into an ambiguous class position. Technological change can be seen as class warfare. 'It would be possible to write quite a history of the inventions, made since 1830, for the sole purpose of supplying capital with weapons against the revolts of the working class,' wrote Marx.[59] And who designs and uses those weapons in class struggle if not the mechanics and engineers? Some are working-class men. Others are drawn from the ranks of the bourgeoisie. Either way they play an equivocal role in the struggle between the workforce and the employer. David Noble noted that, 'As those charged with supervision of the industrial labour force, engineers found labor organisations difficult and disagreeable, and as professionals, they viewed unions as a measure of mediocrity.'[60] So, whether they were members of elite unions, whether they were non-unionized and actively anti-union, the technologists' close identification with the machinery and those that owned it was always in danger of standing between them and other workers. Women workers, whether in industries producing consumer goods or, as increasingly occurred in the twentieth century, in the capital goods industries, were always among the 'others'. Men's power over women continued to exert itself, in this way and in others, within the changing relations of capitalism.

Women's relationship to the machine

The preferential place that men have carved for themselves in production has survived from the earliest days and through several revolutions in economic organization. Perhaps most striking of all, men maintained their unique grasp of technological skills when capitalism exploded apart the ownership of the instruments of production from the skills they entailed and unleashed an unprecedented epoch of technological development. We now have a kind of genealogy for the maintenance technician, the systems technologist, technical manager and professional engineer as we will encounter them in the 'new technology' workplaces of the 1980s.

We also have the beginnings of a similar genealogy for the women 'operators' we are going to encounter. We know that women have continuously contributed a large proportion of total production and that a very sizeable part of that has been in food and clothing, whether for immediate consumption or for sale. In addition, of course, women have been the ones to perform almost all the 'reproductive' tasks associated with child care and housekeeping that are not normally classed as work.

Women were also employed, particularly when single, in the heaviest types of manual labour, were exploited as domestic servants, as 'servants in husbandry' working in the fields, and even carrying coal, washing lead and breaking ore in the mines. More women were forced into labouring (or pauperism) as the break-up of the old feudal relationships dispossessed the least secure. Female cottagers who had scratched a living from vegetable patch and grazing rights on the commons were made landless by the enclosure movement that 'rationalized' the land into large-scale farms. More and more of the women working as independent or family producers in towns lost their livelihood as competition from outwork and factory work organized on capitalist lines in the rural areas destroyed urban craft production. At first many women, like men, became outworkers in their own homes. As industrialization advanced they followed the work to the factories. Women were unpractised in craft organization and many had the docility that results from subordination within the home. The new class of male employers could benefit by this – in a sense they stole a march on men of the working class.[61]

The effect of the industrial revolution and the special uses of women, as perceived by the new captains of industry, were contradictory for women themselves. Some results were clearly adverse. Women and children were terribly exploited and abused in the frenzy of capitalist production. Industrial methods wiped out women's small businesses – bleaching and brewing, for instance. Women's types of production were brought more firmly under the sway of a male principle. Making clothing, food and drink, for instance, as it was socialized and mechanized, became more institutionally subject to men's special knowledge of machinery than women's domestic production had been subject to individual men's knowledge of tools.

As industrialization increased and more and more women were drawn into work, a powerful adaptation of the old ideology of 'a woman's place' evolved to ensure that women's relationship to work and earning was no more than provisional. A basic theme of this ideology was the assumption that woman's proper role was that of wife and mother. 'Remaining in the home was central to the maintenance of a woman's sexual purity and respectability.' The theme of this ideal Victorian lady, says Sarah Eisenstein, 'developed in some complexity and with uneasy insistence, in the early nineteenth century, in literature, popular magazines, religious tracts and public debate'.[62] As she points out, these were middle-class ideas that had little real relevance to the situation of working-class women, yet 'they informed the ideology of the period so thoroughly that they dominated prevailing attitudes towards working women and shaped the terms in which those women interpreted their own experience.'[63] Women, as a consequence, worked but could not aspire to the great achievements dreamed of by many Victorian men.

More positively, however, the development of a female

industrial labour force did bring practical opportunities for women to evade both this gender ideology and the more material aspects of male dominance. First, it meant coming out of the enclosed sphere of the patriarchal family into the more public sphere of the patriarchal firm. This is not so simple a move as it sounds. The feudal and the early capitalist domestic system of manufacture had made the home a far from private place. In a sense the home became truly a private sphere only once production had left it. The constitution of 'home and work', the 'private and public' as we know them was in many ways a cultural artefact of the industrial revolution. The more significant factor was that an increasing number of husbands and fathers lost some of their control over their daughters and wives, as they came to depend in part on an income earned by these womenfolk in the domain of another man.

Second, many women started to earn an independent wage. Though often enough it was quickly subsumed into household income for the disposition of the head of the household, nonetheless it increasingly gave some women independent means. The population of women was greater than that of men throughout the nineteenth century, and the surplus increased from 1851 to 1901.[64] Not all women would be able to marry and many would be widowed. By 1911, 54 per cent of single women would be working for a wage.[65]

Writing in 1915, and looking back over the previous century, Elizabeth Leigh Hutchins concluded:

the working woman does not appear to me to be sliding downwards . . . rather is she painfully, though perhaps for the most part unconsciously, working her way upwards out of more or less servile conditions of poverty and ignorance into a relatively civilised state, existing at present in a merely rudimentary form. She has attained at least to the position of earning her own living and controlling her own earnings, such as they are. She has statutory rights against her employer, and a certain measure of administrative protection in enforcing them. The right to a living wage, fair conditions of work, and a voice in the collective control over industry are not yet fully recognised, but are being claimed more and more articulately and can less and less be silenced and put aside . . . Among much that is sad, tragic and disgraceful in the industrial exploitation of women, there is emerging this fact, fraught with deepest consolation: the woman herself is beginning to think.[66]

The third change was that women were not only following their own traditional kinds of work into the factories. They were also diversifying their roles in production. Though they were found in their greatest numbers in the spinning and weaving mills, and in jam-making, confectionery and other forms of large-scale food production, soon they were also producing other kinds of commodity. Even in the early 'domestic' years of capitalist production women had begun to do 'unskilled', heavy and dirty work in metallurgy, making nails, nuts, bolts, screws, buckles, locks, bits and stirrups. Defoe wrote of the West Midlands area in 1769 that 'every Farm has one Forge or more',[67] and these forges were producing not for farm consumption but for capitalists. When these 'small iron trades' began to be organized into a factory system, women followed. In 1841 the number of women in the Birmingham district employed in metal manufacture was estimated at 10,000. Twenty-five years later there were 2,050 females returned as employed in Birmingham pen-works and others were employed in the light chain trade, in lacquering brass, and making files and pins.[68]

Women, then, were spreading into new spheres of production as production industrialized. What now became significant, however, was the particular role they played *within* these new industries. Women clustered within three types of occupation. Hutchins noted, from visits to non-textile factories early in this century, 'that men and women are usually doing, not the same, but different kinds of work and that the work done by women seems to fall roughly into three classes'.[69] Her first class was 'rough hard work preparing and collecting the material, or transporting it from one part of the factory to another'. A second was finishing and preparing goods for sale: examining, folding, wrapping and packing. It is the third group of jobs, however, that is the most interesting for us. They are the routine production jobs on machines that we shall see women doing in the 1980s. This work is 'done on machines with or without power, and this includes a whole host of employments and an endless variety of problems. Machine tending, press-work, stamp-work, metal-cutting, printing, various processes of brasswork, pen-making, machine ironing in laundries, the making of hollow-ware or tin pots and buckets of various kinds.' Hutchins did not of course note that the mechanics who kept these machines going were *not* women. It could be taken as given that those jobs belonged to men.

The response of male workers

The final significant effect of the industrial revolution on women was that it threw them, in many cases, into direct competition with men for work. Some of the new machine-based occupations of the late eighteenth and early nineteenth centuries, while they demanded great stamina, no longer called for sheer muscle. Employers could and often did replace men with women and children. Whereas the craft guilds had been organized mainly in exclusion of other men – the exclusion of women being more or less taken for granted – the skilled trade unions were obliged to direct their energies to keeping women out. Men could do little to prevent capital engaging women to work in the new industries. Men's efforts therefore had to be geared to segregating women and maintaining sexual divisions *within* the factory. Consciously and actively, male workers hedged women into unskilled and low-paid occupations. In printing, for instance, the male compositors and machine-minders confined women to book-binding and other print-finishing operations where they were severely exploited by employers.

It is the most damning indictment of skilled working-class men and their unions that they excluded women from member-ship and prevented them gaining competences that could have secured them a decent living. Virginia Penny wrote in 1869 that women's lot would be greatly improved if only women might enter the trades and professions monopolized by men. 'Apprentice ten thousand women to watchmakers,' she said. 'Put some thousands in the electric telegraph offices all over the country; educate one thousand lecturers for mechanics' institutes . . . then the distressed needlewoman will vanish, the decayed gentlewoman and broken-down governesses cease to exist.'[70] Men were not misled in perceiving women as a weapon in employers' hands by which their own wages could be kept down. Where they were misled was in their response. Instead of helping women to acquire skills and to organize their strength, they weakened women (and in the long run the entire working class) by continuing to exploit women domestically and helping the employer to exploit them as a secondary labour market. Not only were women barred from men's areas of skill but women's particular skills came to be universally undervalued in comparison: undervalued and underpaid. 'There is no reason, save custom and lack of organisation, why a nursery-maid should be paid less than a coal-miner. He is not one whit more capable of taking her place than she is of taking his,' wrote Elizabeth Hutchins.[71]

So great a gulf had men in earlier centuries fixed between women and technology, however, that the ASE was not obliged to see women as a threat to the engineer throughout the nineteenth century. The kinds of semi-skilled work brought into being by the mechanization of engineering (in the main, machining metal) were not seen by employers as appropriate areas in which to try to substitute women for men. The stratum of 'handymen' infiltrated by the employer into engineering works was just that: men. The Victorian and Edwardian women's movements did not include in their demands technical skills for women. It was not until the First World War, when they were brought into munitions and other heavy industries to release men for the Front, that women began to approach the masculine sphere of technical skill and consequently to be feared for the first time as 'dilutees'.

The *Labour Gazette* in 1917 estimated that one out of three working women was replacing a man.[72] Women went into a number of industries besides munitions:

> They planed, moulded, mortised and dovetailed in sawmills;
> drove trucks in flour and oil and cake mills; made upholstery
> and tyre tubes; bottled beer and manufactured furniture;
> worked in cement factories, foundries and tanneries, in jute
> mills and wool mills; broke limestone and loaded bricks in
> steel works and worked as riveters in shipbuilding yards.
> They could be found in car factories, in quarrying and
> surface mining and brickmaking . . . only underground
> mining, stevedoring and steel and iron smelting were still all
> male.[73]

Women, says this author, shattered the myth that they were
incapable of skilled work.

A serious challenge was made to male exclusiveness in the
ASE by the radical shop stewards' movement of the war and
post-war years. Progressiveness on the woman question was a
logical position for the shop stewards, whose aim was to turn
the ASE from a craft union into an all-grades industrial
union.[74] Nonetheless, the pledge the government had given the
union to lay off dilutees at the end of the war was honoured.
Many thousands of women were ejected from their jobs. High
unemployment among women resulted, made worse by the
slump of 1920.

The ASE became the Amalgamated Engineering Union in
1922, but still did not admit women members. Meanwhile
women's role in the engineering industry expanded fast in the
inter-war years, as they became the characteristic semi-skilled
assembly-line labour force in the industries producing the new
electrical consumer goods.[75] In the Second World War women
again replaced men in many engineering jobs, both unskilled
and skilled. This time the situation for the traditionalist men in
the union was past saving. Women were, with bad grace on the
part of many members, finally accepted into the union on 1
January 1943. The women's section had 139,000 members by
1944.[76]

Acceptance into the union, however, did not mean that those
women who had acceded to skilled jobs in the war were able to
consider them theirs for keeps. After the war, women were once

more expected to retire gracefully to domestic life, and for the most part they did so. Those who stayed were reduced to unskilled or semi-skilled work. Women found themselves addressed by an intense ideology of 'femininity' and 'domesticity'. The media, advertising, fiction and film all ludicrously reinforced gender differences, flying in the face of women's lived experiences. The ideology identified men with work and earning, women with home and caring. To associate women with technological competence now seemed as ridiculous as it had ever seemed.

Yet the situation of women was to change once again in the 1950s and 60s as the economic boom caused a demand for their labour and women themselves, even married women now, began to aspire to independence, work and careers in greater numbers than ever before. By the time the recession of the late 1970s hit the British economy, women had grown to be 42 per cent of the labour force.[77] Statements by Conservative ministers to the effect that women were expected to do the decent thing and return home, leaving the shrinking supply of jobs to men, were this time ignored by women. Women's consciousness had changed radically since the post-war period and this had influenced 'public opinion' more generally. Supportive legislation of the early 1970s had strengthened women's hand. This time they held on to work, though it was often part-time and low-paid. While the number of male employees in employment fell by 14 per cent between 1971 and 1983, the number of women rose by 7 per cent. The recession, and its handling by the government, has caused a dramatic increase in unemployment during the 1980s, but women have experienced it less acutely than men to date.[79]

The way out of the recession for British capital, fervently promoted by a monetarist government, is by shedding labour, reducing the wages of the remainder and investing in super-productive new electronic technology. In such a situation, with men objectively weakened in the labour market, employers indifferent to or even positive towards employing women, and women themselves showing a new confidence in their right to work, we might expect to see women entering technical training and skilled occupations in new technology in equal numbers with men. If, as will become apparent, this is not happening, it should alert us to ask more penetrating questions about how male dominance is renegotiated and how the sexual division of labour continues to be reproduced over time.

2. A wave of women: new technology and sexual divisions in clothing manufacture

Clothing manufacture is often called the Cinderella of British industry. It has a reputation for paying appallingly low wages, for being technologically conservative and reluctant to invest capital. In the late 1970s this Cinderella, besides, fell on painfully hard times. Like other sectors of UK manufacturing, the clothing industry was hit by the world-wide recession. In the four years 1978–81 the number of firms fell by 16 per cent in a rash of bankruptcies. People employed in the industry declined by 43 per cent in this period, on top of a steady decline in clothing employment since the relatively prosperous period that had followed the Second World War.[1]

These catastrophic figures are the net outcome of a complex series of adjustments within the industry as it struggled with its difficulties. One of those difficulties was competition from clothing imported from low-wage economies of the Third World. 'Import penetration', as it is known, increased from 39 per cent to 49 per cent in men's and boys' clothing and from 66 per cent to 76 per cent in women's and girls' clothing between 1979 and 1983.[2]

The restructuring of the industry is the sum of the different strategies with which firms have responded to this pressure. The industry's giants, vertically integrated corporations like Courtaulds, have been able to rationalize their way out of trouble, shedding their less profitable components and moving capital from one part of the world to another.[3] Some UK firms (like Burtons) have cut down on manufacturing in order to concentrate on retailing clothes purchased from other manufacturers. Other companies have closed factories in Britain and played the competition's own game, relocating in low-wage alternative sites. Meanwhile, the big retail chains, such as Marks & Spencer, have increased their influence upon the clothing industry by buying direct from manufacturers, bypassing wholesalers. Those clothing firms that could meet their rigorous standards took shelter under the wing of one of these demanding customers. It made them perilously dependent on one client, but it ensured a predictable and stable demand for their products.

The structure of the UK clothing industry has always been one of a mass of small firms at one end of the scale and a relatively few larger enterprises at the other. In 1981, 98 per cent of firms employed fewer than 100 people.[4] The restructuring process has increased this tendency to 'dualism' in the industry.[5] The last few years have seen the ascendance of a relatively small number of 'modernist' firms prepared to take the risk of committing themselves to big retail clients, if necessary supplementing their home production by commissioning off-shore. The other side of the coin is, of course, the informal and often 'sweated' production of the mass of small enterprises that still constitute the bulk of the industry.[6] Some of the modern sector firms sub-contract work to these small workshops, so allowing themselves flexibility and forcing the risks onto their suppliers. It is of course the employees of the latter, mainly women of ethnic minorities in the inner areas of big cities, who pay the final price in rock-bottom wages, poor conditions and frequent lay-offs.

The technological strategy

Some of the 'modernist' firms, struggling upwards out of crisis, have chosen a high-technology route. It is these that are of special interest here. Government had been urging, since the 1960s, that 'the industry should give a great deal more attention to the application of existing technology as well as the potential of new developments'.[7] An Economic Development Committee for the Industry was formed in 1975 and £20 million of government assistance was earmarked for firms willing to invest in advanced machinery and equipment.

There have always been technical obstacles to the automation of sewing. Engineers have found it impossible to invent a machine that can handle soft and floppy fabric without the intervention of a skilled hand. Besides, with female labour relatively cheap and abundant, there has been little incentive to employers to innovate. In place of advanced technology, therefore, the clothing manufacturers in the post-war period used work study techniques to rationalize and speed up the manual operations. Where once a single machinist would 'make through' a complete garment, today in the bigger firms a garment passes through the hands of 20 detail labourers, each contributing a seam or two at high speed. Machinists are paid using 'measured time' systems in conjunction with piece rates and incentives. Sewing machines are continually refined by their manufacturers, and for some operations, such as button-stitching and embroidery, machines can today be programmed in such a way that a single machinist can operate more than one. An actual replacement for the sewing machinist, however, is not yet in sight.

The work processes in cutting and pattern rooms had for a long while defied innovation too. However, in the 1970s the trade journals began to publish articles about an invention that stirred the imagination of the clothing manufacturer. It was born of a combination of developments in electronics and developments in the economy. Electronics had produced systems of computer-aided design and manufacture (CAD/CAM) for working metal in the engineering industry. These had now been adapted for use with cloth.[8] Meanwhile the recession had focused the attention of employers on productivity and had weakened the will of labour and trade unions to the point that their resistance to innovation need no longer be feared.

The earliest installation of computer-aided design (more strictly it was computer-aided *pattern processes*) in clothing manufacture in Britain was in 1972, in a menswear firm. By 1980 there were an estimated 20 systems in operation here, and by 1983 the number had grown to about 60. The users now range across the trade and include makers of every kind of clothing. The technology in question is unusual in one respect. Whereas many inventions are economical only for long production runs, this one favours short production runs of a multitude of rapidly obsolescent styles. As we shall see, its use has been to lift the manufacturer who uses it into a different kind of market and marketing operation.

There are a number of suitable CAD systems available here today, although none originates in Britain. The two that have acquired the greater part of the market are imported from the USA. The cost of such a system in 1984 was around £120,000. A computer-driven knife (the CAM component of the new technology package) cost approximately £300,000. The prices have fallen since the mid-1970s, bringing the systems progressively within the reach of smaller firms. Nonetheless, the acquisition of such technology is certainly the largest single investment in equipment that such firms are likely to have made, and its use means a shift from a manual method of working reminiscent of the eighteenth century to space-age technology, all in a single leap.

This technology was to enter workplaces patterned by a strong sexual division of labour. While dressmaking was always characterized by female seamstresses, tailoring was a male preserve, and it was tailoring that was the basis of the modern garment industry. The tailor with needle and thimble, the cutter with hand shears: these were men. When the sewing machine arrived, men continued to sew outerwear. In what was known as the 'set system', a craft machinist himself did the skilled phases of the job while supervising a bench of assistants on less skilled tasks. It was during the inter-war period that the craftsman tailor began to be swept out of the sewing rooms by factory methods employing women machinists at lower pay. By the 1950s there were few male machinists left, except for those of immigrant communities in traditional workshops.[9]

It was the cutting room that now became a refuge for skilled men in the industry. The cutter still required special know-how, and entry to his trade was controlled by means of apprenticeship and trade union organization. For a while, therefore, the cutter continued to retain a degree of craft control of his job, control that had been lost in the sewing rooms of the industry along with deskilling and feminization. The tradition was for the apprentice cutter to begin by assisting the craftsman, contributing his unskilled labour while gradually testing his ability with the shears on canvasses and linings. From that point on there was a steady progression open to the aspiring lad, through cutting, grading, marker-making and pattern construction. The pattern-maker, in which this on-the-job learning process culminated, was thought of as 'king of the trade'. A few craftsmen who progressed this far could even hope for jobs in line management in due course.

Manufacturers, however, in order to get round craft rules and expectations and the relatively high wages of the skilled men, had been continually seeking to rationalize and speed up the cutting room in the same way that they had Taylorized the sewing rooms. The unitary craft occupation was gradually broken down. Cutting was increasingly separated from pattern processes (sometimes being hived off to a separate site), and each was again separated into several distinct functions. As the work was deskilled and fragmented in this way, parts of it became physically lighter. The introduction of light-weight artificial fabrics in place of wool and cotton, the introduction of hoists and mechanized rollers to aid spreading of the cloth, and air flotation to ease the shifting of the spread cloth upon the tables, have enabled employers to replace the craftsman on these parts of the labour process by less skilled women at lower rates. The process began first in the ladieswear trade. The women appeared in the cutting room first as bundlers, tying up the piles of cut parts. Then they took on spreading, laying down the cloth. Now they are moving onto cutting itself. Some operate the mobile electric Eastman knife and a few are even found on the bandknife, considered to be more dangerous. They are gradually encroaching up what remain of the skill levels. Today, though accurate figures are not available, it seems that while men do retain for a moment longer in time a majority position in the cutting and pattern rooms, women have already gained an unshakeable foothold there and their presence is growing year by year.

Despite this fragmenting and deskilling process and the substitution of women for men, the expense of cutting, pattern-work and fabric continue to dominate clothing costs, representing around half the ex-factory cost of the garment. It is not surprising therefore that more forward-looking clothing manufacturers have been willing to consider the very considerable technological leap to CAD/CAM, with implications for cutting and pattern-room workers that we shall see.

Two clothing manufacturers

For purposes of examining this new technology and its effects on men and women workers in the industry I looked at one firm using the old manual processes and another using the new computer system. The two firms' strategies in both product and labour market and the two sets of labour processes they employed were clearly contrasted.

The 'old technology' firm, which I will call Steadywear Ltd., is an independent public company engaged in the design, manufacture and sale of women's outerwear on the home and export markets. Its products include ladies' coats, suits and casual clothes, dresses, blouses and co-ordinates. It is not one of the high-flying firms, but rather holds a respected position in the middle ground, with a company turnover in recent years of around £40 million and with about 4,000 employees, mainly women machinists. Steadywear Ltd. used to favour selling through its own chain of high street boutiques. As department and chain stores have threatened the viability of small shops, Steadywear has shifted its marketing strategy to 'concession selling', renting space in big department stores in which to sell clothing under its own brand name. The company also turned to purchasing some of its manufacturing capacity in the Far East. By such techniques Steadywear has survived the recession well and doubled its profits in 1983, the year of my study. This type of operation, however, was considered by observers of the industry to be at particular risk. 'For the middle range producers the prospects for the next few years still remain far from rosy,' wrote the experts in one industry sector overview.[10]

When I first visited Steadywear, in 1982, management were sceptical about CAD/CAM. Two years later they were actively researching the market with a view to converting to CAD. Fortunately for my purposes I was able to see the old manual techniques still in use there – and these are described below.

The second firm, which made the computer technology decision as early as 1978, I will call Newstyle Ltd. It is a large, buoyant clothing manufacturer somewhat larger than Steadywear Ltd., operating on a score of different sites. Rapid growth and expansion had occurred in Newstyle Ltd. over a decade or more and although profitability was set back for some years in the late 1970s the company quickly rallied. Employment grew steadily, increasing to five times the original number in the ten years to 1983. Turnover increased by 200 per cent in the four years to 1982. Profits and profit margins, unlike those of many firms in the industry, improved annually in the three years to 1983, the year of my study.

The strategy chosen by Newstyle Ltd. for handling the economic crisis and pressure on the UK clothing industry was a daring one. It did not follow other manufacturers out to the Third World, but instead actually increased its manufacturing capacity in Britain. It took on more designers when other firms were laying them off. It went steadily up-market in style and to some extent in price so as to enter a product market in which it was not in direct competition with low-wage countries. Above all, it linked itself firmly to one very large retail chain in order to achieve a stable and predictable demand for its product.

New technology in the cutting and pattern rooms was, for Newstyle, part of this positive response to an adverse environment. Only computer-aided pattern-making, grading and lay-making could give the firm the quick turn-around of new styles. Only the computer-driven cutter could give it the throughput of cut work to keep busy the growing number of machinists.

Newstyle Ltd. has a reputation for 'progressive' leadership, always being quick to take up new ideas. It is also known for promoting its managers young, paying relatively well and in turn expecting high performance from all its employees, from the management team to the sewing machinists. Among its repertoire of personnel policies is the idea of the 'quality circle', a co-optive process pioneered in Japanese industry whereby the workers, under management not trade union tutelage, participate in the monitoring and achievement of quality output. Quality circles have been urged on the clothing industry in recent years by the Clothing and Allied Products Industry Training Board (CAPITB), which has promoted instruction in the method. But its workers say of the firm, 'It's a decent employer compared with other factories.' 'It's classed as somewhere to get on.'

Newstyle's design and cutting functions are centralized on one site, one of the largest centres of its kind in Europe. It acquired its CAD system and its first computerized knife in the late 1970s. Around £1 million was invested in CAD/CAM but the company invested approximately £10 million in ten years in a wide range of new technologies, revolutionizing materials handling and computerizing inventories and work in progress.

We should now compare the nature of employment, the old and new technologies and the labour processes they give rise to in these two firms. I will concentrate mainly on the initial processes of pattern work, giving less emphasis to cloth cutting. It is necessary however to summarize the implications of technological change in cloth cutting since the effects of CAD and CAM are so closely related.

A deft hand and a keen eye

The work process and the equipment in use at Steadywear Ltd., though it had to some extent been rationalized and subjected to a division of labour, would not have been out of place in a pre-war clothing factory.

The three main pattern-room occupations are those of pattern-maker, grader and lay-maker, and the flow of work passes from one to another in this order. The work arrives with the pattern-maker in the shape of a paper pattern produced by the designer for a new style. It is much like the pattern that an amateur dressmaker might buy in a shop, in an envelope with a sketch of the garment on the outside. The pattern-maker takes this original, which is often somewhat idealized, and turns it into a working pattern for a saleable garment, reflecting the proportions of ordinary mortals. Retained in the pattern room are several score of master patterns or 'blocks' cut out in card, representing the basic standard dimensions and shapes of every likely *type* of garment: 'lady's blouse with set-in sleeve', 'lady's blouse with raglan sleeve'. The pattern-maker sets about adapting the designer's pattern to accord with the requirements of the block yet without losing the special character of the new style. She or he works at a long flat table, using rulers, set square, pencil, eraser, scissors. First a length of squared paper is dispensed from a roll. The card pieces of the block are placed one at a time on the drawing paper. And working with a considerable degree of initiative, calling on both manual deftness and long experience of garments, the pattern-maker creates each new pattern piece on the paper, taking account of every working detail: gathers, darts, seams and so on. All the pattern pieces must be strictly compatible with each other so as to build up into the finished garment.

The pattern-maker's job, it will be clear, involves artistic flair and manual technique. It also requires supreme orderliness: 'You can't be too meticulous.' It entails a good deal of first-hand contact and verbal negotiation with others.

If, after discussion with the client firm, orders are now placed for the new style, the patterns must be produced in a range of sizes. A size difference is not uniform in all dimensions for all parts, since the human body gains size differentially at hip, waist, bust and in height. These variations are formalized in 'grading rules'. Every block has a 'grade rule table'. Each table has a set of 'grade rules' relating to many 'grade points' around each pattern piece. These rules specify just how many millimetres each step in size must involve. The data are recorded on charts. A competent grader, however, knows them by heart from long experience and may sometimes indeed 'bend the rules', using discretion, acting on hunch.

The method of grading favoured at Steadywear is 'stack grading'. If seven sizes have to be produced from one sample size, the grader will take seven pieces of thin card and lay them one on the other, lining them up to a single straight edge. Starting fom this edge the grader lays out the master pattern piece on top and steps the other pieces out from the edge by the required number of millimetres. She or he draws round the outline of the further side of the pattern piece, tracing from the original sample size. Stapling the card pieces together to hold them steady, the grader then cuts through all of them together, using scissors. The pieces are than unstapled and the process repeated for the second dimension of the pattern piece. The end product is seven pattern pieces, each the appropriate amount larger or smaller than the one adjacent.

An experienced grader usually starts with the back of the garment, working through adjoining pieces, keeping a mental picture of the increments as they are made, conceptualizing the garment size structure as a coherent whole. The lining and interfacing pieces are graded last of all. The curves, finally, are smoothed out by freehand with a pencil and scissors. Each pattern piece must be stamped with its size, style number and part number. Grain lines must be indicated, seam lines and darts too. As the grader completes these tasks she or he groups the pattern pieces for each size and hangs them up with string. When the set is complete a final check must be made against the original pattern. A grading job on one style may take anything from half a day to a whole day to complete.

Next to the pattern-maker, the grader is considered the most skilled of the pattern- and cutting-room employees. Most graders have been lay-makers and before that cutters. Though the grade rules could be taught and learned in a matter of hours, the job as a whole is one that allows a continual improvement and it takes some years before a hand grader is considered to be doing his or her best work. Apart from deftness and 'eye', and an ability to calculate, a particular character and approach to work are required in the grader:

I think accuracy is very important. Accuracy. And I suppose, keenness. You've got to be keen, sharp, got to keep your wits about you. There's more to it than meets the eye, really. You can make a lot of mistakes and if you do make mistakes you can cause a lot of trouble.

The next step in the pattern process is lay-making, determining the optimum position of the pattern pieces along the cloth prior to cutting. Once the cutter did this himself. Now a paper marker, prefiguring the lay, is prepared to guide the cutters. The tools and materials of the traditional lay-maker are rolls of heat-seal paper and carbon paper, pencils, rubbers, scissors, chalk, shears, tracing wheel, metre stick and T-square. She or he works at a long flat surface, rolling out a number of lengths of the drawing paper, interleaved with carbon, which represents the length of the cloth to which the lay is to be planned. The laying-in is a matter of dealing with certain constraining variables: the grain direction, width and length of the cloth, its nap or pattern. With all these variables in mind the lay-maker plans the lay, beginning with the bigger pattern pieces – skirt or back, – laying the pieces of card onto the paper marker jig-saw style, and taking care to see that the direction lines on the pattern are parallel to the edge of the marker and thus to the warp of the cloth. Small pieces are fitted into the spaces between the larger pieces. There is no accurate measure of cloth utilization, but the lay-maker can tell by eye whether the lay is economical or wasteful, in or out of cost. Frequently the lay needs bettering and the lay-maker must remove all the pattern pieces and start over again. Trial lays must be memorized while an attempt is made to improve on them.

Lay-makers feel their job to be creative and interesting. Each style represents a new problem to be solved and there is scope for continual improvement in performance. The occupation demands knowledge and experience and also a person with an orderly mind who pays close attention to the work:

> You've got to be thinking all the time, making sure you are marking in the right sizes, that they are going the right way, at the right angles. You have angles marked on the patterns that you must adhere to, or else, for instance, the sleeves won't fit right. You must be checking and re-checking every bit of the time as you are marking in.

Like the grader and pattern-maker, the lay-maker has a long

job cycle of several hours. All these personnel are relatively free to move about the room, which they share with the cutters, and they spend some of their time discussing the job, consulting and fact-finding.

The cutting process, too, is relatively traditional at Steadywear Ltd. The only division of labour is that between those who cut the cloth and those who iron on the adhesive interfacing. First the cloth is spread and built up into layers, dispensed from bales mounted on rollers. The paper marker is applied to the top of the pile of cloth. Then the main sections are cut out with a hand-held electric shear, the Eastman knife. The more detailed cutting is passed over to the operator of the bandknife. Bundling up the cut parts for removal to the sewing room is also part of the cutter's job here.

The pattern and cutting rooms at Steadywear thus work more or less as a team, and pressure comes from the responsibility of playing an adequate part in that team rather than directly from supervision. There are many elements of the old craft still left in these manual processes. But there is one big difference: the fragmentation of the tasks has allowed women to be introduced into both areas. There is one woman pattern-maker: she would not have been there had the job today required a progression up from the cutting-room floor. There was one woman trainee grader and one woman lay-maker. In the cutting room the penetration of women had gone further. All the pressers were female and one-third of the 27 cutters were female. Management of all these processes was male. Men alone operated the bandknife. The maintenance engineers who kept the simple equipment running were also male.

Cleverness in the computer

At Newstyle Ltd. computerization had reinforced this trend towards employment of women in pattern-room work. While management of the unit remained male, two supervisory posts were filled by women, and there were seven women pattern technicians (as pattern-makers were now called), three female lay-makers and one woman grader. The only men were one ex-manual grader and a younger 'utility man', learning the system overview.

The area containing the new computerized pattern equipment is in sharp contrast with the well-worn workaday environment at Steadywear Ltd. Behind glass and closed doors, designed to keep out dust, the personnel involved in pattern work looked at first approach rather like fish in a bowl.

At Newstyle, while grading and lay-making are performed by computer, the firm had not yet gone over to computerized pattern construction. Their system however was 'wired for' PDS, as it is known, and they have since embarked on it. The PDS labour process I describe here, observed elsewhere, is that which is now in use at Newstyle too.

We have seen that the basis of pattern work is the 'block', the master for each type of garment commonly produced by the firm. All new styles must be compatible with the proportions of an appropriate block. In a CAD system these blocks have been digitized. That is to say, the size and shape of each part have been converted into computer language and the blocks are now held in the computer memory. No more cardboard pieces hang in the store. When the pattern technician begins work on a new style, therefore, instead of getting out the pieces she or he now taps the style number of the job onto the keyboard of the computer terminal (the 'scope' as it is called) and brings it to the screen. On screen now appears, among other information, a list, in words, of the pattern parts in the block. Using an electronic tablet and stylus (a 'light pen') she points to the part she wants, say 'skirt front', and this promptly appears before her eyes, in miniature outline, on the screen. Referring to the designer's original, she now makes the required adaptations to the block. To do so she uses the stylus to indicate the position and the keyboard to specify the function to be performed and the amounts in millimetres she wishes to add or take away. In this way she can 'tell' the computer to perform certain functions: to split the part in two at a certain point and add in seam allowances either side of the cut; to shorten or lengthen a skirt panel; exaggerate a flare; insert fabric into this position or that to accommodate gathers and pleats. Immediately, the altered shape is visible again on screen. The operator can see the alterations she has 'made', change her mind, or move on to the next part.

The final set of pattern parts, once made to the technician's satisfaction, is input to the computer's memory. The set can also be produced as a complete master pattern, printed on paper by a computer-driven plotter. Or it may be automatically cut out in card by a laser-cutter, also directly activated by computer. The pattern, either way, is absolutely dimensionally accurate and quickly available for the cutting and sewing of sample garments.

Once the style is agreed and ordered, a full range of sizes is needed. In a firm using PDS, it will be evident that there is no grading job, as such, to do. The grader's craft knowledge has been given to the computer ('they pick the brains of the senior grader') and is immortalized in its electronic memory. Personally, he (it was usually a he) is no longer required. The computer memory contains the grade-rule tables and the grade rules. While making her sample pattern, the technician has already given the computer all the information it needs concerning the new pattern pieces and their grade points. Applying the rules, the computer can now at a single command very rapidly produce on screen a set of graded sizes for each pattern part, one superimposed on the other in a 'nest', or one at a time. These can quickly be checked by eye for accuracy, and then promptly drawn out on paper by an automatic plotter.

At Newstyle, however, when PDS had not yet been introduced, the job of grader did still exist in an attenuated form. All that was left for the surviving grader to do was 'digitizing': that is, she or he had simply to tell the computer of the shape of each pattern piece and inform it where to apply its grade rules. This is carried on at an angled board onto which the pattern pieces are positioned one at a time. Using a cursor equipped with button controls, the grader moves it around the outline of the cardboard piece, informing the computer of the co-ordinates of each grade point together with the position of notches for darts and sufficient intermediate points around the piece to enable the computer to record and reproduce an accurate representation of the pattern part. Once digitizing is complete, the computer performs all the calculations necessary to apply the grade rules to the pattern.

The result of the grader's work is then safely tucked away in the computer memory ready for lay-making. There are two methods of lay-making by computer: interactive and automatic. At Newstyle and in other mass-production situations the lay-maker still uses an interactive routine. She sits at a computer terminal and makes certain computer-assisted decisions concerning the lay. First she inputs on the keyboard the style number, calling up onto the scope the details of the job to be handled. This might involve, say, all the pattern parts for a ladies' nightdress in four sizes. At the top of the screen appears a list of all the pattern parts to be accommodated in the lay: size 10, back, yoke, sleeve, etc. The operator keys in the width of the material that she knows the lay must fit, and lines appear on the screen simulating the spread of cloth. Using tablet and stylus the operator selects each pattern part in turn. One at a time they appear as images on the screen. Flipping, rotating, lifting them at will, she 'positions' each in turn within the imaginary length of cloth. The outline pieces nudge and bump each other but the computer routine does not allow them to overlap. It eliminates all unnecessary space between. It ensures that the operator does not abuse certain constraints such as grain lines, nap or pattern in printed fabrics. The computer informs the operator, by means of a figure appearing on the screen, of precisely the length of cloth used in the lay and the percentage of wastage. If she is not satisfied she can hold that solution in the computer-memory while attempting another laying-in. When an optimum lay has been achieved, she stores it in the computer memory as her final choice, scrapping earlier solutions. A plotter is now activated which prints out a paper marker – full size or one-fifth miniature. More significantly, it can also, as it does at Newstyle, produce a magnetic tape to drive the off-line automated knife in the cutting room.

The interactive use of the lay-making program as described above can gradually lead to automatic use. As markers are constructed this way interactively, the computer builds up a set of marking rules. It remembers the moves made by the operator as she optimizes each lay. When sufficient rules have been established for varying styles, size combinations and material widths, the computer can apply these to new lays without operator involvement. Her brains too have been effectively picked. The computer now knows the best solution to each problem without further help. In the gentleman's made-to-measure trade it is now possible to go from the customer's measurements, tapped into a computer terminal by the shop assistant, direct to a personalized pattern, automatic lay and cut, without human intervention.

It will be clear from this description that so long as the lay-maker is a person, working interactively with the machine, some experience and 'eye' still helps in doing the job well. Nonetheless, the lay-makers at Newstyle have been imported from the cutting-room floor and trained on the job in a matter of weeks. Lay-making is considered the least skill-demanding of the three main tasks of the new-technology pattern room.

Lay-making this way is such a quick and easy process that cost estimates can be produced and revised many times in the course of seeing a new style into production. In addition, the new systems are equipped with programs that enable 'cut planning', the balancing of such variables as orders, priorities, styles, size ratios, marker and cutting table length, depth of ply and type of fabric, to determine the most cost-effective sequence of work for the cutting and pattern rooms.

Where CAD is accompanied by CAM, as at Newstyle Ltd., the cutting room is also transformed. Here, from a vast high-ceilinged space, is produced the cut work to serve 20 sewing factories. New technology has been accompanied by rationalization of materials handling and movement. A team of young male labourers lift the heavy rolls of cloth onto the spreaders. A team of girls, many just out of school, ride the big mechanized spreading machines up and down the tables, laying down the lengths of cloth, guided by electronic controls. The piled-up lengths, ready for cutting, are transported across and along the room on motorized tables. In this way the cloth can move to the automated cutters where once the team of human cutters would have come to the cloth.

Newstyle Ltd. has a pair of computer-driven knives, each of which can travel along a gantry to serve more than one table. The cutter is essentially a motorized and automated cutting head, carried on a conveyor system up, down and across the cutting table. It bears a reciprocating blade capable of slicing its way through a ten-metre length of 200 layers of cloth in a matter of five or six minutes. It is activated by the magnetic tape produced in the CAD system and simply follows the predetermined path of the lay. The paper marker is now technically redundant. The cutter is no longer a manual worker but a machine minder. She or he merely feeds in the magtape from the pattern room, checks the settings of the cutting head and the accuracy of the spread of cloth, positions the knife at its start point and thereafter switches on and watches the machine run. Newstyle find men and women equally suitable for this occupation and the manufacturer's agent reports that the sexes are used interchangeably by most firms operating such cutters.

Although unskilled women bundlers still have to follow behind the knife, removing the cut work for despatch to the sewing units, there is less bustle and movement than there was before automation. 'People used to float about more. Move from table to table to do things. It were a big throng of us, like,' said a former cutter. 'Now it's things that move, not people.' By 'moving things' in this way, Newstyle have doubled output from the cutting room. Forty per cent more sewing machinists are kept supplied. A job that once took three hours and a team of four Eastman and bandknife operators can now be done in eight minutes by one machine and a single minder. That represents 72 times the original output per head.

The high-technology decision

It has been estimated that CAD/CAM in clothing has resulted in a capital intensity (capital invested per employee) 100 times that of the sewing units.[11] Would such a risk pay off for Newstyle? Return on capital invested dropped sharply to 4.78

per cent during 1978, but quickly picked up and was a healthy 20 per cent by 1983. How was this achieved?

First, there was some labour saving. A large number (exact figures are not revealed) of cutting-room personnel were redeployed, taken up by growth elsewhere in the firm or underemployed, awaiting natural wastage. In the pattern room, however, the number of personnel increased during the late 1970s and did not fall with the introduction of CAD. The gain here was achieved by increased output and productivity. A lay-maker can produce 50 markers a shift in place of two or three. Intensification of work is, besides, still in its early days. Shift work has begun, a morning and evening shift for better utilization of equipment. And there were, at the time of my visits, plans to double the installation of computer pattern equipment without increasing staffing.

It is a peculiarity of this particular kind of technology, however, that labour saving is not the main advantage either promoted by those who sell it or cited by those who buy it. The technology promises a set of related gains, among which the consideration of the wage bill plays a part but does not dominate. One widely recognized advantage of CAD/CAM is enhanced control: control of both employees and of materials. 'It puts management in the driving seat,' one senior manager told me. For instance, it is possible to check the computer record and retrace every step in the production of pattern, lay and cut to detect the source of an error. Employees' time-keeping and output can be monitored. The computer reduces the employer's dependence on his employee's memory and co-operation. The average cutter could remember perhaps nine different ways of laying out the pattern parts of a suit. The computer may have nine thousand possible solutions within its memory, and the number is continually expanding. These are known as 'learning' systems. The employer is delighted to shake off his dependence, as one Newstyle manager put it, upon 'the time-served man who thinks he is a cut above the rest' and to operate instead with a flexible, semi-skilled team, responsive to management demands.

As to cloth, the computer affords an accurate measure of

fabric utilization on every job and is speedy enough to allow for several attempts to minimize wastage on any one marker. More generally, computerization of stock files and the flow of work in progress allows control of material throughout production. Jobs can be costed accurately and easily many times in the course of producing samples and size trials. The installation of new systems is often accompanied by centralization of cutting and pattern rooms and this too aids control of labour and material. Space saving is another factor in management's investment decision. The huge tables used for pattern- and marker-making by hand are no longer needed, and the stores where thousands of card patterns used to hang contrast dramatically with the few shelves required for computer discs. Quality and accuracy are important considerations. The human factor, the small errors in cutting and pattern-making that used to cause havoc in the sewing room, can largely be eliminated by the computer.

Perhaps more than anything else, managers benefit from the speed and flexibility introduced by the new systems. A rapid response to customer demand is particularly important for firms competing for contracts from the large chain stores. Now that a new style can go from sketch to marker in a matter of hours instead of weeks, Newstyle is able to keep up a highly interactive and responsive relationship with its major client, producing a dozen new styles for its consideration in place of one, and making design changes to satisfy their merest whim.

Newstyle are not alone among British clothing firms in using the new technology to change the nature of the goods produced and the market in which they operate. The strength of Third World manufacturing lies in cheap labour; its weakness in its distance from European markets and trends. Large-scale British manufacturers of this kind cannot hope to compete effectively at the low-cost, low-quality end of the clothing market. What the go-ahead firms have done therefore is to push on up market, aiming to generate a demand for clothing with a higher value-added content in the form of garments employing two or more kinds of fabric, difficult materials like jersey, or styles that have interesting fashion features such as embroidery or Lady-Di frills, appealing to impulse purchases by the customer. 'It may seem very silly', said one manager at Newstyle, 'but when things are a little bit depressed and housewives, you know, are feeling low, the thing that probably cheers them up a little bit is either a new hair-do or a new garment. A dress perhaps. So we thought if the price was right and if the styling and quality attracted her – this was the philosophy.'

The result is not necessarily an increase in the quantity of garments issuing from the factories, but an increase in the number of different styles and adaptations of styles passing through the pattern room in relation to final output. There are more trials, production runs are shorter, style-life is shorter. This strategy for dealing with the recession and with competition from foreign imports is perfectly served by the CAD technology.

One thing is certain. CAD/CAM is only just beginning what will be a full-scale penetration of a pared-down modern sector of the clothing industry in Britain in coming decades. The employers know it. It's move out (abroad) or move on (to new technology). 'If you want to be here in ten years' time you have to bring the computer in, basically.' And the existing craft worker accepts it as a 'least worst' outcome. 'Oh yes. It's 1983 and you can't stop still. It's got to come. Got to.' 'I don't think my fear is the machinery so much as Hong Kong.'

The skill equation

For Newstyle's ownership the investment in new technology has paid off. For Newstyle employees the outcome is more contradictory. On the plus side, those who are still there have by definition kept their jobs. But those jobs cannot be seen apart from the jobs lost in the restructuring of the industry as a whole: technology cannot be held entirely unaccountable for a loss of nearly 200,000 jobs in four years. Even for those who remain, the effect in high technology firms has been ambiguous. The ambiguity lies in the vexed question of skill, which in turn is related to a person's prospects and enjoyment in the job.

We've seen that the most extreme effect has been in made-to-measure menswear, where the skills of the craft tailor and cutter were found at their peak. 'If you were to talk to people in our factory,' said the manager of one such firm, 'they would say that they had more routine and boring jobs now than they had five or ten years ago.' In mass-production situations, however, typically in ladies' and children's wear firms such as Newstyle, some competence does continue for the moment to be asked of the operators of the CAD system. Here, as in other industries, the introduction of the computer has had a contradictory effect and one which arouses a good deal of confusion in the workers themselves.

Newstyle's system manager insists that there has been an increase in the skill demanded in the work that he oversees. He would point out, with good reason, that the pattern technician, working on computer, still needs prior training, still has to make decisions to know what is a good pattern and what is not. One skilled grader is still required to give the computer its rules. Even the operative grader needs a technique of a kind. 'It takes something away, yes,' said one, 'but it gives you skill in computers.' And a scope operator, making lays, said, 'They think, "Oh, it's computers, it's dead easy". But it isn't. You have still got to look. It's like a jigsaw, lay-making. Some can spot it, some can't: that will fit there. You have still got to sit at that screen and think how to put the pieces in. You can't just think, "Oh, that will be all right, sod it." Because if you do, you will go out of cost. You are looking to better your lay all the time.'

Neither grading nor lay-making, and least of all pattern construction, is a job for a thoughtless person. You still need 'someone who concentrates, someone who actually likes doing the job. Someone who's bright. Not specially intelligent. You just have to have a bit of *content* to you, really.' Another scope operator put the skill factor this way: 'I feel quite proud when I have succeeded in fitting things in, making a good marker. I think to myself, I don't think anyone else could have done it better than that. In fact, I know more often than not that no one could better my lays. So I do feel quite proud of myself doing it.'

The pattern process can be a bottleneck in clothing production and new technologies in their early days are fallible: they need continual back-up by human skills: 'We are more important than we've ever been.' In fact, operators at Newstyle complained of how often the system went wrong. Besides, since the worker to some extent identifies with the quality of the product (this was a characteristic of craft but not only of craft), she or he finds a degree of satisfaction and takes personal pride in the cleverness of the machine. 'You could say there is more skill to it because the computer gives you feed-back on just how good a job you have done.' Better patterns, more accurate cutting redounds to the worker's credit. 'It saves a heck of a lot of time and it improves the actual standard of your work.'

As with all craft occupations, the old skills were undoubtedly over-rated and mythologized. They were used as a trade union strategem in defence of labour and the wage. They were also used as a male strategem in the relative depreciation of women and women's work. The struggle to maintain the male pay differential has been a characteristic of this, as of other skilled crafts.[12] Women's skills in clothing manufacture, particularly sewing, have as a consequence been grossly underestimated and under-rewarded. It is true that women have entered sewing rooms and cutting rooms concurrently with fragmentation and speed-up, yet the jobs remaining require more skill than is recognized or paid for. The starting point, the benchmark, in measuring skill and deskilling has therefore to be assessed with a little scepticism. And we should be aware that new jobs may be slandered and derogated simply because women are seen to do them.

Is the system manager right, then, in his assessment of the skill equation? A craftsman would reject it. Skilling and deskilling is a subjective matter and the way each is experienced depends in part on the sex of the person in question. If some women would say they had gained a skill and many men would say they had been robbed of one, that would not be surprising. They have come from different places. From the point of view of the craftsman's experience, the old knack and deftness with pencil and paper, the ability to calculate and visualize, the 'feel' for cloth, the 'eye' for a line, all that has gone. The computer now contributes the cleverness and 'the job is deskilled because you haven't been involved in what has gone into making *it* work.' Besides, the work neither requires nor does it get the prolonged training the craftsman had, training which teaches not one but many detailed competences in a unitary craft and which, most importantly, gives an overview of the whole production process. 'We used to be trained to know *why* you did a certain thing,' I was told. 'One of the problems of modernization is that people are trained to do a specific job and people don't see the whole process any more.'

These are ways the labour process itself reveals a tangible loss in skill. There are, though, historic criteria, that must be taken into account too. Skill is partly a political phenomenon.[13] The craftsman used the concept of skill to reinforce craft control, forcing the employer to leave much in the hands of his skilled workforce. The union governed induction to the trade and access to work. In these senses, too, the jobs are deskilled. The garment workers' union, the National Union of Tailors and Garment Workers, has been deeply affected by the recession and the decline of the clothing industry in Britain. Chastened by closures, it has been in no position to resist any measure that seemed likely to keep firms afloat.[14] Describing the balance of class forces in his world, a trade unionist said, 'In recent years it's been five per cent take it or leave it', and the NUTGW has reluctantly taken it. As a result, there are few new-technology house agreements of the kind that can be seen, for instance, in the printing industry, where unions accede to new technology in exchange for pay increases and shorter hours. At most there is a 'no redundancy' agreement in force. Even at Newstyle where there is a post-entry closed shop the union can do little more than act as social worker for its members, otherwise flying along in the wake of management initiatives.

One measure of the loss of craft control is the degree of pressure to which workers are obliged to submit in their labour process. Essentially, the shift to computerization is a shift away from a worker-controlled pace of work. As one article in the trade press put it: 'numerous changes are likely to be required in management personnel and scheduling practices to adapt properly to an environment in which the most important variable becomes machine utilization and "up-time", instead of worker efficiency.'[15]

There is not, in the pattern room, the relentless pressure of piecework payment that rules in the sewing units. But this very fact may lead managements to achieve throughput by other means. Newstyle is leading other firms in the clothing industry in breaking with tradition to introduce shiftwork. Management consultants have been urging this for some time. In other ways, too, many of those I talked with in the computer area were aware of increasing pressure. The new pattern-room jobs may appear like office work, but they are experienced as factory work. It is not the kind of job in which you are allowed to spend ten minutes in the toilet or knock off for an extra cup of coffee when you feel like it. There is a 15 minute break for tea and half an hour for lunch in the course of an eight-hour shift. One male grader described his former manual job in a menswear factory, where he worked in a room with 1,000 other employees and was able to call across the tables, or walk here and there for a chat. 'Going to work, with people, that was the thing, rather than working.' He contrasted this with his present work at Newstyle in a small secluded computer room, where the operators sit at their scopes back to back, more cut off than before from each other and from the rest of the world. 'Basically, it's a fairly boring job, it's very similiar, you do the same thing every day. You don't get to meet anyone. It's just you and your computer and that's it.' Sociability is ruled out in the interests of throughput.

'The system produces so much more than we ever could, but the orders keep growing to match' was the feeling inside the firm. And an outsider commented, 'The atmosphere there is different. To me it's always panic stations. This is going on and that's going on, they are expanding all the time. But it's not just there. Everywhere they seem to want more and more out of the computerized system. Once it is in, they don't seem to compare it with the speed they were doing things before. They want to increase the pace all the time. It is lightning fast compared with how it was, but it is still too slow for them today.'

There has, then, been substantial deskilling, and any residual doubt is dispelled by a reading of the intentions of both engineering firms and clothing firms clearly expressed in articles in the trade press.[16] They gloat openly about the power new technology gives the clothing manufacturer to shake free of the skilled worker, to move from human to machine control. And the deskilling we have seen to date is only the start. There will be a steady attrition of many of the semi-skilled operator jobs and a gain in a very few hyper-skilled occupations. Newstyle is only at a half-way station between the craft tradition and the logical outcome of computerization. Ultimately we may see the complete reunification of all the fragmented tasks in very much more clever and comprehensive computer programs. There will still have to be a person, probably the designer, who 'talks to the machine', designs in 3D and full colour on the scope, feeds the computer its parameters and nudges it through its routines. This will be a skill-demanding and interesting occupation but it will be one surviving among many dead and gone.

Sexual divisions in a class struggle

To this point we have focused on the struggle between clothing employers and clothing workers over skill. But it will have been clear that something strange has been happening within this class context. During the last half-century the industry has been undergoing a sex change. A slow but perceptible surge of women, entering by the sewing-room door, has been seeping across the cutting room and is now washing into pattern-room jobs. What precisely is the nature of the change in the relationship of men and of women, seen as distinct groups, to the production technology and to each other?

As cutting-room processes in the bigger firms have been routinized and fragmented concurrently with the entry of women, a rupture has occurred in the skill progression that used to ensure a promotion path for men and a steady supply of reliable craftsmen and supervisors for the employer. Simultaneously with this interruption in normal recruitment, the pattern rooms have begun to be staffed in part from an alternative source: from colleges, where students qualify by means of the exams of the City and Guilds of London Institute or the Business and Technical Education Council. These courses are primarily oriented to fashion and design rather than to production and technology. Managers in the industry complain bitterly that they turn out impractical kinds of people, full of fancy ideas. 'They think they know it all', 'they come in here expecting top money', but they are not what the manager expects or desires. The rub of course is that they are female. These colleges attract a much higher proportion of young women than of young men. On qualifying, they compete for the relatively scarce design jobs and many finish up instead in the less prestigious occupations of the pattern room for which some of them do undoubtedly feel themselves overqualified. The upshot is, however, that the feminization of the pattern room is to some extent independent of the progress of women into the cutting room. New technology pattern rooms in the immediate future are therefore likely to be a mix of men and women coming up from the cutting room floor and new entrants, mainly women, some of whom will come from college courses. This flux is producing in both pattern and cutting rooms an unusual situation for British industry, one which seems to run counter to the persistent sexual segregation that, as we saw in Chapter 1, characterizes employment in Britain. Men and women are to be found working side by side in similar jobs.

The evidence, however, is that we are watching a moment of transition. The jobs are certainly destined to become entirely female. My postal survey of clothing firms using CAD showed that even though sex-*typing* of the jobs was in confusion, sex-*segregation* was continuing. Most firms were actually operating single-sex departments or teams. Thus, in pattern making, while four firms had mixed-sex teams, seven had all-male teams and four had all female-teams. In grading, one had a mixed team while eight had all-male and three all-female teams. In lay-making, two firms had mixed teams, while eight reported all-male and two reported all-female teams. Even within mixed teams, a more detailed enquiry revealed an arrangement, often conceived as temporary, whereby women were doing one kind of detail task and men another. Women might be cutting by Eastman knife, men by bandknife. Women might be working on the scopes, men operating the plotters, but both of these might be termed 'lay-makers'. Fragmentation of the jobs helps the tricky process of sex change.

A number of factors may slow down the trend towards women. One is the beginning of a tendency to night-shift working. Another is the social conscience that some (male) employers feel today about the plight of unemployed lads. Besides, clothing is, ironically, a largely female industry of misogynist male employers, solidly patriarchal in the upper echelons. The decline in the proportion of male recruits at shop-floor level is leading some managers to worry about securing a proper male progression to management.

On balance, however, the advantage for the employer lies in sex segregation. It is easier to evade the Equal Pay legislation if women work in jobs that cannot be compared to men's. The advantage also lies in employing women in as many occupations as possible. Women are held to put less pressure on the wage than men. Though they constitute 90 per cent of the membership of the NUTGW and a high proportion of its shop stewards, women are poorly represented at influential levels in the union, holding only three out of 38 officer posts. Perhaps because of this the union has tended to give priority to the interests of skilled, i.e. male, workers and has pursued a policy of maintaining formal pay differentials.[17] In the past, men have actively organized to keep women out of the trade.[18] It is not surprising therefore that as women have entered cutting- and pattern-room jobs, relative earnings in those jobs have slipped. The men have been hoist with their own bad practices and both men and women have suffered. Employers have been the ones to gain.

A second advantage to the employer of women lies in the fact that, through the unpaid and unrecognized apprenticeship of a domesticated girlhood, a woman has acquired qualities which the employer can set to profitable work. She is an excellent seamstress, an accurate cutter and has the diligence and niftiness that makes for a good keyboard or scope operator. At Newstyle, the system manager found that women learned the new job more quickly than men. More women stick at their jobs these days, but employers can sometimes reap an advantage from the fact that many women do leave before they climb up off trainee rates of pay, to be replaced by other cheap school-leavers. Employers can use women's particular characteristics without having to recognize women's special needs. Neither Steadywear nor Newstyle had employment policies geared to helping women cope with work and home. Neither favoured part-time working, and neither were specially tolerant of compassionate leave or had a day nursery. Among these women, high unemployment allows employers to be choosy. A shop steward said, 'They think because there is so many unemployed they can reasonably do what they want. They don't come straight out and say that. But they think "We'll pick the cream", you know. But it's a bit sorry for them as en't the cream.'

The employers of course explain the feminization of the industry by a shortage of skilled craftsmen. 'The people we are getting into the trade,' said a Steadywear manager, 'are neither as efficient nor as intelligent as the ones who retire.' And 'you are not getting people coming into the trade now with the skills we require, and the ones that do have the skills are so expensive, obviously it must be more viable to put in a computer'. The male craft cutter, however, knows full well that the jobs have been pulled from beneath his feet. The product has changed. He made good suits, and today he can't compete with women running up jeans and bomber jackets. Factories in his area have closed. Work has moved to underdeveloped countries. At home the industry has shifted its geographical location, abandoning its traditional labour communities. In short, the skills are still there, or could be, but industrialists are not prepared to pay for them.

There is no doubt also a push from women. Women acquire

new job openings through the new division of labour and the new technology. They may not be well paid, but any job is a gain when other occupations are in decline and when many women are breadwinners for families in which the man is absent or unemployed. For women the clothing industry has compensations. 'You are interested in the garments. You like to see the new styles. You know what you would buy.' The more routinized work of pattern rooms, with or without CAD, may be a step down for the craftsmen, but for some women it represents a 'step up off the factory floor'.

But it is not only by employers' initiatives and women's choice than men have been removed from many roles in the clothing industry. There is evidence that men have lost faith in the industry and abdicated from some jobs. Many, like the male grader I talked with at Newstyle, felt out of tune with the new technology. 'The younger you are, well, the computer's a way of life. To somebody who is 40 a computer is something to be a bit wary of.'

A factor pushing men out of the industry is their own sense of what is right and proper men's work. The feminization of clothing manufacture is ruining its reputation as an employer of men. Even under the old regime there was a dubious quality about the clothing industry. An elderly man, near retirement, looked back to the difficult time he had had in defending his choice of a job to himself and his family. They were in the manly trade of building. 'The fashion trade,' he said, lip curling, 'was a little bit, "the other way", you know.' *The other way?* I pursued. 'Well, you know. Effeminate.' This craftsman had chosen menswear as being of the two sectors the least compromising of his masculinity. He did so in spite of what he knew to be the narrower opportunities within it. Several men gave the impression that they felt they had, as one of them put it, 'washed up into ladieswear'.

An NUTGW official recalled to me the difficulty he had had in persuading young men, labourers in the cutting room, to consider taking the short training for more skilled work that would have helped their prospects in the firm. 'Their arguments were ridiculous really. They would have been on bonus, as well.

The thing is, *they thought it was a woman's job.* Just imagine yourself, say in a room with 500 hundred women. Which we do have. And say there is half a dozen boys sat in with them. You know, there is a queer feeling among them.'

So men don't want prospects as semi-skilled workers in what they see as a female industry. I was told more than once: men will only come into the industry today when they can see their way to the top. It seems that women, or more precisely female sex-typed jobs, now block that way.

So far and no farther

There are two kinds of job that men are still happy to have in the clothing industry: those that govern people and those that govern technology. Neither are occupations from which the trade union draws much of its membership. Indeed they tend to be filled by men whose orientation is more towards ownership than labour.

Although pattern-room employees I talked with at Newstyle felt there was little scope for them to move upwards to management jobs, there are precedents for such a move. In fact Newstyle is probably one of the employers offering better than average prospects for women in this industry. Elsewhere the upper ranks of management are almost all, even in ladieswear, solidly male. 'It's a very unbalanced operation,' said one senior manager who would have liked to see things otherwise. 'You have a lot of men managing a lot of women, basically.' Newstyle, on the contrary, is proud of its reputation for 'looking after its women'. Women represent 65 per cent of the bottom management grade, mainly supervisors of female workers. In the next two grades the proportion falls to 25 per cent and in the grades above that to 18 per cent. There is one woman executive director.

The officially open policies of a firm like Newstyle, however, are inevitably modified in practice by the attitudes of existing managers. 'We do find that women have a great difficulty in being emotionally unattached when they are managing groups of women,' one explained. And he added, his judgement quite unclouded by such emotion, that women did not really require assistance in obtaining equality. 'There's only two types of women. Dominant women who get their own way. And soft cuddly women who get their own way. . . Yes, there's only two types of women.' The attitude of senior management at Steadywear was yet simpler. 'My job is to know when a woman is the kind who wants her bottom pinched, or whether she needs her bottom kicked.'[19]

When I asked a woman pattern-room worker at Newstyle, *What jobs do men do in this firm?*, she laughed and said, 'I think men are all the bosses! Or tend to be.' She might have added: and the technologists.

What has happened in the process of technological change in the pattern and cutting rooms, of course, is that men that once produced their consumer goods by means of simple tools (scissors, pencils) entirely under their own control, have been turned into operators (or, more commonly, replaced by women operators) working on machines that are under the technological sway and authority of men with technical skills. The cutting room at Newstyle has a team of three maintenance technicians. The job is growing in importance. A manager said, 'The computerized cutters are looked after like babies. With only two machines serving all those factories a breakdown is disastrous.' He explained that the firm was much more dependent than hitherto on its technical team. Today they needed 'someone with a bit of brain', 'the best set of engineers possible', operating flexibly without demarcation. Although the occasional girl sewing-machine mechanic has been heard of in the industry, recruited under special 'positive action' schemes to introduce young women to technical skills, it seems that they seldom stay in the work.[20] In the maintenance teams of cutting rooms, where the machinery is larger, costlier and more varied than in the sewing units, a woman is the last thing in the mind of a personnel officer advertising for electrical or mechanical fitters for his jobs.

These occupations nevertheless hold out far more prospect than the routine occupations designated as female. A writer on new clothing technology in the trade press reported that there is:

... not a great deal of difference in the initial skills needed by youngsters coming into the industry, with one big exception – *the mechanic*. The role of the clothing mechanic has changed so much in recent years that the [training board] set up a committee of enquiry to look into the way in which clothing machine mechanics are trained and employed in Great Britain ... Its recommendations will dramatically alter the way clothing industry mechanics are trained both in college and companies. The increasing use of electronics, computerisation and the introduction of robotics means the existing City and Guilds course is no longer adequate to meet the needs of the industry. The ability required to cope with modern machinery is at least equivalent to that in any other branch of engineering. The image of the clothing machine mechanic as a poor man's engineer has gone on too long. The report outlines a complete career structure ... to degree level. It is expected that the majority of trainees will remain at 'clothing machine technician' level, but it is important that avenues are open to reach senior management level through engineering. . .[21]

The most important technological job connected with the CAD/CAM system at Newstyle is that of system manager. Some firms also employ software managers, computer processing technicians and other forms of technical specialist. As the craftsman leaves the clothing industry, baffled by the computer, a very different kind of man arrives, one who thrives with it and by it. Someone commented of the system manager at Newstyle, a young man in his mid-20s, 'I would think he would be priceless for a company. There's no one, there's never been a precedent for his skill in the clothing industry.'

It is worth examining the system manager and his job in a little more detail. In enquiries made of 18 firms with CAD technology I did not find any in which this post was held by a woman. The Newstyle system manager is in a sense 'self-made'. He had been a bright lad with a leaning to technical and science subjects, but was impatient at the idea of further education. He sensed, 'automation, look, that's something I ought to be looking for.' He got a job in the clothing industry as a trainee lay-maker on a CAD system. But being one of those people who 'wanted to know what makes things tick', he soon got out of this rut. He found that 'because I was nosey about it they took advantage of that and they said, "Well, really you are learning about the software off-hand, and when we have people going off on holiday we would like you to help out." ' And so he did. He was still only 18. He came into Newstyle as 'utility man' in the computer pattern room, a staff post, and was soon promoted to the bottom grade of management where he was then poised to climb. He was one of the team of technically keen men who got the CAD system fully operational at Newstyle. (It is worth noting that the present 'utility man' at Newstyle is also a man. He is the only man at operating level with the exception of the ex-craft grader.)

The way he recounted his story, it was possible to detect a flow of knowledgeable men from one firm to another and between the clothing industry and those firms that supply the new technology. A former senior colleague at Newstyle, for instance, was now technical manager of the firm whose CAM system Newstyle had installed. He and his engineers were now continually in and out of Newstyle. 'They virtually end up living here,' said the system manager. 'Sometimes we ask them why they don't have an office here.' He clearly enjoyed his relationship with such men. Indeed, in some ways his special knowledge made him closer to them and to computer technologists elsewhere in the industry, than to his own colleagues at Newstyle. Certainly he is personally very well placed with contacts when looking for his next job, his next step up. And the job itself offers, as he says, 'a vast new field' to the man with the initiative to up-grade.

I asked the system manager, 'Could a woman do your job?' He felt that while the job itself did not preclude women, it was unlikely (and it appears he is right) that a woman would acquire the confidence, the knowledge and the contacts to achieve it. These attributes were unlikely to belong to a woman in the operating job at Newstyle. Women quickly picked up the operating skills on CAD but they were not encouraged to go further, to build up their knowledge of the hardware and software on which they worked, 'because they are too valuable doing what they are doing'.

'The future is with the technician,' I was told. 'He'll be the highest-paid man in the factory.' Today at Newstyle the maintenance technician earns 60 per cent more than the spreader whose machine he services. The system manager earns nearly twice what the scope operator earns. While the operators' jobs are threatened by succeeding waves of technical change, those of the technician and engineer are developing and growing. They have a chance to learn and progress. New technology has brought its ambiguous new operator roles within reach of women but it has not brought them *technical* training or competence. The wave of women into the industry is lapping up against twin cliffs of male interest: senior management and skilled technical posts.

3. Running, walking and standing still: new technology in mail order warehouses

The foregoing chapter dealt with a classic process in which craft control was destroyed by modern industrial management methods and where technology, and technologically informed men, enabled capital to introduce women workers to the disadvantage of men. The drama centred on skill. A craftsman's technology involving simple, ancient tools was made obsolete at one stroke by the computer, and the skills that replaced it were no longer direct producers' skills but technical competence in governing *other people's* instruments of labour and work processes. This chapter, in contrast, is about unskilled work, and the technology in question is a mechanization of crude physical processess of materials handling. The gender divisions here are linked to differences between heavy and light work, mechanized and unmechanized work. The story unfolds in the mail order sector of retail distribution.

There can be few of us who at one time or other have not bought some garment or household utensil through the post. For some people, particularly those who live in remote districts, catalogue buying is more convenient than a visit to a department store. Besides, the goods are often cheaper bought by mail order and may usually be obtained on credit. The typical mail order customer is a working-class woman. It is estimated that nearly half the women in the UK make a mail order purchase at some time during a year.[1] In 1982, the year prior to my study, mail order business turned over £2.9 billion, which represented around 4 per cent of retail business in the country as a whole.

Firms doing business by post are of three kinds. First there is a handful of giant catalogue mail order houses whose practice is to sell through agents. Agents are ordinary members of the public who request a copy of the large colour-printed catalogue of goods issued by each firm twice a year. They obtain a small commission on whatever merchandise they are instrumental in selling, usually to other members of their family or to neighbours and workmates. Catalogue mail order houses are grouped in the Mail Order Traders Association. This is one of the most concentrated sectors of British capital. The top two firms in 1983 held 70 per cent of market share, the top five held 98 per cent. It is this kind of mail order house with which we are mainly concerned here. It is, however, in competition with a second category, known as 'direct mail'. Direct mail firms do not operate through agents, but they do produce smaller catalogues of a narrower range of goods which they mail direct to potential customers, often undercutting the big agency houses in price. They are represented by the British Direct Marketing Association. The third category is 'direct response' firms that advertise individual items of merchandise in newspapers and magazines. They compete effectively with the agency houses at the quality end of the merchandise range.

The mail order concept originated in Chicago in the mid-nineteenth century, when Montgomery Ward and Sears Roebuck began to supply the families of farmers scattered across the USA's Mid-West, far from shopping centres. In the UK it began in the 1920s and its forerunners were the credit clubs and doorstep-selling tallymen of working-class communities, especially in the North of England.

Mail order might well be called *male* order. Each of the catalogue houses is a massive pyramid of women, built and dominated by men. More specifically these are pyramids of working wives and mothers. The firms' workforce in office and warehouse is made up mainly of part-timers, married women. Their hundreds of thousands of agents, out there in the housing estates and streets of town and country, are also mainly working-class women. And women workers service the women agents who in their turn sell to millions of women customers. At the pinnacle of these pyramids are male executives and managers, and a board of directors who are also, with few exceptions, men.[2]

The typical mail order firm operates in the North of England, often employing women who have been put out of work by the decline in the textile industries. Such women offer the employer the asset of a ready work-disciplined labour force, and one that comes cheap. The firms often use an old textile mill as warehouse, and sometimes women who worked in the mill as textile workers have stayed on in the same building as warehouse hands. Often this has meant a step down in skill and certainly no gain in earnings.

The particular challenge in the mail order business most evident to the outside observer is the handling of orders and invoicing, credit and cash. This office-based process is indeed a huge logistical problem and has been the first part of the mail order exercise to receive the attentions of the computer specialist. But the warehousing side of the mail order operation represents a unique problem too, and that is the one we are concerned with here. The firm carries tens of thousands of lines, each in several sizes and colours. Many thousands of orders must be filled each day. Any one order may involve six or seven 'options', goods as diverse as a child's vest or a set of spanners. They must be collated, packed and mailed out to the customer. Goods come into the warehouse in bulk and must be kept in reserve stock till needed. Then bulk must be broken and the goods distributed to 'picking faces' from which the order fillers, or pickers as they are known, can select and assemble them. Because items are normally sent on 14-day approval, with postage paid by the firm, a high proportion of goods is sent back and must be checked and replaced in stock.

The mail order warehouse has always been a highly labour-intensive operation. Almost everywhere the manual jobs that make up the major categories of occupation in a mail order warehouse – picking, packing and handling 'returns' – are done by women.

Into the maw of the machine

First I want to set mail order within the context of technological developments in warehousing more generally, because what is happening to the mail order firms is only one instance of an historical trend. Warehousing has been a backward area in British industry and commerce. The typical warehouse, even today, is a mere store tucked away at the back of the works, stacked with boxes and pallets which are moved by hand or by forklift truck in and out in response to delivery and despatch of goods. The warehouse labour force, normally 100 per cent male, is in most enterprises looked on as the least skilled and the roughest. The warehouse manager, too, often has low status within the management team.

Pressure from overseas competition, and the onset of the recession in the 1970s has, however, gradually brought about a revolutionizing approach in British management, a search for efficiency and savings which has slowly filtered down to stimulate change in the storage and handling of materials and products. The aim of the current technological innovations in warehousing is not one but several related kinds of gain. First is the saving of space. This involves maximizing the utilization of what is called warehouse 'cube'. Second is the saving in transport costs to and from the warehouse. Third is a saving in the levels of capital tied up at any one moment in stock. Reorganization of warehousing is often associated with a massive de-stocking that frees capital and space simultaneously. A fourth aim is speed and efficiency in handling goods and filling orders so as to be able to increase the pace of production or offer a better service to the customer. Fifth is control: a more precise knowledge of the whereabouts of goods and personnel. Finally, and very important, is what is euphemistically expressed as labour 'saving'. The labour strategy involves a reduction of dramatic proportions in the number of employees together with an upgrading of the few who remain. As one informant told me, 'Labour is seen as the Achilles heel, the factor in production that is unpredictable, intractable.' The aim therefore is to convert from 'rough and ready staff, difficult to manage, to more intelligent and loyal ones'.

The trade unions, in particular the Union of Shop, Distributive and Allied Workers (USDAW), the Transport and General Workers Union (TGWU) and the General Municipal, Boilermakers and Allied Trades Union (GMBATU), have been energetic in organizing warehouse workers during the last ten years and trying to increase their traditionally low wage levels. Often warehousing policies are designed to diminish this new influence of the unions on the firms' operations.

Both pushing and pulled by the warehouse revolution are the many firms that now produce warehousing systems. The leading countries in this field are West Germany and Switzerland, followed by Britain and other European countries, including Italy, France, Norway and Sweden. The USA and Japan, though highly developed within their own markets, do not yet compete effectively in Western Europe in this field.[3] These firms may produce one component of warehousing systems, such as racking or mobile trucks, or they may produce entire systems including the computer programs that control them.[4]

Ironically, although Britain has been an innovator and producer in the materials-handling equipment market, British industry has not in the past proved an enthusiastic customer. A certain native caution gripped British capital in the post-war period. In particular, a fear of confronting labour over technical change and its associated redundancies made British firms hesitant. A manager in one materials-handling engineering firm told me, 'It's been discouraging for me seeing the pace of change in Germany, for instance. And here firms getting cold-shouldered by the unions.' 'But,' he added, 'it's not like that today. For years and years companies have known they had too many staff, they have wanted to rationalize. Now the Thatcher government has made it possible. Before the recession you couldn't have laid off 100 workers without the rest walking out. People accept it now and companies are cashing in on this atmosphere.' Cybernetics itself brings management problems, however. Managers, said this same informant, 'fear the few residual workers in the system who may smash the monitor lights or go slow on the job.' Once on the technological trail there is an incentive to follow it through till the human element has been eliminated.

This, then, sets the class scene for this particular 'new technology'. A mini-boom in warehousing innovation has been occurring in these early years of the 1980s, brought about by capital taking advantage of a working class firmly pinned down by a government that is monetarist and anti-union.

The automation of warehousing is a complex phenomenon that may mean all or some of a battery of possible changes. It is usually part of a rationalization of a more general kind. Sometimes it includes centralizing the warehouse function, closing numerous outlying sites in favour of an operation consolidated into one warehouse. Sometimes it means relocating to be the better placed for transport from suppliers and to markets. Sometimes a green field site is chosen in the hope of recruiting equally green labour, 'a workforce that know nothing whatsoever about it, have no preconceived ideas and are not unionized', as one manager put it. Most frequently, developments in the warehouse are associated with computerization in the office or with the introduction of electronic systems in production. These percolate downwards to the warehouse in the form of a computerized stock file.

The computerizing of the stock file is of great significance in warehouse organization. In the past, every warehouse stored items of particular kinds in particular sections of racking. It was a kind of common-sense spatial filing system. The warehouse assistant knew that shoes style Buffalo Bill, size 10, colour brown, could be found in Rack A Level 3. With the computer it becomes possible to put any item in any space, thus making dramatically better use of cubic volume and shortening journeys to deposit or retrieve goods. As one warehouse consultant put it, the warehouse is no longer 'honeycombed with fresh air'. Now it is only the computer that knows where things are stored, and its memory is phenomenal. Humans do not need to remember. The warehouse assistant's order forms will instruct him or her not to look for a pair of Buffalo Bill shoes, brown, size 10, but simply to fetch the item s/he will find in Rack A Level 3, or Rack Z Level 2.

New hardware now accompanies the computerization. Racking goes skywards. The highest racks in the new high-bay warehouses are 60 feet above floor level, and they have to be so strong that the architects began to say, 'Why bother to build a building round them? Let's use the racks as the structural frame.' And so the biggest warehouses today are indeed just 'clad racks'. As the aisles became narrower and the racks higher, the hand 'yaks' on which goods used to be trundled about gave way to forklift trucks, then to turret trucks. Eventually the cry was 'get the driver off the truck', and soon he was indeed entirely redundant as the most advanced warehouses installed driverless cranes on rails. They move at great speed up and down narrow aisles, their retractable forks positioning and retrieving pallet-loads of goods in response to computer demands.

The warehouse now becomes a closed system. At the time of writing there are 30 or 40 such total warehouse environments – turn-key systems as they are known – in the UK. There are many hundreds in West Germany.[5] There is no longer any need to heat the warehouse or to light it, because no human beings work inside. It is itself a machine, operated from without. The characteristic warehouse employees in the new regime are, first, a woman sitting at a computer terminal checking goods in and out; second, a maintenance engineer. He (it is invariably a man) alone has the key to the warehouse. To enter the warehouse-machine, he must first switch it off.

Why innovate?

Whether a firm is surviving or failing in the current recession it may find compelling reasons to modernize its warehousing. A company that is doing well and looking forward to a coming upturn in the economy may seize the moment to prepare for it by increasing warehouse efficiency and capacity. A company that is suffering from the economic climate may be forced to rationalize and cut costs or go under. In this case, modernizing the warehouse may be the last throw of the dice. Either way, investment in the new technologies is a risk, but it offers a chance of a way out of the recession.

So it was with the mail order sector. In the 1970s mail order houses had tended to lead the whole retail trade in annual rates of growth. They acquired an enviable reputation among investors as a sector that was capable of weathering recessions. During the period 1975 to 1979 some of the big mail order houses began to lay out capital on computers and conveyor systems and they did so in a spirit of optimism. However, 1980 proved a traumatic year and investors' confidence was brought up short. The catalogue giants were proving to be unexpectedly vulnerable to a deep crisis although they had been immune to a mild recession.

During the period 1981–83 growth in mail order stopped entirely and the traditional retail business sector quickly accelerated into the lead. High street retailers had been engaged in fierce competition and price wars. Shops that would formerly have required cash on the nail from their customers were now giving credit. Certain crucial advantages offered by the mail order houses, therefore, were no longer uniquely theirs. Besides, capital invested in mail order encounters a curious contradiction: for the success of its credit sales policy it requires a working class with secure jobs. The sharp rise in unemployment produced by the recession and the monetarist policies of the Thatcher administration, intended to help capital in general, proved damaging to mail order in particular. 'Until there is a clear change in government policy, which is currently leading to an erosion of the typical mail order customer's relative living standards, the sector is likely to remain economically depressed in share price terms.'[6]

Those firms that have invested in new technology since 1980 have therefore done so in order to be able to steal customers from each other and from retail competition by offering a quicker, better service. Computerization in the office, for instance, was accompanied in some firms by a new 'phone in' ordering facility that is quicker for the agent and reduces the paperwork in which she is involved. It was a gamble and firms with inadequate reserves were at risk. As the *Financial Times* surmised, '. . . differences in financial strength may be beginning to tell in the medium term, as it becomes necessary to invest heavily in new technology in order to remain competitive.' In this new phase the aim of the new technology was far reaching. As the *FT* saw it, the intention was to develop the means 'to turn a customer's order list into a parcel without human intervention'.[7]

Mail order picking: the new systems

As we shall see, the mail order sector is still a long way from this promised land. It has, however, been sold some fancy new techniques in pursuit of it. In this account I am going to concentrate on the job of picker and show what has happened to it with the advent of new technologies, how it fits in with other jobs in the warehouse, how women experience it and how men see it. It will be the central focus of a collective labour process that is strongly patterned by sex.

I saw the way the job used to be by visiting Gamma Mail Order Ltd. Here, though the computer had reached the office functions, it had not yet touched the warehouse. The pickers' job was still as it had been in all mail order firms in the 1970s. Orders, as they arrive from the office, are distributed equally among the women pickers. Each woman collects a batch of order forms and an equivalent number of plastic 'laundry bags', which she arranges on her arm, each to contain the merchandise required for a single order. She examines the orders and plans her own walk around the warehouse, using her wits to collect everything needed for all the orders in the quickest, shortest walk. When the batch of orders is complete she places the goods in trolley bins and wheels them to a collection point, returning to start the cycle again with a new batch of orders. In this way she picks, on average, perhaps 40 or 50 items per hour. The job involves a good deal of carrying and many miles of walking every working day. It is not surprising that most women were part-timers: four hours was tiring enough. At this stage of the mail order warehouse's evolution no machinery was involved at all. The only equipment was racking, the only moving parts were wheeled bins.

The computer and machinery have brought dramatic changes. The two firms with the most advanced picking systems today I will call Alpha Catalogues Ltd. and Beta Warehouses PLC. Alpha Catalogues organize their picking on a 'consecutive batch' basis. Twenty minutes is the unit of work time. Pickers choose the pace at which they wish to pick and are accordingly allocated a grade which governs their basic pay and determines the number of orders they are given to fill in a 20-minute stint. To earn a moderately decent wage it is necessary to work very fast. Goods are presented on fixtures to reach-height in a variety of kinds of open carton. (Meanwhile, women or lads with bins are continually replenishing these forward stocks.) The picker walks the fixtures (she may even run) carrying computer-printed orders with the items printed on them in sequence by location. Her walk-route is thus determined for her. As she picks each item she places it in a bin which she wheels along. It has colour-coded sections. A conveyor with colour-coded carriers is in continual movement through the picking area. After 18 minutes of a cycle this conveyor comes to a standstill and the women hurry to empty their bins into an appropriately coloured carrier during its two-minute pause. They then set off on their next 18-minute picking phase. The goods meanwhile are carried along the conveyor to a transfer point where the carrier bottoms are electronically tripped open to deposit the items on a particular conveyor belt that will carry them on to their appropriate packing stations.

A top-grade picker at Alpha today picks 144 items in her 20-minute cycle; that is 432 an hour, ten times as many as before the new technology came in. The process demands unbroken activity. Since a great deal of walking is involved, it requires a degree of physical stamina. The degree to which this is a base-line exploited job can be seen in the fact that if a picker needs to go to the toilet she must call for a relief picker ('yell for a wee') to take her place. Wee-time is calculated. In this warehouse, women used to get five minutes maximum, men two and a half minutes. Where managements are this mean-minded, workers play them at their own game: after the Sex Discrimination Act men demanded the two and a half minutes per wee they thought the management owed them. And they got it, with back pay for the period of arbitration. Everyone enjoyed this joke, even the women. 'The powder room boys we called them.' But the incident symbolizes something of the passion for measurement and control of these employers. As a union rep put it, new technology had sustained profitability and so had saved jobs, but 'they are boring ones. Like robots. No one's happy.' Her perception is the mirror-image of that of her management, who say that the aim of new technology is 'so that we know what goods are in the system all the time and have control over whether people are doing the job we are paying them to do . . . We are moving from a fairly free system to a fairly controlled system.'

At Beta Warehouses PLC the system is different but, if anything, yet more tightly paced by the machine. The picking department here covers several floors of an enormous warehouse. It is served by an overhead conveyor system, almost half a *mile* in length. It runs through each of the picking floors, coiling down from top to bottom and back up again in a continuous loop. Each floor is equipped with racking for the accommodation of forward picking stock, some of which, holding the faster-moving lines, is equipped with gravity-fed dispensers.

The picking system is highly rational but highly complicated. As orders are received and fed into the computer system, the computer prints out three kinds of instruction. First a despatch note is sent to the packing department to await the arrival of the goods. The second is a picking slip to go to the picking department to instruct the pickers. And the third is an allocation of one space on the conveyor to that particular order. The half-mile-long collating conveyor is continually running between the picking faces. It carries an unbroken sequence of 'gondolas', each with space for three plastic tote boxes one above the other. Each space on the gondola carries a number. Each time it circulates, that space and its number are allocated by the computer to one order and it will 'collect' all the goods required for it during the course of one pass around the warehouse. The conveyor travels at 30 metres a minute, completing one circuit of the whole warehouse per hour.

Each picking slip carries 23 self-adhesive labels, each one an instruction to the picker to pick one item. As the picker picks each piece of merchandise she peels off the appropriate sticker and applies it to the goods. She works at a picking face, confined to her 'zone', covering only certain kinds of goods. In other words she has become a bit of a specialist. A little like the sewing machinist in clothing manufacture who now contributes only a seam to a garment that she would once have made in its entirety, the picker no longer fills whole orders but contributes only a part. The picking zones are balanced so that each generates a similar amount of work and the 'girls' are evenly loaded.

As each picker, responding to a batch of picking slips, walks up and down her picking zone collecting items, she takes with her a shelved trolley on which she places the items in a position exactly determined by the computer instruction on the sticker. This trolley serves as an aid in transferring items to the conveyor system. When her trolley is full the picker wheels it to this conveyor and leaves it. A second woman, a 'putter', works at the foremost trolley. As the numbered gondolas and their boxes trundle by on the conveyor, never stopping for a moment, she takes the items off the shelves of each trolley and, watching the sequence of numbers on the passing boxes, puts each in its pre-ordained box. If she 'misses the boat' and the gondola travels on without the required item, the pick is aborted, dealt with as an error and goes back through the system for a second pass. An inefficient putter will be identifiable to production monitoring in the computer room.

When the tote box on its gondola reaches a transfer point, it is automatically pushed off onto the conveyor that will take it to the packing department. Here the order is matched up with the despatch note. It is automatically replaced by an empty tote box, given a new number, and will circle the picking area once again.

The key features of Beta's system are that the collating is

done not by the picker or by the putter, but by the conveyor system itself. As in the case of Alpha, the women are now machine paced. Walking and carrying are reduced but pressure is greatly increased.

The revolutions of a carousel

Meanwhile, a revolutionizing thought that has occurred to many firms has been 'Why not avoid the time-consuming, labour-intensive walk process and bring the goods to the women?' While this solution had by now been applied in many other areas of the distributive trade, only one mail order firm had introduced it by 1983: Delta Maternity Ltd. Delta are suppliers of maternity, babywear and children's clothing by mail to the home and export markets. In 1975 the firm's owner, an old-style autocrat, decided to reduce warehouse costs by a reorganization involving new technology. He was assisted in this by a new warehouse manager who recognized the existing system as inefficient and approved of rationalization. A start was made on hand-picking. 'If you can save a second on a single job that is repeated by many women many times, you make a big saving.'

The following year the firm called in a group of consultants to help them plan future developments. Storage and Handling Consultancy Ltd. were fed certain criteria by the boss: one was to 'minimize staffing'. In particular they were asked to 'solve the picking problem' and to favour methods that would reduce walking. SHC came up with a plan which, by the time of my interviews at Delta in 1983, was already in effect. There was a new warehouse building, including a high-bay area equipped with pallet racking carrying bulk stock in cartons. Two pallet trucks and four picker trucks capable of operating in and out of narrow aisles furnished with guide rails had been purchased. A conveyor belt, which at intervals becomes three-tier, had been installed to connect picking, packing, export and despatch departments. Finally, picking itself had been transformed. The warehouse manager's dream of 'bringing the goods to the women' had become a reality. The consultants' preferred solution to the picking problem was a system called a carousel (neither as pretty nor as festive as its name suggests). It is essentially a 'cartridge and magazine' system. The magazines are the carousels themselves. Delta purchased eleven carousels, each containing 30 carriers travelling around an electrically powered elliptical track. The cartridges that slot into the carriers are standard cardboard boxes with open fronts. Each contains a different merchandise 'option': plastic panties size 1; baby's cardigan, pink. The women pick the goods from one end of the carousel; the cardboard boxes are replenished from the other. The system is not computerized. In its present form it is a simple, even crude, mechanical arrangement. At first it broke down frequently owing to switch faults and chain links snapping. It could, however, very easily be a step towards a computer-driven system that could routinize the women's work even more.

There was no consultation over the introduction of the new technology here at Delta Maternity Ltd. It was just imposed on the women. At first they dragged their feet over the change-over. The consultant in charge admits, 'They didn't want the system there at all. Totally opposed. Totally.' The women were saying, the former warehouse manager told me, ' "We don't like all that machinery. It'll never work." Women tend to think machinery will bite them.'

There were many operating problems in those early months, and they were mainly due to the machinery, not to the women. Before long, however, they had gone from filling 2,000 orders a day, in the uneasy starting period, to 4,000 orders a day. At this point the warehouse manager held a champagne party for his employees.

Let's look at what the new labour process involves. A conveyor belt runs between the two lines of carousels. The women are positioned back to back, between belt and carousel, one to each carousel work station. All can be seen at a glance by the supervisor at her bench. Each of the carousels carries 120 'options' or items of merchandise. Each has a console of button controls. Order forms arriving from the office upstairs at the beginning of each half-day shift are separated by the supervisor who places them in individual plastic tote boxes. The carousels are lettered A, B, C, D, etc. On top of the order form in the tote box the supervisor places a card carrying the letter of the carousel from which the first item on the order form is to be picked. The tote boxes set off, circling the endless belt of the conveyor.

A woman at any one carousel removes from the belt as they approach any tote boxes that carry the code letter of her station. She stacks the boxes, with the order forms waiting within them, beside her on the floor and begins filling orders. She takes the form from the first box, sees the number of the location within her carousel that holds the goods required, presses the appropriate button and waits for the carousel to circle round and present the relevant box. She then pushes open the safety door and withdraws the item from the box. Referring again to the order form she selects a letter card to indicate the next carousel to which the tote box must progress for the subsequent item on the order to be filled, returning the box to the conveyor belt. An average order involves 6.7 items. The picker that completes the last pick places the box on the upper level of the belt to send it direct to 'packing'. When a cartridge on the carousel is nearly empty the operator removes a card which will instigate replenishment. The cartridges are replenished by another work team from the rear of the carousel installation.

So the picking job at Delta has completed the trend to shorter and shorter walks and more and more detailed division of labour (in this case specialization by merchandise option) observable at Alpha Catalogues and Beta Warehouses. It has become static. Women stand on one spot and their actions are now reaching and bending, taking and lifting. Their imprisonment is symbolized by a little compensatory 'gift' from the owner: a small square of carpet for every woman. No one was deceived by this cosmetic gesture. Carousel picking is not an easy job to do for long. 'There's not so much walking on this job,' a picker said, 'but you are moving your arms. You get a lot of arm pressure. Arms drop off, you know, by the time you go home at lunch time.' Others said, 'A lot of the others don't like working on our job because it's too hard. You are keeping going all the time, pulling boxes off, putting them on.' 'It's hectic and noisy. You have to concentrate on what you are doing, with the buttons and that.'

One young picker described her labour process this way:

Although you've got that much space between your machine, your bench and the belt, you've got to turn round all the time. You do get a bit (pause, while she searched for the expression she wanted – then, with a laugh) a bit *funny in the head*. Turning round and coming back. You have to turn round to press the number you want on the machine. Then climb up one step, reach for something out the bin, the top, then the bottom bin, then come back out the door again. You aren't just stood there. You are in the one spot but you are still moving. And the belts, you have to stretch to put a box on the top belt. Bend under the bench to get things. I'm a fit person. But (she paused again for thought) – the only thing is I do get *dizzy* on there sometimes. The lights are bright and glaring. Yes, I get dizzy. There's a couple of girls complains of that. And headaches.

All the women remark that the conveyor makes a continual racket, baffling conversation and adding to the stress of work.

The question is, of course, how does this labour process compare with hand picking by the old methods? One woman said, 'We all say that we far liked it much better upstairs.' Several endorsed this:

Yes (enthusiastically) that was great. I liked it. There was a lot of older women, retired. We was all picking by hand and walking, with the bags on our arms, and it was very tiring walking, you felt that your feet was dropping off, but it was great fun you know. As you passed a person you could have a laugh and a joke. Which we miss now. We did used to have a nice laugh and a joke upstairs. You know. Here you have got to watch your orders and your belt all the time.

Certainly it was hard work upstairs. But 'if you got them a little bit heavy you could always bung them in a barrow, you know, suit yourself. Here you have the belt, the continual belt, you got to keep the belt going.' It is of course the belt that keeps the women going.

One of the consultants of Storage and Handling Consultancy Ltd. who had been involved in this modernization summed up the implications of the new system this way. The boss's

> sole objective in life was to get a given output for the cheapest cost. He would do the cosmetic things like carpet, flower vases and a nice little tea bar. But that's not what the system was all about. When it was put forward as a concept he didn't say, 'What will be the effect on the human?' No. He wanted control. And he wanted an order to be picked with the minimum cost and the minimum error rate. Things of that nature. The controls put on [the women] before were very loose. Now it was a governed cycle of a machine and things whizzing round. You couldn't have a quick chat against your picking station with Minnie or whoever. You were stuck there until you got a relief. It's the old, old story.

Under the former regime there had always been a little bit of scope for skiving. 'The difference was that you had the gangways, you walked up and down and in and out. You might pass someone and have a chat for two or three minutes. The forelady, she'd holler blue murder if she saw you standing still. "Get those feet walking" she'd go. So away you went and did the next bit. You got your feet walking – for two minutes anyway (happy laugh).' There is also the delicate matter of pilfering. Neither management nor women would have wished to mention such a thing to me, but the consultants had no such scruples. They said frankly that pilfering is everywhere a problem in the mail order warehouses' picking areas. The very low wages in warehouse work may explain this. The carousel system is favoured by consultants and employers partly because it encloses the goods behind metal and plastic casing and so provides only one point of access to the merchandise under the surveillance of the supervisor.

Certainly, it is not all women who would wish to go back to the old ways. Several preferred the machine. Hand picking had been subject to rationalization, to a tightening up, even before the machine was thought of. At first there had been a pile of orders and you just took them and when you had done them you went back and got some more. Then it got so that there was a set number of orders you were personally supposed to fill. This prefigured the arrangement today where the pressure comes in part from the fact that one order is filled by many women. The picker has become part of a crew and one can hold up the work of the rest. Besides, workers are not immune from the priorities of the firm itself. The new system does get orders filled with less delay. In the old picking area the orders were always days or weeks behind and the more responsible of the women, harassed about it by the warehouse manager, continually worried about this. They felt that they were to blame. That is why they prefer the new system. Of course management gain by this feeling of responsibility among the women. As the warehouse manager puts it, 'the girls' output increases without us doing anything about it. They just up their game.'

In so far as the new work is bearable, the women make it so by their own efforts, their own personalities. The effect of continuous monitoring is moderated by the fact that the supervisor is a much-loved woman: 'We work for *her*.' All the women have developed their own ways of easing the labour process and speeding the work. 'My supervisor told me the other day, she said, "Why have you done those orders first?" I'm a bit cheeky (laugh). I says, "Oh, I got my own system, thank you" (happy laugh).' The women make work tolerable for each other. 'I've always liked the company. The girls. I *like* work (dubiously). But I think it's if you like your mates. With me anyway. I've had a big family and as they leave home, you miss it, you know.' 'A great lot of girls they are.'

What sex means to management

Delta Maternity Ltd. sees itself as having 'fantastically good relations with its staff'. This means, frankly, 'we have no trade union here'. There is indeed a great deal of loyalty on the part of Delta's women workers. I saw many wearing badges on their overalls, silver for ten years' service, gold for 20 years. In the bad old days the firm had employed many temporary workers whom they laid off without compunction on a Friday afternoon. Now the workforce was smaller but more stable. Management was, however, tightening its grip. The new warehouse controller was less lenient than the last. The see-through glass wall newly installed around his office, though *he* said it was so that the women could see him beavering at his desk, the women interpreted as an aid in his surveillance of *them*. The proposed creation of a new post, 'warehouse systems manager', was also a sign that the mechanization of the warehouse was now one of its most important features.

In spite of having a policy of equal opportunity, the segregation by sex in Delta's warehouse is almost 100 per cent. The following warehouse jobs are filled exclusively by males: management, maintenance engineering, goods handling, truck driving, assembly of bulk hardware orders, heavy work in despatch and warehouse cleaning. The following are filled exclusively by females: clerical work, assembly of bulk clothing orders, picking, packing, returns, stock control and light work in despatch. Basically, sexual segregation is seen by management as a fact of life with which you do not argue. They say, 'We don't *do* any segregating here.' And yet somehow segregation happens, as it always has. 'If it's a man's job it's a man's job and vice versa.'

When pressed further, the warehouse controller put the separate spheres of men and women down to two factors. First, the element of machinery: 'These women are not mechanically minded.' Second, demands on strength: 'It's just that men do the lifting. You don't expect the average female to be a butch kind of person. That's one difference that remains, that men are the muscular people on the whole. For instance, I wouldn't expect my wife to pick up a bag of potatoes and put it in the car. *I* would expect to do it.' One of the male truck drivers put it this way: 'The majority of the blokes in there are five foot seven upwards and the majority of the women are five foot six downwards and the physical strength is quite different between the two.'

This does not of course explain why you don't find men in the basic female jobs of picking and packing, in which pay is 20 per cent down on the basic male jobs. The warehouse controller put this down to the fact that it is only women who apply for them. The explanation is always social conditioning somewhere else, before, earlier in life, anywhere but in the warehouse. It is supposed also that men and women prefer working in single-sex groups, and there is some truth in this. 'Married women like to work together. So do men. The men like to talk about Joe Bugner and football and what have you. They don't want to know who is knitting what pullover.'

In fact, there is a strong age as well as sex patterning in Delta warehouse. The women tend to be older, often married with children. The men are predominantly young lads. This reflects what management acknowledges to be two distinct personnel policies, one for men, one for women. This is rationalized as, 'We just recognize people's needs. That's what it is really.' 'It is a conscious decision on our part. Women are mainly people who have had a family that has grown up and they have come back to work. They are very loyal and conscientious. They know what the customers feel like and what they want. They treat the orders with a "feel". That is why we like women of that age.'

It is assumed that women do not want burdensome responsibilities. 'The women like to be easy in their mind. The main thing in their life is bringing up a family.' However, the firm offers no concessions to women's domestic responsibilities. It has no creche, no policy on time off to cope with family crises. Since women 'don't want worries', it matters little that 'promotion paths for part-time ladies are quite frankly nil'. Supervisors are drawn only from full-timers 'because of the continuity from one shift to the next'. For a full-timer to be promoted to supervisor also depends, in place of skill or experience, on the quality of trustworthiness. 'It's the *type* of person we are looking for.' Once on this giddy pinnacle, a woman sticks.

As for men: 'The men are a different kettle of fish. It's my conscious feeling about men,' said the warehouse controller. The management's aim, operating as it is in an exceedingly flush labour market, is to 'identify the potential and take the best'. The firm thinks about career possibilities for its men. 'The thing about young men, it's pointless to say, "That's your job and you are going to be left in it for five years," ' explained the controller. 'He'll up and leave. If you take people [i.e. men] on you should put time into them and you owe them the flexibility and opportunity.' Unfortunately, however, this good intention with regard to men comes unstuck on the relative scarcity of supervisory posts to which to move them and on the unbridgeable gap between supervision and management. 'They'd have to go a *long* while as supervisor to be suitable for management.' For the last post that became vacant they had considered both of the male supervisors, but 'they just weren't up to it'. As a result, young men tend to 'just vanish' from the firm at around 25. They either get bored and look for a spell on the dole or, if they are lucky, spot greener pastures.

Notwithstanding this disingenuousness about sex-typing of jobs, both sex differentiation and sex segregation are in fact intrinsic to methods of control in Delta's warehouse. The interests and qualities of married women part-timers are such as to make them ideal pickers and packers. They are, because of their domestic experience, on the whole diligent and serious people. 'We seem to be more bothered about our jobs,' said one. 'More than the men are. They *do* the job and that. But they aren't what you'd call madly in love with it.' The women described their own various, unskilled and repetitive jobs as requiring thoughtful, careful workers. 'You've got to want to *work*.' 'I don't think you'd want someone slap-dash.' They pointed out to me that it is the women who do the incessant, unremitting slog in the warehouse while the men and lads have more casual and sporadic roles.

The product of Delta Maternity, mother and babywear, is seen by the management as attracting a woman's interest and commitment to the job. All mail order firms have 'seconds shops' from which women can buy. And management is right in the belief that a relationship exists between the women and the product. As one packer said, 'We find when each new season's catalogue comes out, when we get a new thing, we show it to each other and say, "Oh, this is a nice thing", "I do like this", you know.' Men on the contrary are, if anything, somewhat embarrassed by working for a firm whose products are so unmanly. The warehouse controller, discussing quality control in picking and packing said, 'If you think about it, here is this parcel arriving through the post to this pregnant lady who may not be feeling very well. It will cheer her up if it is well presented. I will get another order. And besides, it's only right.' The women too feel this is right. 'I like to pack it the way I'd like to get it myself.' They draw on their own experience and identify with the women customers, doing the work extra well so as to fulfil both management's demands and their own standards. I commented to one packer that it seemed odd to me that the goods were sent out packed in plastic bags without air holes. Didn't that create a risk of suffocation for children in the homes the merchandise was delivered to? She looked sideways at me and laughed. And she showed me how, with her sharp thumbnail, she punched a hole in every bag as she packed the parcel. No one had told her to do this. She had never mentioned it to anyone. She simply took the responsibility on herself. This is one of the reasons why managers employ women.

In a similar way the firm thrives on the masculine self-identification of young men. Goods handlers described the strenuousness and mobility of the job as attractive to them, in its way. Men will strain their backs rather than admit weakness in front of their fellows or women. Truck drivers get a kick out of driving, sometimes alarming the warehouse manager who mistrusts 'Stirling Moss types'. If you can't satisfy the demands of masculine identity in any other way, little physical heroisms must suffice.

While sex differences are exploited by managers, they experience *sexuality* as a minefield. Mixed-sex working among young people is always approached cautiously by management. For instance, the older average age of the women in Delta was a factor in their calculations. The warehouse controller complained that in the one 'hot' area, the stock location control section, where men and women worked in the same space, you were likely to get 'tomfoolery, hanky panky behind the racks'. In the same way a maintenance engineer at Steadywear had described as his most disastrous experiment putting girls and lads onto a cleaning stint together. He found them 'kissing and cuddling, finding hiding places in the factory where nobody is allowed to go'.

Men: muscle and mobility

Two qualities are combined in men's work at Delta Maternity and in other warehouses: physical competence and technical competence. The men bind these two together and appropriate both qualities for masculinity. Each affords a little power. Not much, just a modicum of power that is enough to enable men to lever more pay, less supervision and more freedom out of management. The 'goods inwards' and 'despatch' manhandling jobs that men do are purely physical; in the operating of forklift and picker trucks the physicality is enhanced by control of the machine; and in the occupations of the maintenance engineering team technical skills become an important factor complementing, though not displacing, physical strength. The sex segregation has material advantages for women. Labouring pays 20 per cent above the women's unskilled rate, forklift driving 28 per cent above and maintenance engineering 66 per cent. In addition, bearing in mind that management is also male, a situation results in which men as a whole influence women's work processes more than women influence those of men.

However rude their labours may basically be, the men's jobs are mobile and are not repetitive. They can thus scorn the static work that women are confined to: 'No way I'd do the carousel job myself. The boredom! You are always stuck in the same spot. Unless you are used to it, it must be terrible, to do the same thing over and over.' Once, two lads were put on the carousel to help out for a shift. One of the boys who did it told me he had found the ladies 'very helpful' and he had come to respect a kind of skill he recognized, with some surprise, in their work. 'You do have to be very quick, or the work all piles up.' But, he said emphatically, never again. 'To be stuck on the conveyor! Driving a truck you are your own boss. On the belt you are like a robot.'

The men rationalize the confinement of women to the static and boring jobs by recourse to a philosophy of essentialism: women are made that way. The truck driver went on, for instance, to say that 'the women seem to be all right on it [i.e. the carousel]. Well, it just seems to be a woman's job doesn't it? I've been brought up that way.' Women's marginally smaller stature and lesser strength combine with the way jobs are defined and done to secure certain of the unskilled jobs by right and by long practice to a male team in which the cohesive force is masculinity. Women 'couldn't do' the manhandling job because, well, it's *man*handling. 'You have three blokes in a row, spanning 30 feet, and they are chucking the boxes to each other. If you don't catch them . . .! (he raised his eyebrows). And they can be *heavy*.'

The theme of male solidarity and teamwork also permeates the area of technologically skilled work. Everywhere I went I talked with maintenance engineering technicians and craftsmen. They characteristically formed teams of three or four men and lads, relating more to each other than to the rest of the personnel, roaming freely around the works on their special trouble-shooting assignments. The effect is similar to that found by Ann Game and Rosemary Pringle in their study of firms making household electrical goods. 'Comically, men see themselves as tigers pacing restlessly round . . . while women are settled serenely' in their section. They point out that because tradesmen move freely around their machines, around the section and around the whole plant, they are the only ones likely to be familiar with the general layout.[8]

Invariably the maintenance men enjoyed their jobs. The chief maintenance technician at Delta said, 'It's very entertaining, really, the variety.' *You find the day goes fast for you?* 'Oh, crikey, yes.' This man and his assistant, an electro-mechanical fitter, described with enthusiasm the kind of faults they were called on to remedy and the relationship they perceived themselves as having with the women on the carousel. At Delta the technology, though new, still involved little more than the traditional spanner and oily rag. But it is worth bearing in mind that it was of jobs like these that a warehousing systems consultant said, 'What happens is that as you automate you build up a different kind of staff, a team of running fixers. They are the jobs that require a higher level of intellectual ability, of intelligence. And they are more interesting jobs. People underestimate that.'

'We cover such a wide range,' said the chief technician, 'from drains, to taps, cisterns and all the heaters on the roof alone. Such a lot goes wrong. Boilers. All that to be maintained. The sprinkler system and its pumps – very comprehensive.' An onerous responsibility is keeping the carousel turning.

> On the carousel we get broken microswitches. The doors are operated by those microswitches. There is a platform on the top that has 63 of them and they go occasionally. The top chain snaps too, sometimes, the drive chain. You have to climb up there. The bigger chains underneath carry the carousel round on the sprockets, they snap as well . . . We have to get inside there and try to shift them with a crow bar or something, to move the link away from whatever obstruction is holding it. It's a devilish task . . . It is really difficult, hard and heavy work.

The assistant fitter took up the story:

> There *is* a lot of heavy work involved. It is a matter of climbing into spaces, especially on the carousels, you have to *manipulate your body* in such a way it sometimes hurts, you know, to get over things. I think in a lot of ways it's, well, if you haven't got the strength it can be a dangerous job. Tom and me, you know, we help each other out. Otherwise you could be in a bit of trouble.

This teamwork would be spoiled, even impossible, if women were included: 'I couldn't really see a woman doing it, not all of it. Don't get me wrong, a lot of the work they could do, but they couldn't do all of it. *They couldn't replace me.*'

The chief engineer continued:

I'm sure they could do some of it, yeah. It's only the physical side, the drawback really. Okay, you can have a girl mechanic, can probably tune an engine to perfection. But when it comes to taking the head off, dropping the gear box, that kind of thing, I don't think they are physically capable of doing it. In most cases. You get a chap, engineer, to do it, he would probably be able to do *the whole lot*, while the girl could probably do the tuning, the simple part of things, but when it comes to the actual manual side of it, it could let her down. [He meant, I think, *she* would let *us* down.]

Then he slipped imperceptibly, as such men often do at this point of the argument, into taking the company's view on productivity, using it as a reinforcement for his own masculine argument: 'So therefore you would have to employ two people to do what one person could do.'

Although the chief maintenance engineer is here choosing to distinguish the heavy physical aspect of the work as the part that is definitive in ruling out women, in fact he sees women as 'naturally' technically incompetent too. The attitude of the skilled technicians to the pickers is one of irritation combined with patronage:

Take the door solenoids. The women don't really know what should happen when the door shuts. The microswitch puts a solenoid bolt through the door as a safety mechanism, so you can't push it open while the carousel is moving. But often the women complain, 'We can't get the door open, it's jammed.' If they could only *understand* . . . When we are repairing them I do tell the women. Usually I break it down very simply for them, you know. I think after I told them they do take notice and understand. Some have got a bit more sense than others.

Where women showed an above average technical intelligence

this was ascribed to the influence of some man. 'Perhaps their husbands talk to them. Some of their husbands are engineers. Yes. That could have a lot to do with it.' In fact, as we shall see, a woman with a technically skilled husband is less, not more, likely than the next woman to have acquired technical confidence and ability.

The engineers' work is undeniably tough, but they get a compensatory pleasure out of the freedom of movement. *Mobility, this is something that men value?* I asked. 'I think so, yes. I do definitely. And I do believe that most of the chaps here would agree with that.' Women sadly agree that 'men must always be on the move', and the men see it as natural that women accept confinement, being 'always stuck in the same spot'. All this, of course, is contradicted by the preference the women had for the old walking-and-picking job. Aware of the flaws in the argument, perhaps, men buttress it by appealing to propriety and morality. The chief maintenance technician, explaining why his job would be unsuitable work for women, mentioned his own daughter as an example. The emphasis on cleanliness was almost obsessive: 'I wanted her to have a job that she could go nice and clean, and come home nice and clean. And enjoy what she was doing. I'm afraid I'm a Victorian in my way of thinking. I think that a girl if she goes to work *should* go looking nice and clean. She should be able to stay nice and clean and come home nice and clean. That's my way of thinking.' At Delta both men and women, explaining the sexual division of labour in the warehouse, showed how improper it was felt to be that women should use their bodies, use muscle. They could not, should not, and, it was supposed, would not want to do a job that involved climbing up, crawling under, lying down, exerting force, sweating. Active use of technology involves all those things at Delta.

Women: inertia and initiative

It is not difficult to see what men gain from this ideology. It is more surprising, at first sight, that women accept and perpetuate it. They recognize that there is something artificial in the sexual division of labour: 'It *is* funny, when you come in here and you see all the women on the carousels and packing and you see all the men on the trucks. You know what I mean. They are all in their own little groups, kind of thing.' But the majority would not strive to change this. The fact is that they do not feel capable of the jobs men do. They are easily persuaded that men are the only ones with the strength for physical labouring. Besides, the lads are on average younger than the women. Anyway, the small gain in pay they might get from transferring to that kind of work would be at the cost of being a stranger in a male world and having to explain yourself continually to both women and men.

Many women accept men's representation of them as technically incompetent. One picker, talking about what she had observed when the maintenance fitter came and repaired her carousel, said with a giggle, 'All wires!' *Would you be interested to learn more about how it works?* I asked. 'Me? No! I'd probably blow it up. No. Oh, no.' Realistically, of course, the technology represents a strict demarcation barrier. A woman could not intervene in the working of the machinery. 'No. You mustn't. Because if anything goes wrong, it's all electric, isn't it. Computer-like. No, you tell your supervisor and she goes to the maintenance men. They come.'

Relations across the sexes are often stylized, even strained. Among your own kind you can talk your own talk, be yourself: 'It's all women's talk up there. I don't think men would be welcome (with a merry laugh). You know what we women are with our women's talk.' Work is exhausting enough without dealing with embarrassment, troublesome or unusual forms of relationship. Masculinity, femininity, may narrow your chances and abuse your potential. But in such adverse circumstances as warehouse work the effort of trying to cross the gender barrier, abandoning the supportive society of women, can be the straw that breaks a woman's back.

The women also have a sense of what is right and proper – less for themselves than for men. A man's self-respect ought to be enhanced by his work. Of those who had been there the day when the management had tried out a couple of lads on carousel picking, one said, 'It's really *for* women, I think, picking. It seems too easy for men. You'd think they'd do a harder job. Just pushing buttons, it doesn't seem right to see a man doing that. I wouldn't want *my* husband to do it.' Another remarked, 'To see them standing there, picking out baby clothes, little girls' dresses, pants or something. I don't know why, but I don't think . . .' Some of the women found it a right laugh, the lads looked so funny: 'We was laffing, we thought it was great. They was more afraid of their mates, of the other fellers in the warehouse, calling them sissies. They got embarrassed.' But they were sorry for them.

Crossing the barriers of sex segregation at work is an asymmetrical experience – more painful for men than for women. This is evident in the scattered circumstances where change is occurring. Beyond Delta Maternity Ltd., in the wider mail order warehouse scene, managements have begun to see advantage in tinkering with the sexual division of labour. Management can gain flexibility in their deployment of labour by doing so. Alpha Catalogues has put a few women on forklift truck driving. As a consultant told me, 'If you are looking for a careful forklift driver, look for a woman.'

Even Delta had trained one woman to operate the smaller and simpler of the two kinds of truck in use in the warehouse. She earned a little higher pay for having this competence, but in fact seldom used it, being treated as a reserve driver only. It was interesting to hear the comments on this woman's achievement. She got a bit of ribbing at first: 'Watch out, woman driver!' But most of the women admired and commended her spirit: 'If you can drive a car, why not a truck?' And the young electro-mechanical fitter explored his feelings about it this way:

When I saw Joan driving the picker truck I was quite *surprised*. But it also gave me a little, er – it made me feel happy for her, actually. I don't know why. Perhaps it's because she was getting involved in the men's work. I'm not sure. It's a funny feeling actually. It came over me. I was quite astonished when I first saw her, but when I watched the way she was handling it – she's a very good driver actually – I felt a little thing inside me, 'Oh, it's very good for the women. Must be a plus for the women.' I'd like to see a bit more of that at Delta.

Managers of firms like these in the mail order business, and the owners to whom they are answerable, are men. They have a sense of what is an appropriate shop-floor sexual division of labour in a male power system and will often support male employees in maintaining certain jobs as male. If the interests of men as a sex, however, conflict with the interests of profitability, managers must act in the interests of capital. They may have to sacrifice a particular group of male employees to the wheels of change. Sometimes too women's own organization and initiative can swing a decision in women's favour.

Beta Warehouses PLC is an example of this. The year after my study was completed, the shop steward (a woman) reported, 'There's been a devastating impact by technology since we talked to you. It's been bloody traumatic. And it's going to go even further.' Among other things, a new conveyor belt had been introduced in the receiving bay. This belt triggered a three-way struggle between management, women and men. Men and women had both been working, though on different tasks, in the receiving bay. The computerization now made four women per belt surplus to need. Management stated the intention of moving them away, inevitably into another female ghetto. This time the women demanded and won the right to apply instead for the men's jobs in the receiving bay, unloading waggons and palletizing at the end of the belt. Encouraged by this success they also obtained the right to apply for forklift truck driver vacancies.

The really revolutionary step was yet to come, however. The management had a policy of offering voluntary severance pay to redundant workers only if no suitable alternative could be found for them in the warehouse. The women learned that some men were obtaining severance pay on the grounds that the only available positions were low-status women's jobs in picking and packing. Men were not expected to do these. The men had been saying it would make them feel degraded. They couldn't bring themselves to work alongside women. One said the idea made him feel giddy. He explained that he had a phobia about heights and in the same way he had a phobia about women's work. But the women said to the company, 'If you allow the men to get away with this, if you give them severance pay just because they refuse women's work, we will take you to tribunal.'

The women won. Some men were even obliged to join the picking line. The women had used their numbers, their unionization and a competent woman shop steward who was not afraid to call women-only meetings to change completely the criteria on which jobs were allocated in the firm. The principle today is seniority, not sex. The woman shop steward recounted, 'The men got really dirty and mean and nasty about it. But we won. We haven't changed the men's attitude. That would take a bloody miracle. But we have changed the management's reasoning.' Later she reported, 'I *think* the men are settling in. The girls on the picking line welcomed them. One of the men had a birthday and the girls did a whip round and bought him a sweater. He were over the moon with it! Men don't do that kind of thing for each other.'

The approach of the robot

To sum up the situation, not just in Delta Maternity but in mail order warehouses generally, there exists a situation of baseline unskilled jobs for a large number of women and a smaller number of men. In terms of class relations it is no exaggeration to say that these jobs are almost totally subordinated to the interests of capital. Pay is minimal. The recession holds the labour force to the grindstone. Every unskilled warehouse worker is conscious of the difficulty of getting alternative work in the local job market today. Many women workers are supporting their families, either because they are single parents or because their husbands are unemployed. In such conditions employers can, and do, ring the changes between part-time and full-time working, young and old workers, permanent and temporary workers, female and male workers, to suit themselves. They are in a position today to implement their preferences.

Unionization is either incomplete or non-existent. In some firms, like Delta Maternity, the union has been unable to get a foothold. '*I'm* their shop steward,' said the warehouse controller firmly, in answer to my question. The unions, particularly USDAW in the warehouses and ASTMS in the offices, have struggled to win membership and recognition in mail order throughout the 1970s and 80s. They have gained ground in larger firms and, as we've seen, women have achieved some gains.

Unions have made efforts to educate their members about new technology and its implications, but they have had to accept it because they can do little else. 'The new technology has come in because of the recession,' a woman shop steward at Alpha Catalogues said. 'We saw it might save jobs and we were afraid to resist, seeing the unemployment all around.' Of course, in the immediate term, the technology has not saved but cost jobs. The closure of some warehouses and the opening of new centralized warehouses makes it difficult to assess the overall trend in mail order warehouse employment and in women's jobs in particular. I visited one as yet unmechanized but already computer-organized warehouse where the manager commented cheerfully, 'We've shifted a hell of a lot in three years.' *A hell of a lot of what?* I asked. 'People.' They had achieved a drop from 5,500 to 3,500, while the only people they had recruited in that period had been 'specialists, technical people'.

At Delta Maternity Ltd. the story is the same. The high-bay warehouse and its equipment cost the firm £1¼ million. This was paid for by productivity gains in less than two years. It has been possible to speed orders, reduce stock levels and save on space. The same operation by the old methods would have demanded 75 per cent more warehouse cube. There were a number of layoffs, first 20, then a group of eight, then a further 12. Thereafter there was a process of natural wastage so that overall the warehouse numbers have fallen from 170 to 98. Of the 72 jobs lost, 68 were those of women part-timers. The overall effect of the carousel system in particular seems to have been a loss of more than half the picking jobs with a doubling of throughput. The 39 women engaged in picking and replenishing under the old system have fallen to 18 today. It was only three years later that jobs vacated by natural wastage began again to be filled and overall numbers to stabilize.

So technology has both cost jobs and transformed the jobs that remain. Women's work was always hard. Now, 'picking and packing are real grafting jobs for diabolically low wages. And it's all women in there. I've never seen a man slogging like that.' The result is 'more people on the picking floors have nerves than ever before.' The work is a daily treadmill to which, incredibly, women bring their best. 'You come in day after day. You know what you've got to do, and it's the same thing, just with different varieties. You know what's coming next. You just get on and do it. Common sense. I say to myself, come on Lynn, *you* know what has to be done next, don't stand there like an idiot waiting to be told. I just do it. It's like a circle really.' There are stories, however, of breakdown and valium-dependency. In some of the warehouses, industrial unrest is evident. One or two companies made it clear to me that this was their reason for refusing me access to interview employees. It is probably precisely because Delta Maternity was not unionized and the control relatively laid back ('We measure their daily output but we don't throw it back at them') that I was allowed to interview there.

Mail order warehouses show women in a stark relationship to technology. The forward stock warehouses in which they work are gradually emulating the bulk store warehouses, taking on the character of giant machines, tending towards the total machine. Caught mid-way in technological change, with job conditions deteriorating and with labour unrest, managements are vexed by their continued dependence on people. Because they still *do* need the human element, especially to cover for the faults and weaknesses of their new force of production. 'If the computer goes up the Swanee, everything stops,' said a shop steward at Alpha. 'Every minute lost loses the firm thousands of pounds. *People* can be fetched and shoved in to deal with the trouble. They are flexible.'

The same thing was echoed by management. They would dearly love a reliable mechanical, computer-controlled system that could do without people. In the advanced warehouses, men's truck driving and handling efforts in the bulk store have already been displaced by the intelligent unmanned crane. Now it's women's turn. In mail order warehouses, as one manufacturer of materials handling equipment said, 'The people we talk to, the people who are running things, are men. I'm afraid women will finish up in the picking jobs and that's all.' And he added, 'It was not so long ago they brought women into men's jobs in warehousing. Now it's these same women's jobs that everyone is scheming to get rid of.' In the picking area the challenge to the technologists today, the thing they love to talk about, is developing a robot hand to replace the hand of a woman. It would use a grasp mechanism or suction pads to lift the merchandise. It has to be strong enough to lift a pair of shoes, gentle enough to handle a lace nightie without damaging it. It won't be long before they get what they want. The engineering firms are working overtime to design and produce such systems.[9]

In the meantime, where machinery and women interact, the result is a social mutilation of the softer partner: the human being. At Delta Maternity Ltd. the carousel and the computer have perhaps been factors contributing to the survival of their firm. The women say to themselves, 'At least we are not on the dole.' And they have avoided the dreaded alternative of the local food factory, cutting off chicken's heads all day. But for the pickers there has been no increase in pay, no gain in skills, no question of 're-training' for a job which after all takes no more than a couple of hours to get the hang of. At Delta, technology has brought women neither the opportunity to develop physical confidence nor technical know-how and ability. It has just brought them a headache and a sense of dizziness.

4. Technology and caring: new developments in medical X-ray

We've looked at the way computer technology has been transforming jobs in manufacturing and distribution. The third instance of technological change is, by contrast, in the public sector: hospitals of the National Health Service. It is a step away from unskilled or semi-skilled manual work in the business world and into the professional hierarchies of medicine. One of the most technical departments of any hospital is the X-ray department, known to almost everyone as the place they were once carried with a fractured ankle or a slipped disc. The chances are that when they had an X-ray taken of the damaged bone it was a woman who operated the equipment. The great majority of radiographers are women and the occupation is widely thought of as 'a woman's job'. But in many ways this is surprising. Probably this occupation involves women in a higher level of technological knowledge and competence than any other female-stereotyped work. It is in many ways a success story for women and one that disproves the myth that women are unsuited to technological work.

X-radiation was discovered by Röntgen at the end of the nineteenth century. It gradually evolved as a medical diagnostic facility over the next 100 years, to the point where, today, 80 per cent of all admissions to hospital pass through the X-ray department for one reason or another.[1] The technique of radiography involves generating a controlled beam of radiation and passing it through the patient's body in order to record an image of internal structure. The image is normally represented on a radiograph, a transparent photo. 'X-ray', however, is no longer an adequate term to describe what goes on in this area of medical diagnosis. During the 1970s there has been a rapid development in imaging technology. The medically useful spectrum of radiation has expanded, from X-rays to gamma rays and sound waves ('ultrasound'). A recent development is the use of magnetism and radio frequencies in the technology of nuclear magnetic resonance scanning (NMR). Increasingly, in all these new processes, the computer has been enlisted to capture and reconstruct the data received about the patient's internal structure and to amplify and intensify the image, making it easier to interpret. Even in X-ray, the radiograph is now giving way to 'digital X-ray', in which the picture is presented on a video screen. Today the bigger hospitals do not speak any more of the X-ray department but of an 'imaging centre', equipped with many different and complementary kinds of diagnostic machinery.

At some point, however, we have to stop history in order to take a snapshot picture of one item of new technology making its impact on the radiographer. For this purpose I have chosen computed axial tomography, usually abbreviated to CAT and more recently to CT. Cancer scanners, as they are popularly known, have come into widespread use in the NHS in the last ten years. They add a surprising facility to the doctor's diagnostic tools: they can produce *cross-sectional* pictures of the human anatomy. A second merit of computed tomography is that it has much greater sensitivity than conventional X-ray to small variations in tissue density, so that as well as imaging bone it can readily differentiate the uterus from the bladder, kidneys and liver from surrounding tissue, healthy from damaged parts of the brain or body.

The scanner works on an ingenious geometric principle. In place of a single X-ray picture resulting in a flat radiograph, the scanner rotates around the body through 360 degrees, taking a series of transverse 'shots'. The outcoming radiation is received by a travelling detector or ring of detectors. The beam, as it passes through the body, is used up, or attenuated, to a different extent as it passes through hard tissue or soft, and the resulting readings are combined and reconstructed mathematically to produce, on a video screen, the cross-sectional picture that is characteristic of CT. The scanner moves not only around the patient's body, to make a single scan, but lengthways, making images of successive 'slices' as it goes. It is only the computer that has made it possible to handle such a quantity of data and such complex geometric calculations.[2]

The technique of CT was invented by Godfrey Hounsfield, a scientist working for EMI in Britain in 1967. Four years later, EMI installed the world's first brain scanner, and in 1976 the first whole-body scanner, both in London hospitals. By 1980 there were estimated to be 2,500 in use worldwide, and at the time of this research (in 1983) there were known to be at least 86 hospitals in Britain with more than 100 scanners between them.

Although computed tomography is used for many different purposes, including neurology, its most common use is in detecting tumours and providing accurate information as to where they are, how big they are and how fast they are growing. It is therefore closely linked to the treatment of cancer. Here again a radiation technology is involved, because one form of treatment is radiotherapy, the bombardment of the cancer cells with ionizing radiation. Data from CT scans can be used to prepare accurate plans for use in radiotherapy, where the technology is also advancing rapidly. Twinned with a CT scanner it is now common to find computerized planning programs and a linear accelerator, a radiotherapy machine of enormously increased power and precision. These 'lin-accs' are also computer-assisted. They will have a place, though a subsidiary one, alongside CT in this account.

Politics in high-tech health

For all its undeniable diagnostic power, computed tomography has its critics. First they cite problems of finance and administration. Resources in the NHS are painfully short and scanners are very costly. The majority therefore have been bought by private donation or public appeal. However, even if the £400,000 to £600,000 capital cost is found by philanthropy, the NHS eventually has to pick up the running cost which may amount to £100,000 a year. Two authors argued in 1978 that:

the situation with whole body scanners has been very unsatisfactory. Health authorities have been presented with a *fait accompli* and have had little choice but to accept these gifts . . . It is not necessary to deny that the whole body scanner is an impressive technological innovation in order to say that the public should be presented with the other aspects of the case: that there are expensive installation and running costs associated with the machine, that clinical evaluation is not yet complete, that there are other technologies which might be equally useful and that the evidence about the scanner's effect on the outcome of the patient's condition is as yet very limited and hardly overwhelming.[3]

This of course was the second problem. Cancer is an emotive subject and to the distress of some doctors (and even some concerned manufacturers) the fund-raisers often dress up the scanner as something that can 'cure cancer', which of course it is not. One doctor explained, 'The accent in some appeals is scandalous. Probably the biggest role that CT really has is to stop some poor patient having mutilating surgery because we are able to show that the cancer has gone too far.' Another added bitterly that what the patient gets from the scanner is little more than 'the satisfaction of dying with the right diagnosis'. A third worry about scanning is the way it appears to ally naturally with a trend, encouraged by the Thatcher government, to privatization of health services. The potential for making money by cancer scanning is illustrated by the USA where a typical hospital charging $200 a scan can net $20,000 a month after taking into account depreciation of the machine.[4] There are already a number of private scan units in Britain.

The escalation of technology in imaging is the archetype of capital-intensive health care. It has been forcefully argued that too much money is directed towards the modern doctor's priority of peering inside the patient's body and too little to understanding the relationship of the patient to the environment and those things in the environment that makes a person ill. 'The scanner may be very much more sophisticated than the stethoscope, but the project for which it has been devised is essentially the same: to look *inside* for explanations,' wrote Jeanette Mitchell. She also points out that scanners represent the success of the most powerful doctors in the hierarchy of medical specialisms in pressing their case for resources and the cynical interests of hospital administrators in achieving the most efficient utilization of bed spaces – most patients having scans can do so as out-patients.[5]

There is always a tendency, once equipment is available, to use it for its own sake. It is all too easy for a doctor to say, 'Let's have a scan.' It adds one more patient's results to the data available for research purposes. It 'justifies' the acquisition of the scanner. The doctor, however, will not in most cases be present to deal with the human reality: a scan can be an uncomfortable and alarming procedure to a very ill patient. The radiographer, who must deal with the patient in interaction with the machine, may sometimes deplore the doctor's decision to use it.

The scanner enters an NHS hospital, then, as an object scarcely innocent of politics. The world it enters is also highly politicized. The scanner, with its handsomely styled couch and gantry and its flashy console, will be installed behind a glass wall that may impede stray radiation but is not impermeable to a seepage of departmental rivalries and ambitions. CT is usually located geographically in the diagnostic X-ray unit, but socially it is mid-way between a number of interest groups. The radiographers are in charge of day-to-day operation of the scanner and the handling of patients passing through the unit. But as para-professionals they are junior in status to the consultants, the doctors, who are responsible for patient management. The radiographer provides a radiographic service for the consultant radiologist who is thus in charge of the scanner's clinical use. A third team, the medical physics department, staffed by scientists and technicians, has a technical overview of all equipment involving radiation, with responsibility for safety and accuracy. Technological change causes tensions and movement in the relationship between these various groups of professional and technical employees, just as we've seen it bring about a recomposition of skill grades elsewhere.

Within the field of co-operation and competition in the hospital there is a gender dynamic at work. The occupations of medicine are a rigid hierarchy, quite closely class-related, in which the ranks are differentiated by uniforms. The pay differentials are very wide. A basic-grade radiographer at the time of my study was on a rate of around £5,000 a year. A hospital cleaner might get not much more than half that, whereas a consultant begins at three times the figure. Among the occupations, doctors, physicists and technicians are sex-stereotyped male; nurses and radiographers female.[6] In practice, however, this image is lagging behind a situation in which sex segregation is increasingly breaking down. Among the doctors, radiology is a specialism that attracts women. This is said to be because it is possible to limit the demands of overtime and so to combine it, even if with some difficulty, with family commitments. Among physicists the intake is now estimated to be one-third female. And 15 per cent of radiographers today are men. The supporting engineering workshops, however, remain stubbornly male.

So the CT scanner enters hospitals in which a certain gender ideology already exists. Men are 'supposed' to be in top jobs and in the higher technical or scientific jobs. Women are 'supposed' to be in the caring and lower-ranking occupations. The new technology can be seen as provoking a contradiction. It is expressed in a struggle by women radiographers to represent their job, operating the machines, as a responsible and a technological job, and by scientists, engineers and doctors to dismiss both its significance and its technicalities. Individuals, as we shall see, bring their own ideas and practices into this drama, sometimes defying expectations.

The work of the radiographer

To see the old and new technologies in use I spent time in two hospitals. One had a diagnostic X-ray department and a small radiotherapy unit, both with conventional technology. I will call it Northshire General Hospital. The other had, in addition to a range of conventional equipment, a very up-to-date CT scanner and a linear accelerator. This was Southerton Hospital.

At Northshire General, the senior medical consultant in radiology is a man. He is assisted by both male and female doctors. The diagnostic X-ray department is headed by a woman superintendent and staffed by a team of 19 radiographers, of whom four are men. The men are spread among the middle and lower ranks. A huge amount of overtime is worked in Northshire's X-ray department, bringing average weekly hours to 80 or more, with the effect of more than doubling basic pay for some radiographers. This is felt by those I talked with to be essential to obtaining a decent living wage.

The labour process of the radiographers, though tough, is varied and interesting. They work on a rota, spending time in casualty, in out-patients, on specialist work, and in taking the portable X-ray around the wards.

The procedure for a standard X-ray – say, of chest or extremities – is as follows. The radiographer receives a clinical diagnosis from the radiologist, with a request for an X-ray of a particular part of the body. The radiographer decides what views will best serve the clinical purpose. She or he receives the patient, explains what is going to be done, answers questions. She or he then positions the patient on the couch or against the stand, drawing on a good deal of knowledge of physiology and expertise in positioning techniques so as to obtain the best possible radiograph. This often means achieving a satisfactory working compromise between the technical ideal and the patient's pain or distress.

Once the patient has been positioned, the radiographer makes use of a 'light beam diaphragm' which is directed to the centring point on the patient's anatomy. The cones that control the divergence of the X-ray are closed or opened as appropriate, so as to define the area to be imaged. A film is selected from among several available grades of sensitivity, inserted into a container beneath the couch and centred on the X-ray beam. The radiographer makes certain technical decisions concerning the controls that govern the X-ray exposure. While these become routine, they do nonetheless call for experience, technical know-how and judgement, and an ability to make simple calculations. It is normal for the radiographer to set the controls that govern kilovoltage (which affects X-ray penetration) and milli-amperage (which affects blackening of the film), as well as the time of the exposure and the focus. With the aim of achieving a sharp image, she or he must judge the patient's ability to hold still and make a decision as to the length of exposure and film 'speed' bearing this in mind. The body mass of the patient also has a bearing on the differential absorption of the X-ray beam, so radiographers must make an intuitive assessment of the patient's bulk, building this into their calculation of exposure. When all the controls have been set the radiographer asks the patient to hold still. From behind the protective screen she or he will then operate the controls that make the exposure.

During the course of a working year the radiographer will also be involved in more complex procedures such as those involved in imaging the arteries, kidneys or bladder. Some of these call for team-working with doctor and anaesthetist. The pressure of patient throughput is often high. One radiographer at Northshire told me she often dealt with as many as 70 patients in a day and, 'I sometimes think,' she said, 'that if I have to tell one more person to breathe in and hold still I shall scream.' In certain situations, such as casualty, each new patient presents a different and often emergency problem.

So the radiographer's job calls for a high degree of composure, orderliness, efficiency and knowledge. Like nursing, it also demands emotional strength. The person who takes X-rays is a bridge between technology and the sick human being, a negotiator between machinery and pain and fear.

The advent of CT scanning

At Southerton Hospital the routine work is not dissimilar from that at Northshire General. What is different is the addition of computed axial tomography. The acquisition of CT has created two extra posts in the diagnostic X-ray department. (There have also been new jobs born of CT in the departments of radiology, radiotherapy and physics.) The newly appointed radiographers, however, are simply additions to the whole team, working like the others on a job rota that involves them in six weeks on the scanner followed by a spell in each of another four rooms.

The head of the radiology department at Southerton is a man, of consultant grade, and the consultant in charge of the CT scan unit is a woman. They are supported by a number of other doctors of both sexes. The diagnostic X-ray department has a female superintendent in charge, seven full-time and two part-time radiographers, a darkroom technician, a nursing sister, a number of secretaries and a porter. Only the porter is a man. The department has, in addition to its CT scanner, four conventional X-ray rooms, each with a generator and a number of pieces of ancillary equipment. The throughput is about 100 patients a day. *The number has doubled in four years, with no increase in staff.*

The process of making a scan is as follows. The radiographer greets the patient and supervises his or her preparation for the scan. This may involve asking the patient to drink down a particular preparation to reveal the bladder clearly on the scan; giving an injection; or, in the case of a female patient, inserting a vaginal tampon. As with conventional X-ray, perhaps even more so, many patients are afraid of the machine and need reassurance. Some are children, many are elderly and some seriously ill. They call for a skilled nursing approach from the radiographer.

First, the patient's personal details (name, number, type of study, doctor's name, etc.) are tapped onto the keyboard. The radiographer meanwhile positions the patient on the couch, usually in a simple flat-on-the-back position. The couch then slides within the circumference of the cylindrical gantry of the scanner. The radiographer retires to the control room, talking to the patient by intercom. Sometimes taped music may be played to soothe the patient.

The initial step in scanning is to produce on the video screen a topogram, or *flat* X-ray picture of the patient's body as seen from above. The radiographer, using the VDU keyboard, taps in the instructions for the program of scans the doctor has asked for. The computer prompts, with questions on the screen, each step the radiographer must take. The program she or he selects will define the number of 'cuts', the interval between them and the breadth of the section from which the data will be averaged. She or he 'tells' the computer the start position by reference to the topogram and a prepared mark on the patient's body, and the decisions are then played back by the computer as white lines across the topogram on the screen: 'this is where you have asked for scans to be made'. The radiographer may then make alterations before going ahead. The quality of the image, too, is checked by the radiographer and the computer may be instructed to enlarge or reduce it, or enhance the contrast or brightness. When the radiographer is satisfied that the program of scans may go ahead, she or he warns the patient over the intercom to hold still, and sets the scanner in motion.

The entire scanning process may take 30 to 45 minutes – though it can be speeded up if the patient's tolerance is low. When the scan has been completed the radiographer helps the patient from the couch and, depending on his or her condition, either sees the patient out or places her or him in the hands of nursing staff. The data produced by the scan have been stored automatically on magnetic tape and will remain as a permanent record. It will now be replayed on the video screen by the radiographer, sometimes with the doctor present, and selected images will be transferred by means of keyboard instruction to a floppy disc to be kept on the patient's file. A set of ordinary handleable radiographs may also be produced from the computer record since they are easier to view. The scan will be used by doctors to guide patient treatment, which may include surgery or radiotherapy. In the latter case the scans will assist in prescribing 'doses' of radiation and the planning of treatment by the physics department.

Losses and gains for the radiographer

CT scanning is more of a push-button job than the older forms of diagnostic X-ray. Once familiar with the method of communicating with the scanner via keyboard and screen, the radiographer quickly becomes aware that relatively little decision-making remains in the operator's hands. Exposure time and kilovoltage, for instance, no longer need calculating. There is not the skill involved, nor the strenuous physical effort for that matter, in positioning the patient's body and limbs for different shots. Once learned it is a rather repetitive and routine process. 'Don't be misled,' said one radiologist, 'CT may be costly but it is *very simple*.'

It is because of this that the inclusion of CT on a rota is a vitally important point. Unlike the situation in the mail order warehouses and in the pattern rooms of clothing manufacturers, where new technology involves a total transformation of the labour process and the scrapping of conventional tools and techniques, in the hospitals CT is supplementary to the traditional technology. It is an additional aspect of the responsibility falling on the radiography profession, something new to learn and, once learned, an extra skill to offer on the labour market.

One very adverse change has been an increase in pressure for the radiographers. The enormously high cost of the scanner means that the hospital must demonstrate that it is used to top capacity, patients herded through. This is one of the factors that contributes to the technical simplicity of the job. A manufacturer told me that, owing to pressure of work in hospitals, only one-third of a scanner's sophisticated possibilities are in everyday use. There is little time for making the most of data produced by the scan. Worse, there is little opportunity for talking with patients, who are besides somehow more distant behind their glass screen. 'Whereas in X-ray you may have to say to the patient, "Will you turn on your left side, sit up, lie down", and each time you do an X-ray you go to the patient, with the scanner you just set the patient up and then go outside and do all the scans from there.' The way the radiographer sees the job, the quality of care and a close interaction with patients are of paramount importance. These are deteriorating.

It is a sub-group of qualified radiographers – radiotherapy

radiographers – who carry out radiation treatment of cancer patients. If a progressive tempering of emotional needs by technological considerations is visible in diagnostic X-ray, it is still more dramatic here in radiotherapy, where the terrible power of the lin-accs and often mortal sickness of the patient confront each other. At Southerton the accelerator in use today delivers 10 million X-ray volts. The one they hope soon to acquire will pack a punch of 25 million volts. Five-foot-thick safety walls box in the equipment. Treatment time is reduced to as little as 30 seconds and a small error either way in treating a tumour can have disastrous effects. Relying on the computer does not reduce the tension: mistakes are always possible whether through the fallibility of person or machine. Besides, it is an unglamorous job: 'People throw up, they defecate, they bleed over you and they die in your hands.' The radiographer wants to have time to talk to the patient, to keep her or him informed, to give support and loving care. The superintendent of radiotherapy radiography at Southerton, a woman in charge of a mainly female team, said, 'The biggest complaint I get as superintendent is that the girls feel they miss out on involvement with the patients. Sometimes we feel jealous of the nurses. Without the caring, the routine drudgery becomes bigger and more difficult to survive.' Handled sensitively, new technology, whether lin-accs or CT, need not of itself drive a wedge between the radiographer and the patient. In a context of health spending cuts, long patient queues and short staffing, however, it will do so.

In many ways, computed tomography has nonetheless been a genuine gain for the diagnostic radiographer. Technologically, while she has lost some direct control of settings she has gained familiarity with computers and their controls. More important, the very clear cross-sectional images of CT bring, literally, 'a whole new dimension' to the radiographer's anatomical knowledge. Clinical interest has been added to the work. Whether or not doctors attend the scan, radiographers are more likely than in conventional X-ray to develop their 'pattern recognition' skills and to discuss the patient's condition with the doctor.

From information received from 60 hospitals using CT, it is

clear that most radiographers are pleased by the arrival of computed tomography. They would, however, definitely not wish to work on it permanently or full-time because that would mean gaining an additional skill and responsibility only to lose the ability to practise those they already possess. At present it seems that most hospitals do in fact include CT on a rota and involve a high proportion of all radiographers in operating it, so there is little danger that CT will damage the profession. When the skilled craftsman in clothing learns the computer routines that replace his craft skill he sometimes says, 'Well, it's another string to my bow, isn't it.' He is deluding himself, for he'll never need scissors and pencils again. But when the radiographer says this of scanning, it is for the moment true. CT is a genuine addition to her or his competence.

There is, however, a latent struggle over the radiographer's skill. The manufacturers of the new equipment are undoubtedly trying to make each successive generation (not only of scanner but of all imaging equipment) more 'idiot proof' than the last. Iontomats measure film exposure and switch off the X-ray machine automatically. Organ programs mean you just press a button bearing the symbol 'head' or 'chest' and the machine does the rest. International competition is tending this way, as the Japanese manufacturers try to break into the world market with scanners that are cheaper and simpler than European models. The 'dinky toy' scanner is aimed first at the growing market for X-ray equipment in less-developed countries where the manufacturers are encouraging the idea of the 'barefoot radiographer'. But it will certainly also find buyers in Europe.

Many doctors and physicists, jealously guarding and promoting their own special brand of expertise, dismiss the radiographer's skill and argue against the increasingly elaborate training they receive.[7] At present the Diploma of the College of Radiographers requires three years' study, combining formal education with on-the-job training in a hospital. The basic entry requirement today is four GCE passes, of which two must be at A-level. The courses lead to exams in such subjects as physics, anatomy, photography, equipment and patient care. There is a higher diploma, too, involving more advanced study and other optional qualifications in nuclear medicine and ultrasound. A specialist short course in computed tomography is now under discussion.

The medical and scientific establishments are not keen on the upgrading of radiography training. One male consultant radiologist complained to me, 'For 60 per cent of radiographers it is totally unnecessary for them to have learned anything except anatomy, positioning and what knobs to twiddle. You see? They don't really need to know anything about how the equipment works at all – most of the time.' He was ferociously opposed to the recent raising of standards of entry to radiography courses and suggested that 'someone to take X-rays' could be adequately trained in six weeks. There was some male rivalry involved here perhaps, for he felt that the average unassuming radiographer (read as female) was manipulated by ambitious people 'up there' in her profession (read as male). Likewise, a physicist said, 'As far as the machines are concerned it is really a question of pushing buttons and, ah – how can I put it without trying to run the job down – it wouldn't take too long I think for anyone to train.' *As a person with no prior knowledge, how long would it take me to learn to use an X-ray machine?* I asked him. 'Ten minutes.' This physicist, the doctor quoted previously, and many like them, would prefer to see the profession of radiography split into two levels: routine technicians quickly trained; and, as one put it, 'people of vision' to head the profession and take the senior posts. He felt, not incidentally, that the former were likely to be women, the latter men.

CT scanning also precipitates disagreement between radiographers and physicists concerning certain aspects of the overall labour process. For instance, measuring radiation 'doses' and planning radiotherapy treatments – steps intermediate between scanning and radiotherapy – are things a radiographer is trained for and would like to do. Yet in both hospitals this work was done by the medical physics department, emphatic that it was within their remit.

Radiographers are sharply aware of being caught up in a struggle over relative competence in the hospital. They insist that advances in technology call for more not less training for their profession: 'We have to be very careful how we go about things. Doctors have the last say and physicists have actual control of the technology. The radiographer could become the pig in the middle, just using the thing.' Of course every job, even that of the scientist or doctor, involves a certain amount of routine. So does that of the radiographer. But, as one said, for them the important thing is 'to expand our expertise, not narrow it down. We don't want to be reduced to button-pushers, which is what the doctors want us to be.'

The profession is well equipped to defend its interests. Radiographers are protected by the College of Radiographers, which governs recruitment, in negotiation with the Department of Health and Social Security. The related Society of Radiographers acts as a trade union, but some radiographers also belong to the Association of Scientific, Technical and Managerial Staffs (ASTMS), which has a radiography advisory committee and negotiates with the NHS on behalf of radiographers. Not so long ago a radiographer could 'interview the hospital' rather than beg for a job. Even today, though the seller's market is less buoyant, there is still no large surplus of radiographers to bring the rest to heel. The status of radiography is recognized within the Council for Professions Supplementary to Medicine, set up in 1961, with which all practising radiographers must be registered. The radiographer's role is defined in law: doctors and physicists, for all their higher status, are not qualified to take X-rays of patients. During the 1970s, trade union consciousness and activity throughout the hospitals resulted in a committee of enquiry which gave a pay boost and improved the career structure for radiographers and other para-professionals.[8] One danger that has been averted is the risk that radiotherapy radiography, with its particular demands on nursing ability, would develop as a second-class group, all-women and lower-paid, within the profession.

It is their professional organization that has so far ensured that radiographers' prospects have not been damaged by advancing technology. It is not surprising that they have done better out of technical change than clothing workers or warehouse hands. Career prospects have opened up, not closed. In the 66 hospitals I surveyed a total of 113 new radiographer posts had been created by CT scanning. The status of hospitals acquiring CT rubs off on those who work in them: 'Having CT means you have an ace team.' Such experience looks good on a *curriculum vitae*. Nor have women, as women, lost out. The new posts at Southerton were held by women, and in other hospitals too 'women have been in there when new technology came and they have moved along with it.' In many ways, for all the stereotyping in hospitals, the NHS provides women with a more supportive environment than industry. At Southerton Hospital, for instance, the employees have a creche and several radiographers have had children and come back to work, bringing them along.

Men in a minority

In the female-stereotyped profession of radiography there is now a growing minority of men. In departments of medical physics there is a growing minority of women, invading a formerly male fraternity of scientists. In such a situation of flux it is possible to see a manoeuvring by men to make use of subdivisions in the work and the structure of staffing in such a way as to define themselves as separate from, different from and superior in various ways to women. Women as a consequence are actively involved in defending and advancing their status. What men and women say about each other in these situations is sometimes cruel, sometimes generous and often comic. An ideology of gender difference is widely expressed. And the technology and the skills needed to control it emerge over and again as themes in the power play that goes on between departments and between the sexes.

The profession of radiography, when it was founded in the 1920s, was the creation of a group of men. As the occupation became less experimental and more routine, women were recruited as operators of the equipment. It came to be thought of as a suitable career for a middle-class girl wanting to get away from the parental home for a few years before setting up a home of her own. This class connotation gradually weakened with the introduction of student grants. The Society had its first woman president in 1935. The number of male radiographers, however, grew in the war years as the armed forces trained their own. The improved pay and status that followed the report of the Halsbury Committee attracted more.[9] The scientific and technical content of the training was now given more emphasis and this too had the effect of attracting men. Today, with high levels of unemployment, many men are forced to overlook their distaste for 'women's work' in this field as in others. Two thousand out of the Society's total membership of 12,000 are men, and the proportion is growing.

Male radiographers tend to follow a different career path from that of women. First, the great majority opt for diagnostic rather than therapeutic radiography: it is less nursing-oriented, has more career openings and a higher earning potential. Radiotherapy offers little overtime. In disproportionate numbers men float rapidly upward to the top of the profession, helped by their freedom from day-to-day domestic responsibility. The result is that in 1984 the president, secretary and more than half of the College's council were men. A disproportionate number of men hold the senior post of superintendent in charge of departments. Men often seek opportunities abroad, in teaching, in research and in industry, as salesmen of X-ray equipment: 'Anything,' say some of their women colleagues, 'to avoid being there when someone is weeping or throwing up.'

There is a practical argument that is sometimes put forward *against* male radiographers in clinical work: when dealing with women patients they must be 'chaperoned' by a woman. Here, as in the warehouse and the clothing factory, sexuality as such emerges from the shadows and becomes one of the employer's management problems: 'You are obviously handling people, feeling them all over their bodies.' One male radiographer complained to me of the discrimination he felt when he was chaperoned in mammography work (i.e., examination of breasts). It is a situation where the individual man has to carry and answer for the relations that result from male sexual behaviour, however, not an instance of prejudice.

There is nonetheless some discrimination against male radiographers. The female superintendent in charge of diagnostic X-ray at Southerton Hospital said, 'I possibly shouldn't say this but I personally would *not* like to employ male radiographers. I have had a couple. Absolute disaster! (merry laughter).' She held that men 'weren't as patient with the patients'. And another superintendent radiographer said, 'If you haven't got the right approach, considering the patients and so on – for men it's more of a *job*.' She was backed up in her attitude by the female consultant radiologist who said, 'I don't blame her. It's a small group and the girls get on well together.'

This, on the face of it, sounds very like the prejudice encountered by women when men refuse to countenance taking *them* into their working teams. We have to look, however, at the reasons women discriminate, for they are quite contrary to the reasons men do so. The situations are not symmetrical. When women enter an occupation its status falls; when men do so pay and prospects tend to improve. The constant in each case is male power. Men scorn and despise women as workers and feel their manliness degraded by the presence of women in 'their' jobs. Plentiful evidence of this will emerge in Chapter 6. What women dislike about men joining them in 'their' jobs, however, is very different. They fear, with good reason, that the more men join the profession the fewer will be the top jobs available for women. The female superintendent quoted above, for instance, explained that it was 'problems of, I think, supposing that because they are male they can take over'. They dislike the superior attitude men bring with them, what women radiographers call the 'failed brain surgeon syndrome'. They resent the way patients, and indeed everyone in the hospital, defers to male radiographers more than to females. 'If there is a male around, even if he's a student, they'll address him as doctor.' 'The general assumption in hospital is that if you have a white coat on and are male you are a doctor. If you have a white coat on and are a woman you must be a lab assistant.'

There is another factor involved here. Some male radiologists and superintendent radiographers also discriminate against men because they personally prefer a female supporting team.

One radiographer called this 'the hareem principle'. It is recognized that, particularly before the Sex Discrimination Act, some consultants recruited women on the basis of whether they had a pretty face or good legs. 'They used weak excuses to reject men, like the lack of toilet facilities.' 'They like to rule their little roost.' Some male radiologists, however, prefer to have a male at the head of the radiography team, someone they can talk to 'man to man' while continuing to relate to the radiographers beneath him as a 'bunch of little girls'.

When male radiographers do appear on the scene, male superiors may feel agitated about ensuring career advancement for them. One male consultant I interviewed was noted for playing guardian angel to the male radiographers, and he did indeed point out to me those men in his department who were studying for their higher exam. He appeared quite unaware of the existence of the three women in his department who were studying for this same exam. 'I think on the whole,' he said, 'a man who is going into radiography will reckon he wants to become top chap, do you see? Whereas a lot of girls go into it thinking, well, nice thing to go into for a little while until perhaps I become a mum. They don't like the *hassle* of running a big unit. They won't ever want to go to the top.' This was in spite of the fact that currently, in his own hospital, the very competent superintendents of X-ray and radiotherapy radiography were both women.

This consultant saw the role of women as 'getting on with the rest of the hospital staff and patients more easily because they are girls. With doctors you know, a bit of femininity going around the place, cheers people up, doesn't it?' Indeed, the question of male radiographers carried contradictions for him because, while he respected those men who showed signs of proper ambition, he feared a male element that might not 'play the game', might let down the male 'first team': 'Looking scruffy, long hair hanging down the back, no tie on, that sort of thing. In the past I have had occasion to pull up some of the men.'

Women radiographers, as would be expected, vary in their individual generosity concerning male colleagues and the degree to which they gender-type them. Some wrote them off as 'hopeless with patients'. Some women were caught up in the conventional ideology of masculinity, either feeling the job to be too inferior for men or conversely feeling that men, if they were daft enough to want such a 'woman's job', must be in some way deficient: 'Male radiographers tend to be not too bright. If they were bright they would have gone into something with more opportunities for them.' 'They are a bit gormless, some of them.' The majority of women, however, totally rejected such ideas and insisted: 'They are every bit as good as us.' 'They have as much to offer as women. They *ought* to be here.'[10]

Of course, it is true, some men do want to achieve high status. 'My ambition is to get to the top,' one male diagnostic radiographer told me firmly. Some men do think they are whizz-kids with technology: 'I think if there was a new machine that none of us had seen before, I probably would pick it up quicker. Because I've always had a bit of an aptitude for making machines work.' Some feel that their supposedly greater physical strength must be an asset badly missed till now in the X-ray department. A slender and rather short 18-year old youth, newly arrived in a department staffed by well-built and experienced women, touchingly described how he would be able to 'help them out by lifting heavy patients'. Some men do undoubtedly feel inhibited by their masculine identity from holding a distressed patient's hand or putting an arm around them. The same young man said, 'I think I wouldn't be as good with a patient as a girl is. Why? Well, part of their instinct is to be mothers isn't it? Where a woman patient was crying perhaps (he laughed anxiously) I would feel a bit lost. I wouldn't be able to comfort them in a convincing way.' He felt male radiographers and nurses would come into their own 'restraining a violent patient'. As we shall see, however, not all men's self-images are so narrow.

Women: a scientific opinion

Though technically skilled, the radiographer is not the person who knows most about the principles and mechanisms of the equipment on which she or he works. That knowledge resides with the scientists and technicians of the medical physics department of the hospital. Medical physics acquired its importance in the hospital as new techniques involving harmful radiation developed. They were the team that took charge of quality assurance of equipment and radiation dosimetry for the radiotherapy department. They also took responsibility for the safe handling of radio isotopes and in many cases actually came to run the function of nuclear medicine – a diagnostic procedure in which the patient is injected with radioactive material and the emissions from the body measured on a 'gamma camera'. Gradually they acquired responsibility for X-ray equipment too. It was natural that, as the use of computers in medicine and health administration grew, much of the expertise was built up among the scientists of medical physics. Now, technical functioning of CT scanners has been added to the department's role. Although there has been a decline in nuclear medicine with the rise of CT scanning, physicists as a group have clearly, overall, gained influence by technological advance. Their trump card is the safety law. This and their scientific knowledge and competence place them in a position where they must now be included in decision-making on the acquisition and running of equipment. Technology has eroded the outright supremacy of the consultant: 'Doctors no longer have the control they like to think they have.' As a result, 'What is happening nationally', said a physicist, 'is, well, *war* would be too strong a word. But the medics are very conscious that they are being nudged hard by the physicists and they don't want to give up power.'

Medical physics is still a male-dominated world. Even though women have begun to get a foothold in the profession they cluster in the lower grades. About one-third of basic-grade physicists today are women, but only 17 per cent of seniors and 7 per cent of principals. In 1984 there were no women top-grade physicists in Britain and no women heads of department.[11] If women climb to senior grade it is normally in the nuclear medicine side of the department's work which involves patient care. Women are particularly favoured in nuclear medicine because, unlike a male physicist, they do not require 'chaperoning' when dealing with women patients. In 39 medical physics departments in hospitals with scanners, I found women to have a negligible role in computing and to be entirely absent from management, research and development and other purely scientific activities. There was a smaller proportion of women among those people in medical physics whose work involved them with CT scanners (2 per cent) than among the staff of medical physics generally, where women were 16 per cent of the total. It would appear that the preponderance of men in physics departments may have prevented women physicists getting the advantage from the advent of CT that women radiographers have acquired.

In Northshire General and at Southerton Hospital women constitute about one-third of the physicists – that is, more than the national average. All, however, were in basic grade but for one senior. The work done by women in these physics teams was similar in the two hospitals: quality and safety work, including calibration of radiotherapy machines; treatment planning; and dealing with patients in nuclear medicine.

Beneath the physicists in status is a corps of technicians. In Northshire and Southerton the technicians are 80–85 per cent male. Hospitals normally have a specific team, drawn from the technician grades, of technicians whose particular concern is the first-line maintenance of the machines. These are in effect hospital engineers. At Northshire the engineering technicians were part of the medical physics department, but at Southerton they formed a department of their own. The struggle we noted in Chapter 1 between different kinds and levels of technologist over control of technology, exacerbated by innovation, can be seen here in connection with the new imaging equipment. A technical manager in one of the big supplying firms said of the maintenance men in hospitals: 'A lot of them are flexing their muscles for more status and say in the hospital.' A maintenance technician did indeed tell me that he thought doctors and physicists were 'a bit bewildered because now they are so dependent on us. I think they find it very galling.'

The enhanced status of the hospital engineer may be illusory, however. The manufacturers of the equipment are actively trying to minimize the intervention of hospital personnel in the equipment in order to extend the control of the firms over their markets. They are doing this by making the machines more reliable, and by designing them so that whole components are removed and replaced when faulty, to be taken back to the factory for repair. It is almost impossible today for a hospital to avoid signing contracts with the suppliers of their equipment, who send their own engineers to the site. The manufacturers engage in a similar struggle with the hospitals' upper scientific echelon, the physicists. 'They want to talk with the computer and play with it,' complained one company's technical manager. 'We don't want that. We've designed it for simplicity in use. They take too intelligent an interest.'

The occupation of hospital maintenance technician is represented as profoundly masculine. At Southerton Hospital the chief technician was beside himself with irritation at being asked by me to discuss the question of the suitability of women for jobs in his department. He reluctantly showed me round his workshop, emphasizing the heaviness and hardness of both machinery and tasks. 'No room for a woman's body here,' he said. In reality, owing to technological change, some of the work in his department was by now light benchwork, repairing electronic parts. It was in such work that at Northshire, where the masculinism was more muted, a young woman had joined the maintenance team. Georgina Hodson was a university-qualified physicist who wanted a chance to learn about electronic technology. Now she was working at a bench, being taught to repair circuit boards in spite of being very overqualified for the job. She was on the point of leaving to return to university to study for a Master's degree.

Among the women physicists, I met several who felt their skills and qualifications to be under-recognized and under-used, and they expressed resentment at the authority of the male scientific hierarchy. Radiographers in interview made it clear that they too felt male physicists to be arrogant in their attitude towards them. And indeed some of the senior male members of medical physics who I interviewed did display quite marked prejudice against women, both those in their own departments and those in radiography. It seemed that women physicists might be right to suspect they owed their job more to the need to have a few women around for chaperoning purposes than to their male colleagues' appreciation of their technical abilities. In the same way it seemed that radiographers in part owed their hold on their profession and their jobs to a systematic undervaluation by men of the technical complexities involved in it, not to recognition of women's technical skills.

One senior physicist saw the women of his department as making rather second-rate scientists. 'I think the girls (pause) – this is to some extent chauvinistic and I am not meaning it to be – in general the girls, a lot of them, come into medical physics and they are *very good* at doing the sort of routine service-type jobs. They have a much better eye for detail, they are better at getting on with people and are often good teachers. They do a *super* job. But there are fewer of them that have that *extra spark*, who say "I can't bear doing things that way, this is a much better way of doing things." You know what I mean?' *They aren't inventive, you mean?* 'Yes. Women may well get an Oxford degree in physics but they still tend to be more pedestrian. They may be academically well qualified, but they still tend to be led as to what to do. Then they do it very well. They won't come up with a spark of genius. The answer to it is – and I don't know whether either you or I are going to like it – is that women are more fitted for the humdrum sort of jobs. Oh well, philosophical points! (hearty laugh).'

Women are seen not only as poor scientists but also as incompetent technologists. Three male physicists described to me how women are no good with machines. 'I can see a woman dabbling around with test tubes, but not with technical apparatus and all that.' *Is it that you detect some different quality brought to this kind of work by men and by women?* I asked another scientist. He answered, 'Yes, I think I do. I can't explain *what* it is. I don't want to be unkind, but I can't quite [he hesitated] – *see* a woman delving inside a computer, getting out soldering irons and oscilloscopes . . . I believe it goes deeper than just being a question of tradition. From all the women I've known, they are not very good at that level. Things that require you to be extremely tidy, careful, take good notes, logical thought, things you can do sitting at a desk – yes. But I think it is more to do with the fact that women don't like dealing with the thing at a grassroots mechanical level. They basically don't like machines.'

A physicist who had become a computer specialist spoke of women's relationship to computers in very much the same terms:

> As a general rule the women are broad based. They tend to be more interested in the applications. The men are more interested in 'playing with toys'. The whole thing is more *fun* to the men. The women are more – not exactly doing it *as* a job, but the job itself is more interesting . . . [As for men], it's partly technical competence. But it is also an interest in *having* technical competence. It is tackling the machine on its own terms, being actually interested in the computer, bending it to do very clever things. It is male chauvinist piggery and all that sort of thing, but as a gross observation, as I see it, it is something to do with the way men and women are born. Yes.

As a result, 'if I was looking for someone to do systems work, to be involved with the computer, I would be very much looking for a man, and would be very biased towards a man. If I was looking for someone who had to be very reliable, providing a service for other people, then women seem to have quite a lot to offer.'

There is a particular prejudice against married women who, as one senior member of a medical physics department put it, had frankly 'got us over a barrel' since the legislation strengthening maternity rights. Marriage is seen as making a man into a positively better bet as an employee and colleague. It gives him stability, a purpose in sticking to the job. It makes a woman a risk, and childbirth clinches it. The whole domestic sphere, women's reproductive role, is seen as contaminating women's good character as workers and even the workplace too: 'I can't help thinking that women are made in such a way that they have got maternal instincts that men haven't got. I see strain and stress here because women are trying to hold down a good job while little Johnny is ill. They are made differently, you know. We are two different sexes. And I wonder if we are monkeying with the whole thing too much.'

For men who pride themselves on having analytical minds and a respect for scientific method, there is a curious subjectivity here. Myths of 'the feminine' are more in evidence than observable fact. One physicist, for instance, explaining why women make adequate radiographers, said, 'You don't need to be technological, you just need a sixth sense for when things are going wrong and that is something you are born with.' These rigorously educated men might as well be citing the Zodiac.

Certainly these attitudes were liable to spill over into selection and appointment. One woman physicist described how, in interview, senior physicists tried to sell her a certain job with the incentive that it was near enough to the town centre for her to be 'able to pop out and get your hair done in the lunch break'. Women who have earned some respect in their own and other people's eyes by obtaining a degree in physics can be quite taken aback by meeting such dismissive attitudes in work, waking up to the fact that 'men think they're wonderful and that women are pretty stupid'.

Fighting back against gender-typing

This crude identification of men with science, technology and successful careers, and women with technical incompetence, dullness and the Florence Nightingale role in hospital, does not go uncontested. There are both women and men who fight against being pigeon-holed. What they aspire to is wholeness.

Three young men were of special interest in this respect. They were all students in the very female world of radiotherapy radiography, one at Northshire General, two at Southerton Hospital. These three were bravely swimming against the tide of gender ideology and they spoke quite poignantly about the gains and costs of doing so.

It is generally assumed that men 'don't like having women in charge of them. Especially young men. They seem not to like it one little bit, having women tell them what to do.' This may be true for some, but these young lads were apparently contentedly learning from women ('They let us do this or that,' one said happily), and in turn women were being kindly towards them, if a little patronizing: 'These two lads, bless them. They are very sweet. I feel sorry for them sometimes. All the chat at coffee time leaves them out.' For Matthew, there was a little anxiety about 'being outdone' by the women. 'I would feel a bit put out if they could do more than I could,' he said. But he also made it very clear that he would have felt even more of an outsider, and even more in need of proving himself, in a workplace comprised entirely of men. He had difficulty accounting for his choice of work to men he knew outside the hospital: 'Sometimes people seem to think I must be a bit simple or something, that I am working with a lot of girls.' As a result he would say as little as possible about his work to men outside. 'You wouldn't make too much of it, yourself. You wouldn't go up to a lorry driver and say what your work was . . . But I think I would be worse off working with all blokes. Because, I don't know, I used to find at school they would always have different interests from me. Whereas here, if they are all doing something different from me, well, they are all female. So I don't feel so much the odd one.' Masculinity is, after all, a hard task-master.

Young men encounter a widespread ideology that defines them as being unable or unwilling to take on the caring role in hospital. For instance, 'I think men and women see the importance of jobs in different ways. It's what you want out of a job. Men are more willing to give up contact with patients and people in order to do a job which makes them feel, I don't know, more intelligent.' This may be true of many men, perhaps the majority. It accurately reflects the masculine gender ideal. But it does not really describe all men as individuals. Peter, another of the young male students of radiotherapy, had first chosen nursing and in some ways was disappointed with radiography because patient care was not a *big* enough part of the job. He was emphatic that the ability to love and look after people 'is a very personal thing. You are either good with people or you are not. It's not related to sex at all.'

Do you feel able to use physical contact to comfort patients, hold a man's hand for instance? I asked him.

Yes. And I always do. If I know that something is going to hurt a patient. I will try to do that. I didn't at first because I felt I was just a student and I didn't know whether it was my place to do it. But for instance, sometimes you have to put in eye drops and it hurts. There was this woman, she hated the thought of coming in. Nobody ever thought of what it was like for her. She hadn't said that she wanted someone to hold her hand. They just left her. And I think I helped her with that. And it pleased me.

The ideology also asserts that 'men are more interested in the technical aspects of the job'. But, as a perceptive woman radiographer pointed out:

The men often do appear to be more interested in the technological side but I'm not sure whether that is because they think they are supposed to be or because they genuinely are . . . The over-riding feelings of society, that it's not a man's work, tends to affect what men think about radiography and how they approach it. It may well *make* them more interested in the technical side rather than the caring side.

Peter saw it as important to try to change the expectations. In this way, as a pioneer, he could help people to understand that men could be more caring. 'If there were more male nurses the patients would come to expect that men could do it.' Some women were much more ready than their male counterparts to admit some prejudice, and they attempted to overcome it. A superintendent in charge of radiotherapy radiography said she had always felt that 'there's something wrong with a man that does caring work ... It's just that I felt it instinctively. I always have done. But I know it is wrong.' The new young man, the first male student in her department, was turning out well. 'I'm glad to be proved wrong,' she said.

Many women, too, run counter to gender image. It is true that some are not ambitious, that some are simply passing time till something better turns up, and this could be marriage and children. But many prove their commitment by staying with the job for a lifetime, often returning to it after getting their children into nursery or school. As one put it, 'We would *all* like to get on. The difference is that men are louder about it.' Most women radiographers and those women physicists who are employed in a role that involves patient care are excellent in this aspect of the job, just as the ideology has it. But not every woman would agree with the one who called this 'my highest skill'. Some do have more of a scientific bent. A woman physicist, for instance, said, 'I prefer *not* to have to go and chat with the patients. I'm quite shy and I don't do it very well. I really prefer to sit in an office and come out with the answers for somebody else. Solving a problem is what I get most satisfaction out of.'

Women are conscious of the derogatory opinion of their technical abilities held by some male colleagues and superiors: 'Most men seem to think if you go into something scientific or technical then you shouldn't *be* there. It should be only men there. "Only *we* know about this. You can't possibly know. Your job is mopping the floor after the patients' mess." ' They fight back against being represented in this way. Many women I talked to expressed enthusiasm for precisely the technical aspects of the job: 'I like radiography because you have to think. I like to work things out.' 'I like to go to every possible seminar or lecture to find out what is the latest technique around.' 'Perhaps I make more out of the job than I am meant to. I want to find out more. I want to know why things happen. I've got an enquiring mind.' 'I find this new technology so exciting. I just want to get into it. Everyone must get enthusiastic if they are the slightest bit involved.' But most are reluctant to sacrifice closeness to the patients in order to get closer to technology or to climb the career ladder. That enables men to say of them, 'Women radiographers lack ambition.'

For all the talk of technical skills, there are, of course, clearly defined limits to the radiographer's technical responsibility. This applies whether the radiographer is a woman or a man. If a machine stops, even if only because the bulb in a warning light needs replacing, and even though the radiographer feels perfectly sure she or he could safely fix it, a hospital maintenance technician must be called. When a radiographer suggests, 'there are certain basic faults I could learn to repair myself', the technician roundly condemns such aspirations. Safety requirements would be breached. Manufacturers' warranties would be invalidated. And even though much of the fervour is born of the engineer's instinct for demarcation and his stubborn underestimation of women, he of course has official authority on his side. The fact is that, exceptional though it may be among 'women's jobs', radiography is nonetheless within the category of operating jobs. It is not engineering. There is a sharp divide in the way the two sets of responsibilities are defined, and not only in hospitals. An operator job and an engineer job have different histories, different associations and are filled from different labour markets.

5. Sources of technology: women's place in engineering

The significance of the role we've found women playing in all three new technologies is simple: they are *operators*. They press the buttons or the keys. They are the ones who do with the machine what it is made for: they produce on it – CT scans, graded patterns and lays, or simply completed orders for the mail order packers to parcel up. Their role is output not input. What women cannot be seen doing in any of these three kinds of workplace is managing technology, developing its use or maintaining and servicing it. They cannot be seen fine-tuning the machinery, setting the mode of its use or the pace of production. Nor, with the lonely exception of Georgina Hodson, momentarily fixing circuit boards in the Northshire Hospital maintenance team, can they be seen taking the covers off and meddling with the works. Women, if you like, are acquiring the 'what' kind of knowledge, but not the 'how', the 'why' and the 'whether' of the technology.

There seems to be an invisible barrier that women do not cross. What holds them back, on the face of it, is lack of the right kind of schooling and training, and the way in which jobs and promotion paths are defined in the workplace. The division of labour that separates the woman operator from the male maintenance mechanic or systems technologist is so obvious it is difficult to question. How *could* a woman aspire to cross it? Yet some women do wonder. A young woman spreader in Newstyle Ltd. said, with salty scepticism, 'We've all got us opinions about the mechanics. I know who I think is good and who I think is rubbish.' She was certain that a woman could do that job. 'If a woman can run a machine she could mend it, couldn't she? If it were her job and she had trained for it. Yes.'

The jobs of maintenance engineering and systems control that we've seen men filling in hospital X-ray, clothing and warehousing are, in a sense, outriders of a larger corps of technologically clever workers found elsewhere: in the engineering industry from which the technology originates. Here in the capital goods industries there are many firms riding the crest of the technological wave, thriving on invention, helping to produce the new equipment, to market it and get it into use. They may no longer be in Britain. Many are multinationals, often based in the USA or Japan, producing technology all over the world, picking and choosing the cheapest labour and the lowest transport costs. But wherever they are and whatever the crisis and confusion 'down-stream' among the firms that buy the engineering industry's machinery and equipment, in the industry itself there are bound to be some successful companies in which technological jobs are being created. I looked at five organizations at this level, 'up-stream' of the warehouses, clothing factories and hospitals. Some were local, some were subsidiaries or agents of overseas firms. In this chapter I will examine the skill structures in these five enterprises and the place of women in them. What are women contributing to the creation of the new technologies that, at a lower level, they operate?

Origin of new warehousing systems

First, then, is a management consultancy, Storage and Handling Consultancy Ltd., that we have met already in Chapter 3. SHC is a group that specializes in warehousing, materials handling and distribution. It advises client companies on the location of their warehouses; on the transportation of their goods; the movement of goods within the firm; and on warehouse organization, design and equipment. It has made a particular bid for a reputation in automation. As a result the firm has gone from strength to strength. A consultant told me, 'We have no recession. There is no recession as far as we are concerned. Automation is coming. It has to. This is the way *out* of the recession.' Another member of the consultancy clarified this by explaining, 'It depends whose recession.' Automation may be the way to survival for capital, he said, but for the employees it is more often the way to the dole office. Storage and Handling Consultancy Ltd. was the firm contracted by Delta Maternity Ltd. to rethink its warehouse. We have seen that it did indeed help Delta to prosper but this resulted in the loss of some women's jobs and the transformation of others.

SHC Ltd. is not without competition, of course. Since the 1960s many management consultancies have started to specialize in storage and materials handling, which was formerly a neglected field. But SHC has done well, taking on new staff each year. It is profiting by the former neglect on the part of British management concerning warehouse efficiency. As firms wake to the need to rationalize operations, to shed staff and subject those who remain to tighter discipline, SHC steps in to tell them how. It is not only a question of bringing in a conveyor system or new racking or even a computer for stock control: 'We have a lot of clients who have problems with operating costs and we are asked to advise on the management structures of the organization and maybe help them to create a new management style and even to build up a new management team.' As we saw in Chapter 1, technology is only a means to an end and it goes hand in hand with reorganization and restructuring of the firm and its workforce. The warehouse consultant is a textbook case of the technologically skilled person who redesigns equipment and in so doing reshapes other people's experience of work, even their life chances.

The consultancy team of SHC numbers 19 people. The firm is owned by two partners. Beneath them are two working directors, and below them again are senior consultants and consultants. They are supported in turn by a handful of designers, administrators and secretaries. The working environment is comfortable and civilized, relationships warm and informal. The project work is team-oriented, cutting across these strata. A team normally involves a number of directors or consultants co-operating under a project leader. Its work involves dealing with client firms, collecting and analysing data on the firm's activities, on production, sales, stock levels, deliveries, locations, distances. The consultants then discuss the client's problems among themselves and with the client, define the requirements and come up with a solution. If the proposal is accepted by the client, SHC may supervise its carrying out. They will order equipment and manage building contracts.

The work at SHC was described to me as 'applying a scientifically trained, disciplined mind' to a problem: 'Breaking the large picture down into individual elements and applying common sense.' But it also involves specialized expertise. Some of the members of the consultancy have engineering degrees and membership of engineering professional institutions. Others have engineering 'higher national' diplomas or certificates. Some bring to the work university or polytechnic degrees in chemistry, maths or physics. More important than all of this, however, is working experience. The consultant needs an extensive first-hand knowledge of management and planning in industry and commerce and a detailed knowledge of the computer systems and mechanical handling systems that are available on the market and what they can do. They must know the technological options. Consultants need a tough streak to be capable of pursuing problems to their solution: 'They have to be pugnacious.' But they also need to get on well with people: 'Personal chemistry is very important. We have to develop rapport.' If you are this kind of person the job offers many satisfactions. It uses and develops a technical expertise. It is mobile, pleasantly stretching, gives one a sense of achievement and has very good career prospects.

Where do women feature in SHC Ltd? Of the 19 individuals, four are women. Three of them are secretaries and one is an accounts clerk. Everyone else, from draughtsmen to partners, is male. The women's jobs do not call for more than the most rudimentary technological literacy, sufficient to enable them to deal with the phone and with correspondence. Five years previously, however, SHC Ltd. had had two women in technical support roles. One had worked in operational research and the other in mathematical programming techniques. It was not that the men at SHC were in any way prejudiced against women as colleagues, they emphasized: 'We are all mature people.' It was just that they felt the contribution of women to the group was likely to be limited. Because of the travel involved, the traditionally rough working-class environment in warehousing and the need to win the respect of 'your average male client', the consultancy normally 'requires a male-oriented team'.[1]

Meanwhile, far from the concealed lighting and tasteful decor of SHC, out on a windy industrial estate, is Steelwork Ltd. – the sharp end of a project partnership. This is the engineering firm that SHC Ltd. commissioned to produce the carousel for their client, Delta Maternity Ltd. It is a very different world – workaday, grubby, an environment of grease and metal shavings. Steelwork Ltd. is a small, privately owned engineering workshop engaged in the design, manufacture and installation of conveyor systems for industry. They make overhead chain conveyors for abattoirs; underfloor chain systems for hauling trolleys around factories; conveyor belts; powered or gravity roller systems for materials or product handling. Knocking up the Delta carousel was a typical job for Steelwork Ltd. Today the firm is increasingly having to acquire the skills to apply electronic controls to these systems, for programmed stopping and starting.

The owner of Steelwork Ltd. began his career as an electrician's mate and progressed to work as a mechanical engineering craftsman, always learning on the job without formal training. In this he is similar to the workers he employs: eight are craftsmen, mainly fitter-welders. Some have, some do not have, formal qualifications. A City and Guilds certificate is immaterial so long as a person is competent. Much of the invention on which this little firm depends is supplied by its executive engineer, who has both mechanical and electrical engineering qualifications and has since taught himself a great deal about computers. The only other employees at Steelwork are a draughter and an office assistant.

To do the job of putting together these one-off handling systems for warehouses and factories, the workshop is equipped with, among other things, lathes, milling machines, cutting and welding gear. Among the workers there is considerable versatility in the use of this equipment. 'Some are more skilled on the machine side, but may have no experience of welding; some are perhaps better welders, or better at electrics. But all are employed on an equal basis for maximum flexibility.' There is freedom of movement around the workshop. Pressure is not heavy, except at moments of crisis before a job has to be delivered. There is no foreman and the men are used to taking responsibility for their own part of the overall job, which often extends to making decisions about priority and ordering of work. 'We try to use people properly,' the owner said, 'and allow people to use themselves to the full.'

All those who find their livelihood at Steelwork Ltd. are male. There was worried concern from some, politely suppressed mirth from others, at the idea of a woman even thinking of applying for a technical job here.[2]

Steelwork Ltd. and Storage and Handling Consultancy are in competition with some giant firms which both produce warehousing and materials handling equipment and, as part of a comprehensive package, advise clients on reorganization. I interviewed senior technical personnel in two of the largest of these firms, curious to get a wider sense of the kinds of jobs being created by new technology in this field and the place of women within them. One of my informants ran through the firm's organization chart and marked off all the jobs that had been created or enhanced by the advent of computerized warehousing and materials handling technology. There were 60 such jobs. None of them was filled by a woman: 'Not unless I marked the odd secretary,' he said. 'It's safe to say that women in this company are almost without exception in secretarial and administrative jobs. Oh, one became a draughtsman [sic]; she had an eye for colour. And two got promoted to management jobs in Personnel, and that was frankly because we needed women to deal with our women employees.'

Likewise, the executive in the second firm I went to could think of no woman technologist or technician in his vast organization either. In fact, he added that in the three materials handling firms in which he had worked during his career, and these were three very well-known international companies operating in this field, there had 'never been a woman higher than draughtsman, and only one of those'. In warehousing generally, among both supplier and client firms, women technologists seem to be a species that has yet to evolve. 'There are very few women in this business. We take it for granted it is men. When we do come across a woman we are quite taken aback.'

Delivering computer-aided design

As with warehousing technology, after looking at computer-aided design in the pattern room of Newstyle Ltd. I again traced the technology to source to see what kinds of organization and what kinds of skills had been involved in its supply. None of the automated pattern or cutting systems in use in Britain today is manufactured here. So I couldn't include in the study an examination of the real primary source of this technology, which lies in the USA and in various European countries. That is where the parts are made and the systems assembled, where the design and development engineering teams are at work. These firms are represented in Britain only by small agencies or subsidiaries that have the contract to import, market, sell and service the equipment here. These, however, are interesting in their own way. I was able to visit two agencies of this kind and find out about the function and staffing of each of them. Let's call them Clotec Import Ltd. and Garmentec UK.

Clotec Import Ltd. has a contract from a US manufacturer to handle the maintenance of its existing systems in Britain. It has also acquired the agency for import and marketing here of a European CAD system. Garmentec UK is the British representative of a US electronic engineering firm, well to the fore in computer-controlled systems in use in many industries. It is precisely the kind of firm that one would expect soon to come up with the robot awaited by the mail order firms. The role of Garmentec UK is to sell its parent company's CAD/CAM system to the clothing industry here, to develop the market among the middle-sized clothing firms and to operate service contracts for those already in operation. These little agencies, then, are the outreaching feelers of thriving high-tech organizations that operate worldwide.

Clotec has a managing director, a technical director and three field service engineers. Garmentec for its part has four managers and 12 service engineers covering the UK and Scandinavia. The kind of work that these teams handle is similar in each case. First, there is the role of managing, marketing and selling the new systems. This involves a good deal of travel, making contact with clothing manufacturers for purposes of either selling new systems or updating older ones. A high level of general technical and operational understanding of the systems is called for and it appears that an engineering background, involving both training and experience in practical engineering, is an important asset for the job. One of the technical directors had started life as a sewing machine mechanic, the other with a degree in electrical engineering. The occupation clearly requires the personality and presence to win the confidence of senior managers in customer-firms and it is also helpful to have a flair for selling and actively to enjoy the competitive world of business.

The second kind of job in these agencies is that of field service engineer. Clothing manufacturers, until recently, had little technical equipment to maintain other than sewing machines. Today the more advanced manufacturers, like Newstyle Ltd., have a considerable range of different kinds of equipment in use, including computers and computer peripherals. Each has its peculiarities and its range of spare parts. Firms therefore now rely very much more than they once did on service contracts with the suppliers of equipment. The field service engineer's job, whether for Clotec or Garmentec, involves a wide variety of technical tasks. He instals the new equipment and 'commissions' it – gets it into operation. He carries out preventive maintenance checks at regular intervals, and comes in response to a call-out to supply spares and fix faults. The work is increasingly electronic, though elements of the mechanical still remain (disc drives and cooler fans, for example). The engineer carries tools and spares for on-site repairs. Sometimes items must be brought back to a central workshop for the completion of more time-consuming repair work, or they may be returned to the country of origin. The job involves a great deal of overtime, absence from home, travelling by car. Most field service engineers will have picked up an HNC or done an apprenticeship, but it is not unknown for this kind of competence to be acquired informally by years on the job.

There is, thirdly, an element of systems analysis work involved in both agencies. What is needed for this is an extensive knowledge of the computers and peripheral equipment on the market, their general capabilities and their specific applications in the clothing industry. Bespoke software sometimes has to be produced – programs for 'cut planning' perhaps, or for stock control or machine inventory – to accompany equipment sold to a client firm. A small part of this job could be hived off to a routine programmer.

The three kinds of role described above, in both Clotec and Garmentec, are filled exclusively by men. It was felt to be very unlikely that a woman would show up with the qualifications or the aspiration to do such work. Anyway, 'I'd be a bit hesitant, I think,' said the technical director of Clotec, explaining that it was a man's world in which such a woman would have to operate, and one in which he felt she would have difficulty in carrying conviction.

The characteristic role of women in Clotec and Garmentec is that of secretary. There were several – running the office, dealing with mail and answering the phone. They act as home-base to their mobile male bosses, keeping the kettle on the hob. There were one or two exceptions, however. Denise Brown, at Clotec, was working part-time as a trainee programmer and therefore had a toehold on the more technical aspects of the work. She might in time, and with encouragement, develop a career on the systems side. It seemed more likely, however, that the other half of her job would be the one to demand her attention. This was to be a part-time 'training and applications specialist'. Garmentec also employed two women in this role and we will see that other engineering firms do too.

The job of 'training and applications specialist' – I'll call it trainer for short – is of particular interest. The trainer follows the salesman and the service engineer 'on site' in order to instruct the client's own staff in the use of the equipment. It is a job with some unusual features for a woman: it involves travel and a respectable level of technical know-how, even of pay. Women are felt by Clotec and Garmentec to be the obvious choice for trainer because, first, they are already in the labour market as operators of CAD systems in clothing firms and, second, they are felt to have the personality to be acceptable as teachers.

To get a wider sense of what goes on at this level of supply of CAD systems, I also talked with senior technical personnel in a management consultancy specializing in the clothing industry. I asked one of these men, who is uniquely placed to know the field, to cast his mind around the dozen or so specialist software firms in Britain currently supplying the clothing industry and to tell me of any women in them in technical jobs. He concluded, after some searching, 'I think there are two. Both programmers.' Again, in this thriving area of technical developments, it is sparse pickings for women.

Building X-ray equipment

Finally, let's move to the world of the electronic engineering multinationals that are spawning the brilliant new computerized techniques in medical imaging. Four very large firms dominate the computed tomography field in Britain. Half a dozen other companies, including a Japanese and an Israeli firm, between them hold a smaller corner of the market. Only one of the large firms is manufacturing X-ray equipment in the UK however, and even in this case only a small part of the total manufacturing process is carried out here. This company, which I'll call Electronics International (EI), is in many ways an interesting case within the electrical engineering industry.

One of the largest and most successful companies of its kind in the world, Electronics International manufactures a diverse range of products, from light bulbs to integrated circuits, dishwashers to jet engines, hair dryers to medical systems. Annual sales are in excess of £25,000 million. Electronics International Diagnostic Systems (EIDS), the subsidiary which produces the X-ray equipment with which we are concerned, is only a small part of the EI business even in Britain. It has approximately 500 employees, 100 in an administrative centre and 400 in a manufacturing plant. I visited both and interviewed people in technical roles within the firm.

In the late 1970s the US firm of Electronics International had been suffering competition in its home market from a British firm successfully introducing its CT scanner there. The response of the US multinational was to take over the British firm and shift the manufacturing process to the USA. The role of its manual labour force in Britain was then reduced to certain semi-skilled operations. Parts and assemblies were now shipped out from the USA to Britain for a limited range of operations to be done on them before they were shipped back for completion of the machine as a whole in America.

While the Diagnostic Systems side of EI grew and prospered, the manual skills required on the shop floor in its British operation diminished sharply. Whereas there had been 30 skilled men employed on manufacture of the complete scanners, the new personnel manager retained only 10 in the fragmented assembly operation. What were needed now were cerebral skills rather than manual ones. 'He said we were dinosaurs,' one of the remaining craftsmen complained. The 10 remaining skilled men were allowed to keep their grading but the jobs they filled were classed as semi-skilled and as each man left he was replaced by a semi-skilled worker at a lower grade. The firm also made increasing use of agency workers. Up to a third of the shop-floor employees at any one time might be employed not by EIDS but by an employment agency. They had no entitlement to sick pay, holiday pay or pension fund and naturally were unlikely to belong to the union. While management claimed this protected the jobs of permanent staff, the arrangement clearly enabled EIDS to manage with fewer of them and afforded the flexibility to lay off agency workers without notice in slack periods.

The Amalgamated Union of Engineering Workers, representing those of the shop-floor workers it could persuade to join, was powerless to stop these processes. The individual skilled men, however, resisted in their own way by refusing to teach any of the new, younger, semi-skilled operatives to use the tools, such as measuring gauges, characteristic of skilled engineering. While management felt the new technology demanded 'technician skills' and began sending some lads on electronic engineering courses, the craftsmen for their part felt apprenticeship had 'gone up the spout'. They would not co-operate in what they saw as a degradation of training and skills.

Off the shop floor, in the higher grade of professional engineering, the employees of EIDS are represented by TASS. Their situation is more promising. In prosperous firms such as EI the growth element is not in the shop-floor jobs but in graduate engineering. One of EI's competitors, for instance, reports that whereas not long ago blue-collar workers represented two-thirds of total employment, today this has fallen to one-third. The compensatory growth has been in graduate engineering. Of 90,000 employed in manufacturing in this multinational, no fewer than 50,000 are people with higher level technical qualifications, and one-third of these work in research and development. The question of women's situation in EIDS, then, has to be considered within this context: a losing battle being fought by craft engineers and a winning streak enjoyed by more highly qualified technical grades.

The divisions in which the technically qualified personnel of EIDS are mainly to be found are three: field service engineering; manufacturing; and sales. First, the field service teams for the UK and overseas involve many of the firm's top-notch practical engineers. Once EIDS has sold a scanner or other item of advanced imaging equipment to a hospital it is the field engineer's job to get it into use. Such people have to be good all-rounders. They have to help prepare the suite of rooms for the scanner, effect its physical transport to the hospital, install it and get it into working order. They then take on regular preventive maintenance and are always on call to keep the scanner running at its optimum performance. They need to be diplomatic and sympathetic people, capable of forging good relationships with doctors, physicists and others in the hospital. They have to travel widely and work independently. They tend to have a lot of pride and interest in the technology and to be continually adapting their competence upwards to keep pace with technical change: 'We no longer want someone who's the kind of person who has a feel for tying things together with string. X-ray used to be "tractor mechanics", you know, relays, valves, hefty switches. If it doesn't work, hit it with a hammer. It's computer knowledge we need now, a new breed of engineer, not just for CT but for all modalities.' For this kind of person the prospects are good. EIDS field service engineering division was to recruit 10 more engineers in the coming few months. Employment at the administrative centre generally had increased 40 per cent in three years, nearly all the recruits being technically qualified people.[3]

Where were women in the field service engineering division? Not one was to be found among the 14 technical managers, nor among the 80 engineers. Seven were secretaries, three were in clerical or administrative roles and the remaining two were, respectively, a statistical analyst and a computer operator. None of these posts required any competence in imaging technology beyond a familiarity with its terminology.

Second, then, is EIDS manufacturing plant. Twenty-five per cent of the work done here is research and development. The remainder is production, putting together assemblies for inclusion in CT scanners and other kinds of imaging equipment. The 400 employees at the plant can be divided broadly into shop-floor workers and engineers.

The shop floor is organized into two areas. In Area A are approximately 50 assembler-wirers, threading and fixing components onto boards, working at a bench, using simple tools such as soldering irons. There are also loom workers, laying wires onto boards. At the time of my interviews these two categories of semi-skilled work were all undertaken by women because the work was seen as having an affinity with needlework or embroidery, as I was told by a male shop-floor worker. There were a number of men in Area A, however: they were in the higher-grade job of inspection and testing of the women's products.

In Area B, though the pay was the same, the assemblies tended to be more complex. One characteristic job here is fixing a power supply to the frame of an X-ray machine. This involves snipping and tie-wrapping wires, a little soldering, screwing and bolting parts to the frame. Whereas in Area A the women's work repeated itself on a cycle of a few minutes, here it took more than half a day to complete one frame. One or two women had recently been moved onto this job. The personnel manager said, 'One of the reasons for bringing women into Area B was that some of the men were getting bored and discontented with their job. We asked ourselves, why are we getting problems in Area B and not in Area A? It clearly wasn't the job as such, because the A-type jobs are even more boring. We obviously came up with the answer.' *That men get bored more easily than women?* He laughed. 'Well, no, but that men have different expectations of their work than women have. They have expectations of what it *should* be.' *So you brought women into the jobs that bored the men and gave the men more interesting things to do?* 'Absolutely. I am interested in the psychology of it. I think it is something to do with what a man thinks is important, what is an important job. He wants to be able to say, to people outside, "I am this or that. I am a fitter" . . . Why do we get less trouble from women?"[4]

Women, then, are present in the production area of the plant in considerable numbers, but they are firmly tied to the lower of two levels of semi-skilled work. Men, when they have served five years in this manufacturing plant, can apply for a green union card from the AUEW which gives them supposedly skilled status. With this they can get a better job in a neighbouring aeronautical firm. Women could in theory make this move too, but they never do. It is assumed that skilled status, even if it is acquired only by time-serving, is, like that next-door aeronautics company itself, a male preserve.

The engineers, including a good many professional engineers, work in the upstairs offices. They are, broadly speaking, divided into hardware, test and software engineers of different grades. Some of them have 'higher nationals' and others, the majority, have one or more degrees.

The hardware engineers are, in the main, the designers and developers of the electronic systems in use in EIDS equipment. Their work time is shared between desk, bench and console, as they solve design problems and make prototypes. The work involves mainly mental activities but also some practical use of tools. All the 58 hardware engineers are men. The 49 test engineers, among whom I include a six-strong repairs team, are involved in manual technical work at differing levels of skill. Again they are all men.

Software engineers are also mainly employed in research and development (R&D). They work at desk and computer console, reading, assessing and writing programs, solving conceptual problems, de-bugging programs, negotiating with the hardware engineers. The work does not involve tools, unless the computer itself is a tool. It is teamwork, largely self-motivating. Twenty-two out of the 23 software engineers are men. As the personnel manager put it, 'There's usually a token woman among them.' And there she is, token or not, a real live woman engineer: Pamela Franks is a celebrity in my 'up-stream' study as Georgina Hodson was a celebrity 'down-stream'. She is the only woman engineer who surfaced either in person or by reference in any of the three technologies considered here. For female company, in manufacturing's engineering section, Pamela Franks has 13 female secretaries and nine women in clerical or administrative roles.

Sales division is the third section of EIDS that employs technologically informed, if not necessarily qualified, personnel. The sales teams must have some knowledge of the equipment they deal with if they are to be convincing to clients. It is not, however, engineering competence so much as a general kind of systems know-how that is called for. The division has 17 sales managers, product managers, senior and run-of-the-mill sales persons. The jobs involve travelling widely and afford scope for a degree of initiative and freedom. One of the junior sales persons is a woman. The remainder of the team are men. There are six secretaries, all of whom are women.

There is, however, an interesting sub-section of sales known as Clinical Support. Once imaging equipment has been purchased by a hospital and the service engineers have installed it and got it working, someone has to go out and teach the hospital team how to use their new acquisition. This used to be done by the salesman or the engineer, in passing. Today it is done in a more conscious way, employing the services – as in CAD/CAM in clothing – of a 'training and applications specialist'. Here once again it is mainly women who are the trainers. At EIDS the clinical support manager is a man, responsible for two male and five female trainers. They are former hospital radiographers, people who have been attracted by the prospect of travel and better pay than the NHS can promise. They are perhaps people who are personally less interested in the patient-care side of the radiography job, more keen to be involved with technology and innovation.

The trainers' work takes them to every country of the world. It involves them in spending a week or two in the hospital, building up a working relationship with the radiologists and radiographers, helping them to get the best images the scanner can achieve and select the most appropriate programs for their needs. The job calls for a good deal of anatomical knowledge, radiographic technique and clinical experience. The trainer must be at home with the technology, and in no way intimidated by it. But she or he also needs tact, patience and an understanding for and tolerance of the often fraught personal relations surrounding the new scanner. As with the CAD technology, women are felt to be the sex more suited to the job, first because there are more women radiographers to choose from, and second because this is a public relations job for which women are felt to have the natural charm. It is convenient, however, to have a couple of men on the team because men are more acceptable, and find life less difficult, in certain countries such as those of the Middle East where there is an adverse reaction to independent women.

Here, then, we have a clear, even stark, picture of the role of women in the production, marketing and servicing of computed tomography and other modern imaging technologies. It is a picture confirmed by information gathered from the other 'big three' firms, where I interviewed product or marketing managers for CT. Low-paid, low-status secretarial and administrative support is women's most characteristic role. Unskilled and semi-skilled assembly work is the nearest women come to hands-on experience of the technology. Women feature as trainers for sex-specific reasons, but women engineers are as rare as gold dust.

One of the senior technologists I spoke with was responsible for developments in the next great imaging invention that will soon join CT in the hospitals: nuclear magnetic resonance scanning. Several firms are now racing to sweep the market with their NMR scanners. This technologist told me that, to his knowledge, there are only two women working in NMR research throughout the world. Both have approached the field via science rather than engineering, one being a physicist and the other a mathematician. In his firm, of the 87 people actively working on R&D on NMR, including mechanical, electrical, computer and software specialists, there was not a single woman. 'We have to take the best,' he explained, 'and there are very few women so highly qualified.'

The cost of the difference

Some might ask: does it really matter that women and men play separate and different roles in these innovative engineering firms? Does the sexual division of labour here really hurt anyone? The answer has to be that the difference is not a difference between equal jobs and equal prospects. Men's occupations and women's occupations are unequal by many different measures, and women have not chosen their situation.

The contrast in pay and conditions of work between the top-flight engineer and the routine clerical or factory worker is obvious to anyone. At SHC Ltd., the warehousing consultancy, the male working directors earn five times as much as the female secretaries; male consultants two or three times the figure. Denise Brown, the trainee programmer/trainer at Clotec Import, earns half what the Clotec field service engineers earn, when a car is taken into account. Engineers at EIDS earn up to twice as much as the women assembler-wirers, and the managers (male) three or four times that rate. One software engineer told me how feather-bedded he felt and how shocked he had been when, looking through the firm's conditions of employment, he noted not only the difference in wages but also the unfairness in pensions, holidays and other conditions of work between those on the shop floor and the engineers. And the shop-floor workers are 75 per cent female; engineers 99.5 per cent male.

I asked managers in all these firms to attempt a ranking of the categories of employee according to certain criteria. Women consistently turned up in jobs ranked among the lowest in responsibility in the firm. They were in jobs considered to be the easiest to fill when vacancies occurred. Clerks and secretaries are two-a-penny today. So are assembler-wirers. Even trainers can be recruited from a flush market of radiographers or CAD operators. In contrast, CT engineers are so scarce that, as one manager put it, the few firms in the field 'can only poach them from each other' with offers of higher salaries: 'There's an astonishing shortage of engineers. A software engineer can name his price. Someone coming out of university with a mathematics or physics degree and a couple of years' experience can get 9K, 10K [i.e. thousand pounds] right away, no problem.' Certainly the terms in which some engineers described their firm implied that they, not the employers, had been the ones to do the choosing.

What it is like to work, whether it is enjoyable or even tolerable, is also something that varies in aggregate between women and men. There is of course an overlap. Secretarial work, it is true, can often be performed in relatively comfortable circumstances. So too can the junior administrative work which women sometimes do. Some men labour at tiring, unskilled and even dangerous jobs: I met more than one engineer with a finger missing. But there is a noticeable contrast in several of the factors that differentiate men's and women's work: length of job cycle, interest of the job, the autonomy and mobility it affords. Consider the difference between a job like that of the assembler-wirer where the work cycle is a matter of minutes, endlessly repeated, and that of the typical male hardware or software development engineer where the start-to-finish period of any one project can be months, sometimes years. Compare the sense of involvement and completion in the two jobs.

An electronics repair engineer at EIDS, comparing his work with that of the women clerical and secretarial workers there, said, 'I don't see myself in *that* profession. I wouldn't have the satisfaction of finding at the end of the day I have repaired something. Creativity. You think of a typist or clerk as just writing and typing and that's the end of it. I suppose men who are used to creating things would find it quite boring to go to that, sat in a chair all day long, keep on typing.' Of course men tend to undervalue women's work just because they see women doing it, and there is an element of that here. But the truth is that the men's jobs do deliver more satisfaction to the men who do them than women's jobs do to them.

On the whole, men are more likely to be self-supervising. The same engineer quoted above described how, if he has an off-day and feels like a break from the bench, it is within his power to decide to sit and read the technical manuals for the day, keeping abreast of the theory. A software engineer at EIDS said of the work, 'There is only very gentle pressure from the team leader to meet deadlines. We tend to get involved with [the work] . . . take bits of code to work on at home.' They do overtime, but more out of loyalty and team spirit than compulsion, since overtime is not paid. 'They have a lot of freedom,' said the EIDS personnel manager of the engineers in his firm. 'It is a creative, innovative job, independent. It is not easily controlled. We reckon to have problems with them. Compared with the shop floor it is impossible to exert the same kind of discipline. They get away with much more flexibility. You know, you hear stories of this one and that one who prefer to work from midnight till eight in the morning, and you have to let them.'

Even at the lower level of electrical and mechanical repair work to X-ray tubes, there is 'no-one breathing down your neck' and the atmosphere is 'relaxed'. It is interesting that the fraternity between technically minded men can secure a measure of this freedom even for low-paid male workers. One of the electro-mechanical repair technicians described his job as 'so simple I could teach a 10-year old kid to do it'. He said that the job was not dissimilar in many ways from the women's routine assembly jobs. Yet, because he knew the manager socially through a shared interest in cars, the supervision for him was minimal. 'It's delicate. It's the actual people. He is pretty good. He doesn't mind, so long as he can see at the end of the day you are doing the job . . .'

If one were to measure, in feet, yards and miles, the radius of movement of each of the different kinds of worker in this study, the narrow confines in which women work and the relative mobility of men would become strikingly clear. Trainers are, for women, in a remarkable job because it allows them to travel. Far more typical of women's work is that it is office-based. The (male) service engineers, the salesmen, roam the country in their company cars with their radio-paging bleepers: 'We run about everywhere, up to Glasgow, down to the West Country, backwards and forwards.' On their travels they radio in to the (female) secretary back at base who is waiting with a welcoming cup of coffee when they return. A working director of SHC Ltd. had this different length of rein clearly in mind when he said of the prospect of a woman consultant joining the group, 'There's no reason why we shouldn't use a woman very successfully – but in the design team where she would be working in-house, under some element of supervision'. Even at the micro-level, it is normal for women to work at a work station, at a machine, whether it is a typewriter, a scope or an assembly bench. This was symbolized by the little patch of carpet the management had given each woman working at the carousel at Delta: she used to walk the racks; now two square yards of the meanest Wilton is room enough. It is characteristic of a technician that he moves around the machine, carrying his tools with him shifting, fixing. Many women and many men say of men: 'They can't bear to be stuck in one spot all day.' It is represented as a quality in women that they can accept immobility. But few women are asked what they prefer.

Finally, of course, the most obvious difference between men and women, taken as groups in this 'up-stream' study, is the sheer gap in technical training, know-how and competence. I asked management informants to tell me what qualifications were expected in each job in the organization and to describe in some relative way the kind and degree of technical knowledge required. Almost without exception women fell into the categories of job that called for no technical training of any kind. The most that had been invested in them was a shorthand-typing course. They had nothing to offer to the employer they were working for to secure their promotion; they had nothing to offer any alternative employer to enable their release. Meanwhile, all around them, the qualification requirements are rising. Today even the lower posts in service engineering, production engineering, design and development are beginning to specify degrees in place of technician qualifications. New technology is continually pushing up the minimum level of technical know-how that is saleable. Women have not yet got access to last year's knowledge, let alone next year's.

There was one apparent glimmer of light for women among these occupations, and that was the success of a handful of women in climbing from operator work to that of trainer. By getting these jobs women had achieved a step up in earnings (to £12,000 at EIDS) and an extension in mobility, building on their basic operator skills. They may even have acquired prospects in industry, for one woman sales person in X-ray had arrived there via the trainer job and one trainer with whom I talked was nursing hopes of a transfer to sales. But how open the upward route really is must be in doubt. One of their employers stated baldly that there were really no prospects at all for his women trainers who, when they were 'burnt out' after three or four years in the job, would 'pack it in, have a spell at home. Get married perhaps. Look for a different career.' The trainer's job is an operator's job writ large. It is not an instance of women entering men's work but rather of female-gendered occupations moving into a new sphere with the change in technology, carrying women along with them.

The CAD/CAM manager was quite frank about his reason for employing women trainers. The women are expected to use their femininity persuasively: 'They have a talent for it. In the case of 60 per cent of our customers we are dealing with the managing director or the production director. And they tend to have a keen eye for a nice young lady, a pretty young girl, say, and they may well say, "We'll buy the system if she's the one who's going to be doing the training".' The trainers are sometimes used to demonstrate the equipment at industrial exhibitions: 'People are more responsive to a woman demonstrator. "We'll have a look at what *she*'s doing." It's a catch, if you like.' Of course, as a trainer, the CAD/CAM manager went on, 'she'll always be backed up by a man.' She is the velvet glove on the rougher hand of the engineer and salesman, an adornment on the machine. I asked for confirmation: *You are describing a partnership between male and female roles, each sex playing a specific part?* 'Precisely.' Not surprising then, that one applications specialist in radiography, in the early days before she had learned to disguise her naturally warm and open manner, found male clients tended 'to assume I came with the machine'.

Apart from the trainers, there were one and a half women in this 'up-stream' study in the capital goods industry with technical training and competence. Against how many men? Around 300. What the men have, what the women lack in technical know-how is an asset that is highly saleable, transferable to other firms in other industries, and incremental: you learn more each day that passes, and you yourself become more valuable. More generally, it is a kind of purchase on the world. Technical competence, if you have it, spills over into domestic and social life, giving confidence and enjoyment and a degree of power. Somewhere, somehow, women are being cheated of these things. How does it happen?

No queue at the open door

Is it perhaps that we cheat *ourselves*? Everywhere I went among
the engineering enterprises I met with the same story. It goes
something like this: 'No. We have no women engineers or
technicians. Shame. It's not that it's impossible. I do remember
hearing of one once. Janet something, or was it Joanna?
Remember her name, John? At Hewlett Packard, or was it
ICL? Must be five or six years ago now. It shows it can be done.'
And then you ask: *Why don't you recruit women here?* 'Oh, it's
not for lack of trying. Women just don't apply.'

A senior manager at EIDS said, 'Our industry is sufficiently
dynamic to ensure that we shall seek out talent wherever it
resides, irrespective of the prejudices which continue to be
found in society in general.' Software engineering was felt to be
especially accessible to women: 'We'd be looking for a graduate
in science, someone who has worked with computers. It's a
desk job, playing on a console. It's not like an electronic
engineer who has to go out on a bench.' Even in hardware,
however, they would consider a woman: 'The *biggest* problem
area for us is recruiting engineers. Any of my managers would
gladly take on a woman with the right qualifications. We'd be
happy to find anyone, man or woman. Us and loads of firms
like us. Women could make a great career for themselves here.'
His colleague added, 'We receive very few applications from
women for the professional jobs. I thought this may have
something to do with our advertising but the proportion is
similar even from the unsolicited applications from employment
agencies.'

'Frankly,' went on the first, 'we are worried why we can't
recruit women. The picture here is very stark. We discuss this a
lot in management meetings. Okay, some of it is fairly flip, you
know, light-hearted. But at the more serious level we do want to
know why we can't get women. Because there is an argument
that if you *do* get a woman she'll really bust her arse, because
she'll be a careerist. She'll be there because she's keen. And that
is the sort of person we need.'

This manager went shopping every year to the top universities 'for the best' of graduate engineers. Of a list of 20 he was recently offered, only one was a woman. He meets with similar response to advertisments. One out of hundreds may be a woman. Because the personnel department leans over backwards to recruit women, a woman applicant will get an interview even if her qualifications only scrape through the basic criteria. It is the same at technician level. The Engineering Industry Training Board offers grants to subsidize firms offering technician places to girls. EIDS would be happy to make use of these grants but no female technicians come forward; 'yet in our unskilled and semi-skilled jobs we have lots of women.'[5]

It is the same in the other firms in this electronic engineering environment. The evidence with which I was continually presented was of willing managers, unwilling or absent women. The conclusion is: 'It's not our fault.' 'We are the tail that is being wagged by the dog. I mean the social and educational thing. If we put on adverts "Women PLEASE Apply" we wouldn't get them. It's too late. We need to reach into the schools.' And this is where everyone places the blame, far away from the workplace. A unanimous chorus repeats: it's the parents' fault, it's the teachers' fault, it's the fault of the careers advisers. And of course, fundamentally, it's women's fault: 'they are their own worst enemies'.

There is some truth in all these claims. Many books have discussed the way in which what happens to boys and girls at home and in school results in a sexually differentiated labour force, different qualifications and aspirations among boys and girls. It makes sense, however, to look at the workplace too and ask: is there something going on here, something in the relations of employment, in work culture, the way jobs are defined and distinguished from each other, that conspires to keep women from even aspiring to technological work? Why do women shy away from jobs and firms like these?

Certainly we cannot discount women's early experiences. Nor can we take the pure white consciences and sparkling principles of the personnel managers at face value. Behind the proclaimed welcome for women there do lie double standards and prejudices. But today we should expect, I think, that capital's desperation for appropriately skilled labour, skills on which the future survival of companies depends, might here and there override patriarchy's distaste for upsetting the sexual division of labour. That is, if women are also willing to give it a try. We have to look deeper at the relations of work to understand what is going on. The evidence points to men's special relationship to technology having something to do with women's non-relationship to it.

6. Gendering people, gendering jobs

In connection with the eleven workplace studies described in Chapters 2–5, I talked with 152 people, including managers, trade union representatives and employees. The majority of these were the subjects of 'in-depth' interviews in which I invited them to describe their job, their workplace and their relationship with employers and each other. They discussed their training and skills (or lack of them), their relationship with machinery and tools and the impact of technological change on their work. They also talked about the way activities are shared up into 'men's jobs' and 'women's jobs', not only at work but also at home, and what they felt about this sexual division of labour.

While people are working, they are not just producing goods and services for their employer and a pay packet for themselves. They are also *producing culture*. The relations that surround technological work are made up of both things people do and things they believe and say. What they do gives rise to what they feel, and of course their feelings and ideas also partly determine what they and other people do. Some ideas are widespread and are able to influence people who are not immediately engaged in the same practice as that in which they originate: they are hegemonic ideas. The ideology of groups that have power tends to be hegemonic – a vehicle of their power. But always there are sets of practices and ideas that run counter to these and resist them, setting up alternative ways of understanding things, of 'making sense'. It is possible to see something of these processes in what people were saying in interview. We've seen what people are actually doing at work; now we can listen to the meaning they give to their situation and their actions. Much of what they said took the form of expressions of gender and gender difference, what it is to be a woman or a man and to do women's or men's work.

Gender, it is by now widely accepted, is not the same thing as biological sex. People are born more or less clearly one physical sex or another, and on this basis they are ascribed a gender. They are then 'brought up' socially to live that gender: masculine or feminine. 'Gender is in the first place a *social* fact.'[1] Of course, quite apart from the sex a person is born, it is quite possible for people growing up to feel and believe themselves to be the opposite. The relations between chromosomes, gender ascription and gender identity are rather loose.[2] On the other hand, most people do come to feel themselves to be what they are told they are and treated by others as being. Parents from the outset behave differently towards boy and girl children. So do teachers and friends. By 16, as a rule, most of the kinks have been ironed out – the tomboy has submitted to skirt and handbag.[3] What is often forgotten, though, is that the experience of adult life continues to mould and reinforce gender. A person works for perhaps four times as long as she or he is at school. As we'll see, *work is a gendering process*.

All known societies have two complementary genders – and a very few also have recognized roles for people who don't fit either. The character and behaviour that are considered to be masculine or feminine, however, vary widely from one culture to another. What is manly in one may be effeminate in another.[4] The constant is inequality between men and women: that, like gender difference, seems to exist everywhere today. We have no choice but to suppose that the social process of gender construction, formulations of gender difference, are important mechanisms in sustaining male dominance. It is an expression of men's hegemonic ideology, and one into which women get swept. If, as Ann Oakley puts it, 'on the whole Western society is organised around the assumption that the differences between the sexes are more important than the qualities they have in common', this serves men and disserves women.[5]

The result of this gendering process is that all behaviour

becomes gendered, and all interpretations of behaviour too.[6] Man and woman become 'a couple' and are seen as complementary to each other, regardless of the fact that in many transactions between men and women (working, training, shopping, enjoying recreation) there is no real need to see them as couples at all.[7]

It is very difficult to stop ourselves seeing things this way, even when we are aware. Gender is part of our tools for thinking, for ordering and understanding the world. Genevieve Lloyd has explored the way 'Reason', the philosophical concept that underlies modern science, technology and industry, is itself gendered.[8] The 'Man of Reason' was conceived of as precisely 'transcending the feminine', and so it is impossible for woman to be thought of as sharing in rationality. It is not a simple matter of excluding women as people, Lloyd emphasizes, it is a constitution of femininity itself. What we can see in the processes of philosophical history, she suggests, is 'the genderization of ideas'.[9]

From the very early days of human civilization, something similar has happened with work: *occupations themselves have come to be gendered*. It is of course a two-way process. People have a gender and their gender rubs off on the jobs they mainly do. The jobs in turn have a gender character which rubs off on the people who do them. Adam Smith wrote, 'the difference between the most dissimilar characters, between a philosopher and a common street porter, for example, seems to arise not so much from nature as from habit, custom and education.'[10] The differences he was pointing to were class differences, but he could have said the same of the gender contrast between a deep-sea fisherman and a receptionist: the jobs they do and the lives they lead both build them different genders and cause us to approach each with different expectations. Our whole world is gendered, from shampoo, tissues and watches to environments as local as the 'ladies toilet' and as large as the North Sea oil rig. Things are gendered materially (sized or coloured differently, for instance) and also ideologically. We can use objects as gender metaphors: a pink ribbon, for instance. Tools and machinery are gendered too, in such a way that the sexes are expected to relate to different kinds of equipment in different ways. An eighteenth-century man no doubt felt effeminate using a spinning wheel, though he would have felt comfortable enough repairing one. Today it is difficult to get a teenage lad to use a floor mop or a typewriter because they contradict his own gender identity. Any woman lifting a crowbar is likely to have some gender-conscious thoughts as she does so.

When a new invention arrives in the workplace it is already gendered by the activities and expectations of its manufacturers and its owners. It may even be ergonomically sex-specific, scaled for the average height or anticipated strength of the sex that is to use it. Even if it arrives apparently gender-neutral it quickly acquires a gender by association with its user or its purpose. The computer was the brainchild of male engineers and it was born into a male line of production technology. The fact that it has a keyboard rather like a (feminine) typewriter keyboard confuses no one for long. When a computer arrives in a school, for instance, boys and girls are quick to detect its latent masculinity. Their own relationship to each other and to the machine quickly confirms it. It is not surprising if, as teachers report, boys soon elbow themselves forward and the majority of girls retire from the field.

In the previous chapters we have seen some of the material aspects of the gendering of work. We've seen how using the computerized pattern scopes and keyboards, filling orders in the warehouse and wiring assemblies in an engineering works – all new jobs – were quickly established as female, while the new engineering occupations kept the male identity of those they replaced. We've seen various confusions and conflicts over radiography where two practical components of the job, caring for people and controlling machines, appear to be in gender conflict. We shift now from the material to the cultural aspects of work. We look at some of the ideological processes that help sustain divisions and inequalities between men and women, especially enabling them to tide over the crisis of technological change. In this chapter the men talk about their skills and careers, while in the next women respond with their own ideas about technology, work and men.

'Man and machine in perfect harmony'
(Advert for the Ford Sierra car, 1983)

Of the 83 men I had the chance to interview about their work, 34 had engineering skills at craft, technician or professional level. Others were skilled in different fields (clothing, radiography) and a few were semi or unskilled. It is mainly from interviews with the technical men that this chapter is constructed, and to those who contribute most I give fictitious names. The men who are not quoted have not been suppressed for having something different to say, however. I have simply used the best and clearest expressions of the range of ideas that came through the interviews as a whole. It is misleading to add them up and say '20 thought this, 12 thought that'. What is more significant is the field of issues with which people are concerned and the tensions that exist between the different meanings they ascribe to them. What emerges here is the hegemonic ideology, a broadly understood and accepted body of masculine ideas, shot through with conflicting and even subversive themes. One man often gives voice to both, since few of us are single-minded and many of us feel uncertainty.[11]

In the main these men identify themselves with technology and identify technology with masculinity. Technological jobs are often more than just a job to those who do them. Many of the skilled and qualified men expressed real pleasure in their work. They clearly enjoyed their labour and took pride in their competence. A good many described how they had liked to 'tinker with things' while still a little child: 'From an early age I was into pulling things apart. I was asking how does this work and how does it come apart. From my *very* early years. So my parents say.' This insistence on technical talent showing up very young is to be found too, for example, in Samuel Smiles's *Lives of the Engineers*, a work of 1862 celebrating the famous Victorian civil engineers, men whom Smiles describes as 'strong-minded, resolute and ingenious, impelled to their special pursuits by the force of their constructive instincts'.[12] Of Brindley, the wheelwright-turned-canal engineer, for instance, it is said that 'one of the things in which he took most delight when a boy was to visit a neighbouring grist-mill and examine the water-wheels, cog-wheels, drum-wheels and other attached machinery and to imitate the arrangements with knife and wood.'[13]

The supposed 'natural' affinity of man to machine was expressed by one of the men I talked with as 'love at first sight'. Another elderly maintenance man had kept his ageing romance burning bright: 'You've got to sort of fall in love with the machines you're working with. You respect 'em.' When machines are abused by careless operators then you feel 'it's like somebody's ruining your work'. Engineers identify so closely with the technology with which they are involved that many will choose their employment less by the salary it offers than by the complexity of the technology it opens up to them. 'We find the way to get a good engineer,' said a personnel manager, 'is to advertise your level of technology, the level you are at. They will come for that, for the interest, not for the money.'

A good engineer loves a challenge: 'To work on machines that can push you to the limit of your capabilities. What is boring is to cruise along on circuitry that's a doddle. It's boring to go down to a lower technology. It's too easy. There's no self-respect in it perhaps.' In the excitement of team work a mutual admiration arises. One sees oneself reflected in the admired eyes of other men: 'It's a tremendous feeling to feel that you are working with hopefully very intelligent and switched-on people' – 'people who have a lot of vision of something they are trying to achieve.' Men's experience of engineering work cannot fail to increase their sense of the greatness of their sex, inculcate a sense of being special.

There is a remarkable book, *The Soul of a New Machine* by Tracy Kidder.[14] It is a factual account, reading like fiction, of the invention of a 32-bit mini-computer by the American firm Data General. Kidder documents the competitive, exciting, happy and zappy relationships existing among a group of men dedicated to pulling off a technological triumph. The author perhaps did not intend a celebration of masculinity, but that is what the book turns out to be. Here again we find the childhood joy in technology: 'I took apart clocks and all kinds of stuff,' says one of the protagonists. 'Lawn mowers. I loved taking things apart. Loved putting them back together too. Just to look inside and see how it works. Hands on, that's what I liked to do.'[15] 'Hands on', 'can do' are phrases used often in engineers' talk. They reflect the delight they take in mastering matter: 'There's some notion of control, it seems to me, that you can derive in a world full of confusion if you at least understand how things get put together. Even if you can't understand every little part, how infernal machines get put together.'[16]

In Kidder's book we can see the self-identification with successful technology: 'Dreams of pure freedom were not uncommon in the basement. For those who had such fantasies, the best job imaginable would allow them to try to build the unattainable, the perfect computer. What, by contrast, would be one of the worst jobs? One that obliged an engineer to build a kludge .'[17] You feel the infatuation with the project, as one engineer after another 'signs up' with the team, to give all he has got to the solving of this entrancing problem. 'You're gonna die, but you're gonna die in glory.'[18]

As we'll see with the engineers in our story, such a life and such a project leave little space for the merely human. Thinking of his neglected home and children, the genius of Data General reflects, 'That's the bear trap, the greatest vice. Your job. You can justify just about any behaviour with it. Maybe that's why you do it, so you don't have to deal with all those other problems.'[19] At more characteristic moments, 'West would sit as his desk and stare for hours at the team's drawings of the hardware, playing his own mind games with the results of other engineers' mind games. Will this work? How much will it cost? Once, someone brought a crying baby past his door, and afterward it took him an hour to retrace his steps through the circuit design he had been pondering. Laughter outside often had the same effect and once in a while it made his hands shake with rage.'[20]

The women in Tracy Kidder's book are few and they flit by at speed, but a diligent observer can detect their passing. There are the wives at home, carrying the human world on their shoulders to free their men for the great project. They have no place bringing their crying babies into work. Even women legitimately found in Data General, however, are in a sense out of place. There is a secretary, Rosemarie, portrayed by Kidder with tender irony as a domestic, out of her depth but happy with the honour of serving in small ways. 'To Rosemarie, the Eagle project was like a gift. She had so much to do every day: budgets to prepare, battles to fight with one department or another, mail to sort when the mailroom was untimely moved, phones to answer, documents to prepare, paychecks to find and deliver on time, the newcomers to attend to. ("Would they have a place to sit – and the conditions weren't the best, you know – and would they have a pencil?") Each day brought another small administrative crisis. "I was doing something important" she said.'[21]

Finally, in a brief moment of bizarre horror, a young secretary working on a word-processor makes an appearance:

A young woman worked for Rosemarie. She was unmarried and, by general consensus, good-looking. Every day for a couple of weeks during the Eagle project, she was 'assaulted' at her desk. She would be doing her electronic paperwork when suddenly everything would go haywire, all her labor would be spoiled, and on the screen of her cathode ray tube would appear cold, lascivious suggestions. 'Whoever was doing it', said West, had 'the mentality of an assassin.'[22]

A pursuit of the evil-doer takes place through the labyrinths of software and circuitry, an enjoyable exploit for the knights of know-how.

Exploits, especially of creative technology, give a man this sense of being above the humdrum, the world of wife and Rosemarie. Barry Furlough, a production engineer at EIDS who had been involved in the early days of the development of the CT scanner, had felt something similar to the elation of Kidder's computer engineers:

You collectively are at the forefront of whatever it is you're doing. And you don't have to be winning Nobel prizes to do that. It can just be that you are working with your company's product line which is at the forefront for them. It doesn't have to be anything really wonderful. The fact that you are at the limit of your company's experience: that's a marvellous feeling. And if it is the case, as it was with me, that you are involved with something which, without being mealy-mouthed about it, is doing humanity a bit of good. The scanner was such a tremendous breakthrough for the medical world. Everybody was so excited, swept up in it. It was terrific.

Sometimes, listening to engineers like Barry, you catch echoes of Francis Bacon, the Renaissance scientist. It is worth remembering the extent to which the creation of science was itself a gendered and gendering process. The task of science was a rational understanding of Nature. As we saw, Reason was a masculine concept, Nature by contrast was female. Bacon used metaphors – 'penetrating Nature's secrets', 'storming and occupying her castles' – that clearly express the masculinity of the scientific project.[23] In a tract titled *The Masculine Birth of Time* Bacon wrote of science: 'I am come in very truth leading you Nature with all her children to bind her to your service and make her your slave'.[24] Genevieve Lloyd points out that these metaphors 'give a male content to what it is to be a good knower'.[25] They also give a male content to what it is to transform and manage matter, to tame forces; in short, to be a technologist.[26]

So men appropriate the technological sphere for masculinity. They also make use of the masculinity of technology to form bonds with one another. They converse about work, technology and sport. 'Our conversation does tend to be very, very male dominated. The obvious things. Not so much politics. More movements within the business field. That keeps us together,' an engineer told me. And another said, 'We are talking about cars, repairing this and that. We talk about cricket.' The effect on women who do try to be part of such a scene is isolation. 'I felt like some kind of an alien or something,' said a young woman who had tried a spell as a computer operator in a roomful of men. 'Because they treated me as if I was a freak or something. It was all guys' talk, cars and things. They don't think girls know anything about cars. They talked down to me all the time.'

The men also, however, relate through competitive swearing and obscenity and a trade in sexual stories, references and innuendo that are directly objectifying and exploitative of women. It serves the purpose of forging solidarity between them. Some men told me frankly that, yes, a woman there, it does cramp your style and spoil the conviviality. The obscenity creates a boundary across which women will fear to step. A maintenance technician told me, 'If someone [i.e. some woman] came into this set-up they would have to accept it and not try to change it. That is my feeling. It would be difficult to explain to a girl the sort of language and behaviour that goes on in an all-male preserve which they would be coming into.' Woman, you are warned.

Tensions between men

Despite the bonding of man with man through this love of technology, however, there are disunities in the fraternity. The complications arise in part from the dependence of technology on wealth and economic power. We saw in Chapter 1 how capital has little regard for masculine self-respect when profit is at stake. It is obliged continually to attempt to bring down and devalue the engineer as any other worker. Men with technical skills must, in response, continually attempt to climb the ladder out of reach. A fitter-welder, who clearly felt himself slipping downwards, said, 'The people that are building the computers, they are organizing engineering work, they are the people that are getting all the work. People with skills like mine are losing it. There was a time when I could just go down the road and get a job with more money, more satisfaction or whatever. But now there's not so many to choose from.'

Engineering is making a significant shift from mechanical and electrical processes and products to 'high tech': electronics, but also lasers, bio-engineering and other developing areas. The British engineering industry is suffering many closures in the process and employment has collapsed. Although unskilled and semi-skilled workers, mainly women, took the brunt, half a million men's jobs were lost between 1978 and 1982.[27] Those with the redundant skills generated by the last technical revolution, or those who never quite made the threshold that lifts one from semi-skilled to skilled work, are being ejected from work. The honourable process of the past used to take a lad through the hardships of apprenticeship to the security of craft status, by which he became a man respected by men and a worker with some status in the working class. This process is now either non-existent or a charade.

Dan Perry, a forklift truck driver in a warehouse, described how he had seen through the 'skill' story to his own satisfaction:

I started the engineering apprenticeship really looking forward to being an engineer and having a skilled job and that was it. I did my first year at college. And then went back to the firm for the next four years. And in the first few weeks I realized that me at 17 was standing there doing a job, and the 57-year-old bloke next to me was doing the same job and he was getting paid far more than I was. And I was going to be doing the same thing for the next four years. It doesn't take long to work out that you are cheap labour.

And this marked a turn in Dan's life. He walked out of there:

I would have taken any job. But I was only unemployed one week. I went to the Job Centre on Monday. Said, 'Look, I've been in engineering. I can't take the apprenticeship any more. I've jacked it in. I haven't got a job. I'm prepared to do anything.' They said, 'We've a cleaning job, a job unloading lorries and one for a forklift driver. What do you fancy?' I said, 'Oh, I'll have a bash at the forklift.' Sounded different. And I started on Monday. On the Friday I left my apprenticeship I took home £21. The next week in the new job I took home £36. And within six months I was grossing £78.

Did you feel you had lost anything in terms of skill? 'In terms of status, to do with the outside world generally, yes. Because you were working in a warehouse compared with being a skilled or apprentice engineer. This is how I felt.' But when he found that his earnings stood him in better stead for getting a mortgage than the dubious status of being on the first step of the craft progression he changed his view. Dan, then, dropped off the skill ladder. But as we shall see later, he is a man who does not hold very tightly to masculine status and power.

The contradictions for men, however, arise not only from the workings of capitalism but also from the hierarchical nature of patriarchal relations. Heidi Hartmann emphasized both the bonds and the divisions when she defined patriarchy as 'a set of social relations . . . in which there are hierarchical relations between men and solidarity among them which enables them to control women'.[28] Male self-identity is won in a costly tussle with other men for status and prestige, and this applies in technological work no less than in other situations. Those men who seek their masculine identity in technological competence find themselves obliged to manoeuvre for position and negotiate their rank relative to other men. There are comparisons of competence: the *cognoscenti* versus the rest. One man explained to me how hard it is for the man whose know-how is not recognized by the others, who doesn't make it into the clique within the firm. There is rivalry, too, between the generalist and the specialist, and between specialisms. The electronics man may look down on the mechanical man as a spanner-and-elbow-grease type; he in turn may be seen as a *parvenu*.

One professional engineer described to me the discomfort he felt in his relations with craftsmen: 'In some ways they may regard themselves as subservient. Or perhaps I think of myself as being on top. I'm not sure.' The relationship expresses something of class, something of patriarchal ranking. But the sturdy self-image of the hands-on man is well able to mobilize masculinity in defence of self-respect: 'If you have five O-levels and five A-levels and then you don't want to get your hands dirty – I think practical experience is far and aways more – I mean if you have it on paper but you can't do it in practice, what is the good of the paper? Twenty-one years of age, some of 'em, and never got their hands dirty. They may have all the knowledge, the trigonometry, God knows what, but it isn't going to benefit them in a job.' One practical engineer I talked to had tried to demonstrate to a professional engineer, whom he suspected of trying to pull status on him, why the latter's impractical ideas wouldn't work. In his indignation he made a misjudgement with the machine that cost him the fingertips of one hand.

We need to remember, then, as we see in the account that follows of men fending off women from the technological sphere, asserting the authority of their competence and knowledge against women, that they are having to cover their flanks against attack from elsewhere. They may impose their definitions upon women with the more ferocity just because the individual and group status of the engineer, or of any one kind of engineer, within the world of men cannot be taken for granted, but is itself continually in negotiation.

Besides, it is self-evident that in actual fact not all men are technologically skilled or knowledgeable. It is not men but masculinity that has this bond with machinery. Not all men succeed at anything and certainly not all succeed in technology. Many men know no more than the average woman of how machines and equipment work and how to fix them. Technological development and choice is out of the control of ordinary people, whether they are men or women. This feeling was expressed by a young semi-skilled technical worker, Terence Dunning. 'Technology is going too fast,' he said, 'and people are going backwards. People are not progressing and becoming better people, but technology is going so fast it's going out the window. People think, God, it's so far in front of me, they won't even think of catching up, they won't even try. That's useful for some people, it sort of keeps the other people quiet. But it – the technical people are going by leaps and bounds and leaving the rest behind.' *So you see a sort of technological elite getting stronger?* 'God, yes.' *And you aren't part of it?* 'No. I don't think of myself as part of it.' This may be a more painful feeling for many men than for women, since women as a sex have till now not aspired to be part of that elite.

Working at careers

As men appropriate technology for masculinity, they similarly appropriate 'work'. There is no male equivalent of the expression 'career women'. You can't be a career man. Such a phrase is tautologous because it is assumed that if you are a man your work will inevitably be a lifetime project. Nonetheless, careers do not come automatically to men. They have to be worked at, with foresight and nerve, and they take a toll.

There is some truth in the fact that technological work, whether at the manual or professional level, benefits from a career commitment. This is because, in the first place, the learning process is lengthy and, given our present way of seeing things, for it to be worthwhile embarking on it a person needs to expect to practise for many years. Secondly, knowledge and know-how are rapidly obsolescent owing to continual change in technology, and so it is felt that engineering jobs cannot easily accommodate a break, as for child-rearing.

The career imperative, however, is ascribed a high value by men. They struggle with each other and measure their status as men by their success in the technological world. Characteristically, a promising engineer will seek employment with a go-ahead firm. Electronics International certainly considers itself one of these. It has a conscious philosophy of creating an atmosphere that is designed to select for the fittest: people who thrive on pressure. 'The firm have deliberately introduced a new work culture, a new ethical system,' said a personnel manager. This system, he explained, had to do with driving people hard:

> If someone gets on here we do it by sticking to our ideals, being strong enough to argue our case . . . What we want is someone who will go at it hell for leather. It is a young management environment here and very competitive. Most are in the 28 to 35 age range, graduate and postgraduate. It's an aggressive environment. Nobody wants anyone else shooting down their ideas, you know. Perhaps we overplay the role, but we enjoy it.

Newstyle Ltd. is another zappy firm, known for promoting young and pushing hard. 'We find it difficult to get people with fire in the belly,' a personnel manager said here. 'It's not a very nice expression. But I think industrial jobs are a lot to do with personality. Personality and enthusiasm. Those sorts of people are difficult to pick up . . . The problem is not necessarily picking up the people with the skills but with the personality and the drive to succeed in our environment.'

Working at EIDS, as in many companies, requires total immersion. 'You'll get a meeting called for six or seven at night. Working over the weekend is not unusual. That is accepted.' Many of the men I met worked very long and irregular hours. Family commitments must come second. Such work is clearly predicated on not having responsibility for child care, indeed on having no one to look after, and ideally someone to look after you.

The business environment of the go-ahead firm is therefore one in which it can be difficult for a woman to see herself fitting. Electronics International, as we saw, claims to be consciously undiscriminating, disappointed and surprised that women are not coming forward. The principles of male supremacy, however, do not need to be built into discriminatory personnel policy, since they are embodied in the relations of the firm, where they are fully effective: technological jobs in practice remain in male hands. How this occurs is hinted at in an EIDS job advertisment: 'Enthusiasm, along with creativity, drive and a clear understanding of your personal contribution are needed in a business where technological limits are constantly being tested and new frontiers broken and explored.' On the face of it, this is not discriminatory wording. But women know how women are usually defined – not with words like 'drive', 'limits', 'test'. However a woman evaluates herself as an individual she is likely to read such an advert as addressed not to women but to men. To many women it will be more of a warning than an invitation.

An engineer in another leading electronics firm, similarly producing X-ray equipment, reported that 'women don't like the industrial research environment'. Of two ideally qualified graduate women he had recently interviewed, one had felt the firm would be 'too tough' for her; she felt 'vulnerable'. The other had said she felt 'scared of such a big company'. He concluded with some satisfaction, 'It's a man's environment here and you're accountable.' It is not suprising, perhaps, that both these women graduates were looking to the National Health Service hospitals as a more nourishing environment for females with technical and scientific skills. Such 'service' jobs, however, were dismissed by the EIDS personnel manager as a 'namby-pamby' choice, in contrast to the 'hard-nosed option of industry'.

Men build their careers by progressing from one such firm to another. It is not just the professional, university-educated man who does so. The technician too can climb up the salary scales – from technical maintenance, say – and, keeping a weather eye on developments, can 'ride the technology'. One of the formulae for success is to socialize. Contacts with other men must be made and fostered. 'It's a close-knit community,' said a technical manager in clothing equipment. 'You tend to know each other. And you can say, "Oh, I'm with so-and-so now. I'm in marketing." And he'll say, "You'd better come over and see me then." That type of thing.' Certainly I saw several interconnections and movements of qualified personnel between clothing manufacturers and the technology supplying firms. Remember the service engineers, for instance, who 'virtually end up living in the firm' that buys their equipment and are well placed to develop contacts.

Here is an instance of a successful male career. Donald Ramsey worked as an apprentice electrician from the age of 15 to 21, studying by day release and block release to get his City and Guilds. He meanwhile also acquired six O-levels at night school, because he had left school without any. He then went to college and passed another City and Guilds in heating and ventilating. While continuing to work in these occupations he next did courses in estimating and critical path analysis, so edging over to the management skills. He got a job as a trainee work study engineer in manufacturing industry, having identified work study as a practice that was well placed to help a person with manual skills gain a foothold in managment. This was the beginning of take-off for Donald. However, as a tactical step he moved to a bigger firm in a related industry to develop a knowledge of 'organisation and method'. Here he began using computer programs and picking up some systems knowledge. He now stepped back into his chosen industry and there gained a management job on the basis of his newly won grasp of computers. Later, using his knowledge of the industry, he took the inspired risk of joining a group of consultants working in his industry. He had now picked up membership of a couple of professional institutions. Currently he is a busy consultant, advising the industry on new technology and organization and, not incidentally, standing in a prime position in the labour market. 'There isn't a month goes by when I don't get an offer,' he says.

Donald Ramsey is characteristic of successful technical men in his delight in his own career. There had been false starts and it had been a hard slog, but now

what is most enjoyable is the total involvement you can have. You are never bored, you are never fed up, and it is so satisfying because you are always helping somebody. You go into companies, and you mightn't be that good, but you do know that little bit more and you can help them, and if you can help them they like you for it. And that itself is job satisfaction. And it is not a mundane job you dread coming in for. I never, ever dread coming to work. Because I know that there is going to be something else happens every day, it'll be something new. There isn't a day goes by without the phone ringing and someone is telling me, 'Have you heard about such and such, which is just coming in?' And I will find out more about it. So you are always learning, learning something else.

Richard Bellamy, another technical manager, said of himself:

There is no doubt my ambition is to make it big. Have a

company of my own perhaps. I would always have something new, try something. Make a success of something, get it out on the market and build it up – that sort of success. I don't think I would like to sit back and continue [as now] and say, 'This is the level, this is what I am going to be doing in ten years' time' (laugh). I hope not. I might still be involved with [this firm] but I hope by then it will be two or three times as big as this. As far as I'm concerned the company has to keep growing and the prospects appearing. If it's a dead-end job I'll look elsewhere.

We should always recognize that these positive expressions by men about their careers are the public face of masculinity. There is no doubt that such careerism is riddled with contradiction and cost. Capital exploits men by means of their masculine identity. Men destroy each other. We are living in a time of economic crisis when jobs are insecure and hard to come by, when men are thrown into ever-more intense competition with each other for their first job, for promotions. Andrew Tolson writes of a crisis of confidence for the professional man: 'More and more men have begun to see the career-structure as futile and impossible to sustain.'[29] As we saw, Dan Perry had turned away from a technological career ladder: he could mock gently what he observed from his lowly position near the bottom of the firm, but he was also bitter about the political economy that produced these effects. For every happy and successful career engineer, therefore, we should expect to find an anxious competitor or a defeated failure, what Phyllis Chesler called 'the countless burned-out male casualties, the male body-count involved in male heroics'.[30]

For all the seeming camaraderie among men at work, men seldom give each other emotional sustenance. Tolson says: 'in the white-hot world of corporate industry, ideological cynicism is reflected in the expression of masculinity at work. The collective interaction of men working together is conducted from a distance; it is a formal advertisement for male solidarity in an essentially false situation.'[31] Work-fellows are good for a jar and a laugh. They are not good for a shoulder to cry on.

Undoubtedly the wives of men like Donald Ramsey and Richard Bellamy would tell us another tale of their careers, one that only they hear.

What men are engaged in, through this pursuit of technological brilliance and successful careers, is *transcendence*. Simone de Beauvoir wrote in *The Second Sex*: 'Every individual . . . feels that his existence involves an undefined need to transcend himself, to engage in freely chosen projects.'[32] And again: 'Man's design is not to repeat himself in time: it is to take control of the instant and mould the future. It is male activity that in creating values has made of existence itself a value.'[33] To transcend is precisely to rise above the mundane, the womanly. The lives of these men 'transcend' those of their wives. They pay a price, but women pay a higher one.

Women: inauthentic workers

Listen for a moment to what men, from the vantage point of their own dynamic careers, have to say about women as workers. In contrast to the way men represent themselves – as striving, achieving, engaging in the public sphere of work – they represent women as static, domestic, private people, as non-workers. Simon Oldfield, a technical manager in a large firm producing materials handling technology, saw women in the workplace frankly as an aspect of the decor: 'Well, women tend to see to the little things. They create a pleasant atmosphere. Women are associated with the nicer things of life. They make a nice show of pot plants and so on.' (This was not expressed as a joke.)

I asked Donald Ramsey, *Could a woman have had a career like yours?* He thought about this: 'A woman would have to work harder at it than I did,' he concluded. I found it difficult to imagine how anyone could have worked harder. He went on:

There are hardly any female general managers [in my industry]. Either because of family commitments or because they don't think they can do it and aren't pushy enough. I only got where I was through being pushy. If I hadn't I would still be a work study engineer. I don't think women have the confidence . . . You don't find the same enthusiasm in the female labour force as you do in the male labour force.

Richard Bellamy, commenting on the absence of women technologists and managers in his industry, said, 'On the whole women are happy with nine-to-five jobs and maybe a family and a home. They are not that interested in being on top, or running things. I wouldn't say there wasn't *any* woman who was. But women are not that committed as a rule.'

Here we are entering complicated terrain. Of course, in one sense the men are quite straightforwardly making meaning of what they see around them. Few women *are* visibly making successful careers, technological or otherwise, in these industries. Most of the women the men encounter at work *are* in 'undemanding' nine-to-five support roles. They themselves have formative relationships with women in domestic roles: mothers, wives. It is not surprising that is how they see women. In another way, however, the men are selecting some things to see and ignoring others. They are overlooking those instances where women do work hard, sustain careers and prove a long-lived interest in a profession or industry. They are leaving out of account the extent to which their own careers have been made possible by mothers and wives who have foregone careers. The terrain is made more complex still by the fact that nothing is altogether 'given'. As the men act and speak they create the world they describe. They are writing a script that will be acted out, one in which men will tend to perform as properly gendered men and women as properly gendered women.

In what men say of women, a good deal of simple stereotyping goes on. Men say the usual things: 'Girls can cope with boring and repetitive tasks, men can't', 'Men can cope with extremes of temperature (the cold store, the foundry), women can't', and so on. To repeat these is tedious. Indeed the men often recognized that they were prejudices and apologised for them: 'just chauvinism I suppose'. They did, however, go on feeling these things, and no doubt acting on them. Let's look at more elaborated statements by men about women as workers that show some of the complexity of their beliefs.

First, there is the question of whether a woman should work at all. Here is a man, Tom Delaware, for whom a man's career is of crucial importance and whose natural instinct is to keep women at home. However, he is by now uneasily aware of the fact that since the Second World War it has become normal for women to work after, and even through, child rearing. About his son, Tom said: 'So long as he doesn't waste his life. That's my only stipulation.' *What would be wasting it?* I asked. 'Well, if he just didn't work, didn't have a job, even with the situation we have with unemployment. Or wasting his time by getting three O-levels instead of eight. (Crisply) And very weak ones. That would be wasting. We have set him, my wife and I, and the school, we expect certain things of him. You could go on for ever like this.' Tom is curiously engaged in this part of the interview, whereas before he hasn't given much of himself. There is emotion now behind what he is saying. *But the wasting would continue in adult life if he didn't progress through organizations and . . .?* 'No. He could be an entrepreneur and work for himself as a fishmonger, as long as he makes a success of whatever avenue he goes into. Not saying he couldn't be a self-employed plumber. It would be a jolly good employment, I should think,' he said bitterly, 'for the year 2000.' *Supposing this 14-year old son of yours was a girl?* 'Oh. (Pause) Right.' Tom takes a moment to catch himself up, surprised by the question. After a moment I try again. *Can you try to think through this question of 'wasting' again? Would the criteria be the same for her? or different?* '(Sigh) No. (Pause) Assuming she has the same academic ability I would still expect her to go through, hopefully, the same cycle. Thereafter of course, not to waste whatever she has gained in experience or academic qualifications, but to use them until she will get married and have the normal family. But then hopefully thereafter she would have such an attitude of mind that work could come back *into her home scene again*.' (My italics)

Secondly, here is Sandy Robertson, an elderly craft cloth cutter and pattern grader in Steadywear Ltd., struggling to explain the presence in the firm of a young female grader, Sushila, a trainee at his bench. So fixed is he in his view of women as domestic creatures, as non-workers, that he can only explain her presence in industrial pattern-cutting as misdirected enthusiasm for 'fashion' and home dressmaking. 'This little girl that we've got, she went to college, she started to learn cutting. But she isn't doing pattern-cutting as such here. I think from a girl's point of view they start off wanting to make their own clothes, don't they? This is the idea of it, like, isn't it? And I don't think grading as *we* do it, if she learned just grading, it wouldn't enable her to make her own clothes . . . I've not really spoken to Sushila about it. But if a girl wants to make her own blouses, if she wants to make a dirndl skirt or something like that, well, what she is taught here won't in any way help her to do that.' *You don't think she wants the same thing out of the job that you want out of it? A life-long job in the industry?* 'I think that perhaps is it. I don't think so. Yeah. I think from a man's point of view it's a job and it's a job whether it's a skill or an ability or just a flair for doing it. I've earned a fairly good wage. I've not done marvellously out of it, but I've not done badly either, you know. I've never been in anything else.' Sandy ends by hinting at the contradiction that is troubling him. In fact, Sushila can't be explained his way, because the industry is coming to prefer female pattern personnel, as we've seen. *So in a way, do you feel it's spoiling the trade, this that you are describing, an almost amateur approach?* 'Well, I suppose in the end it would, wouldn't it. And I haven't seen any boys for years coming into it.'

For many men it is unthinkable that women could possess a technical competence equal to their own. Those women who show a glimmer of ability are spoken of like performing seals: 'I've never *seen* one do it, though there are *some* clever women about that can mend fuses, mend plugs and do things like that. Round the house.' A field engineer said of women trainers: 'We do even train them up a bit. For instance give them a pair of pliers to carry in their pocket so that if someone wants an image adjusting they can give it a tweak.' Women would have to be paragons of competence to be accepted by male colleagues.

Another maintenance man warned, 'She'd have to be capable of going off and wading into the brute [he meant the machine] and giving it stick. Coming out bloody but unbowed, coming out *joking* about it. Like the rest of us . . . Here, if you are a bit of a dead-end and you are not safe to be let out on your own, you won't be part of the clique as it were. We spark off each other.'

Where women do give the lie to men's conception of the normal, and feature among the professional and technical *cognoscenti*, there arises a 'seek the man' syndrome. For instance, when a man refers to a woman technologist of his acquaintance, even if she is known to him through work, he'll often add: 'Her husband is such-and-such', 'She's married to a physicist working in the same field.' In fact, one added, quite gratuitously, 'When they are together at night they can talk it over.' It is as though the woman can only do the job because she is informed by her husband's know-how.

The woman who does stick with it and attempt to do equal work with men represents a problem for the man. By definition she can't be the old familiar domestic woman, nor can she be the working subordinate – secretary or operative – with whom he has long since developed forms of relationship that are comfortable to him. She is not easy for a man to work with; a regular bed of nails, in fact. Being competitive 'makes them not very good colleagues, not an easy part of the team. They tend to get a bit Thatcherite if you know what I mean.' With such women, said Barry Furlough,

> You can't get on their wave band. They take their defensive attitude to the job to the point where they are unnecessarily close about what they are doing. They feel if they give you any little chink into what they are thinking about, that somehow will be a crack in their armour . . . It tends to make them very officious. The problem is that women strive too much. They spoil it for everyone.

Dominance by head and by hand

Let's explore a little more deeply the problem that these men are encountering. When women enter a masculine occupation a collision occurs between two incompatible values. The way gendering works is by ascribing a series of polarized characteristics, complementary paired values, to the 'masculine' and the 'feminine'. Ruth Schwarz-Cowan pointed to some of these dichotomies when she wrote:

> While we socialize our men to aspire to feats of mastery, we socialize our women to aspire to feats of submission. Men are hard; women are soft. Men are meant to conquer nature; women are meant to commune with it. Men are rational, women irrational; men are practical, women impractical. Boys play with blocks; girls play with dolls. Men build; women inhabit. Men are active; women are passive. Men are good at mathematics; women are good at literature. If something is broken, daddy will fix it. If feelings are hurt, mommy will salve them. We have trained our women to opt out of the technological order as much as we have trained our men to opt into it.[34]

Normally men and women, things and jobs, comfortably reflect these complementary values and when women step into male work they upset a widely accepted sense of order and meaning.

We'll see below how men use one of these pairs of complementary values – hard/soft – to explain and legitimate their exclusion of women from technological work and careers. Yet there is a point beyond which any such ideological construction is liable to encounter a crisis. One occurs for instance, in the form of a credibility gap in men's claims both to manual and to mental superiority. At one moment, in order to fortify their identification with physical engineering, men dismiss the intellectual world as 'soft'. At the next moment, however, they need to appropriate sedentary, intellectual engineering work for masculinity too. Ideological complementary values such as hard/soft must therefore always be seen as provisional. The values called into play in the hegemonic ideology will vary from time to time and from one situation to another. This parallels the variation we noted in the way the genders are differentiated from one society or culture to another. The values and qualities associated with the two genders are strictly contingent on the demands of sex supremacy and on nothing else. Male power is the bottom line.

The concept of women as the soft sex and men as the hard dates back to very early days. Isidore of Seville, in the sixth century AD, linked the terms for male and female to strength and frailty by a pun. The Latin word *vir*, he suggested, is related to *vis*, meaning strength. *Mulier* (woman) is related to *mollitie* (softness or weakness).[35] The association was strongly emphasized in Victorian ideology: 'Physical delicacy, relative intellectual weakness, timidity in the face of harsh contacts or conflict made it necessary for a woman to look to a protector who could defend her from the world . . .'[36] A glance at the collection of photographs of Victorian working women collected together by Michael Hiley[37] shows an impressive array of sturdy, muscular and work-stained women and girls. They work on the waterfront, in markets, in factories and mines. They wield shovels, picks, riddles. But the strong woman was denied or rejected in ideology then just as she is today. The women surface workers of the collieries provoked a violent debate about the suitability of certain occupations for women in which it was complained that the pit-brow lasses didn't resemble women at all, dressed wholly or partially in male attire. They were 'degraded womanhood', 'torn from [their] natural sphere'. Women should be soft; if they are hard they are not women.[338]

The dichotomy between hard and soft is pervasive in the way engineers represent jobs and people. A male technology student in a Swedish polytechnic is quoted by Boel Berner as saying:

One would perhaps think that the love of women is weaker among those who have given themselves up to cold technology than among any other young student. But the handling of hard, linear tools breeds a desire for softer, more beautiful, curved ones, and after long days of calculations the technologist looks for the utterly incalculable.[39]

The men I interviewed, expecially those in the manual kinds of engineering work, made the manly association with hardness very clear. Here is Jack Tyley, a young apprentice maintenance engineer, talking about his work: 'You've got to be (sigh), a very *hard* person, in engineering, to work with mechanical or electrical things. A very hard person.' *How do you mean, hard?* 'You've got to be tough. You get a lot of knocks as an engineer. You've got to take the knocks, a lot of cuts. It's very dangerous really. Even if you do know what you are doing. I sometimes go in, knowing I'm going to hurt myself, but I know the job's got to be done, so I've got to do it. I don't know that a woman would have the same attitude. I know we're built differently, physically. And I think it would put a lot of women off, knowing that they are going to get hurt.' *You've got to be courageous?* 'Yes, you have really. Yeah.'

Metal plays a special part in these representations. It contributes the hardness factor: 'The handling and fitting of metal, that is 90 per cent a man's job.' The tough, weight-lifting, nerve-demanding, metallic aspects of practical engineering are confidently assumed 'to weed women out right away'. Yet I asked many of the men two questions. If you had a back injury would it prevent you doing the job? And, do you have a minimum size and strength requirement when interviewing men for the job? Nearly always they answered the first: I would find a way round the problem, get help, use aids, split things down into smaller units, reorganize the job. And in answer to the second I never heard of any physical criteria used in selecting men. 'The fact that you are a man is enough. You're going to cope,' one engineer admitted, honestly. The quality of strength, like the quality of surviving dirt and hurt, is so deeply gendered it is impossible for men to think of women as strong or as survivors.

In conversation with practical engineers about their work I was aware time and again of a '10 per cent formula' being wheeled into play. That is to say, a man would describe some small aspect of the job that would definitively prevent women doing it, even if (a big 'if' of course) they could do the remainder. This is the way a maintenance technician, Joe

Wedderburn, described a job that was in large part, in fact, electronic benchwork, light and relatively clean:

> You see, at certain periods of time we will get involved in lifting up the floor, going down the pit at the bottom of the couch ram [on an X-ray machine], where there is motors which have to be got off. They literally have to be manhandled. Now it is a filthy, dirty sort of job. Because of the lift of the couch you need about a six-foot ram which goes down into the ground. And it needs a motor to drive it, which is fixed at the bottom. And any part of that ram or the motor at one time or another may have to come out, which means physical work.

You don't use lifting tackle?

> Oh yes, the ram itself, you *would* use equipment to lift it. It is well over a hundredweight, perhaps two or three. The motors are 30 or 40 pounds, which is not in itself too heavy. But it is the awkward situation they are in. You have to lie on the floor, block it up, undo the bolts and then you have to get your arms underneath while you are lying on the floor to get it out. You can only get one person down the pit at a time, but once you have moved it to the side, you can get help to get it out, someone up top. It is so constricted that it usually has to be manhandled. Someone will put a rope down to haul it up ... We get involved with vacuum problems, too, which may mean the oil pump and you start getting oil sloshed about. A girl might be prepared to do the electronics side which is nice, clean, comfortable, sitting at a bench [but] I think it would be rare to find a woman who was prepared to do the whole range of things. It's difficult enough to find men to do it.

Joe Wedderburn wound up by saying, 'Perhaps 90 per cent of our work a girl could do, but the situation will crop up when that 10 per cent has to be done ...' Then I asked, *Are there any men in the department who are less competent than the rest of you, slightly built or weaker?* And he said promptly, 'Yes, we do

194 / Machinery of Dominance

have one.' He spoke in an undertone while telling about this shameful but revealing matter. 'He is elderly and we are having to carry him, to be honest.'

A major contradiction in this ideology of hard versus soft lies, of course, in the fact that most senior engineers are not, by the time they reach senior status, 'hands-on men' (if they ever were). A crisis of continuity occurs for male authority in the career rift between the practical engineer and the technological manager. There comes a time in many a practical engineer's life when he has to make the decision to seek or accept promotion to a sedentary job. Age as well as personnel policy can prompt this: as a man grows older he finds manual work tiring, his health may not withstand the strains. If he succeeds in making the leap to a desk he may be able to exchange one kind of potency for a greater one. If he fails to do so he will undergo a rapid decline in relative status and earning power.

The difficulty lies in the fact that such a man has tended to rely for self-respect on an identification of his masculinity with physical effectiveness. Often this has meant running down the desk-bound intellectual. The practical hands-on engineer has often found a way round the problem of considering women as potential colleagues in his manual style of work (especially if he wished to avoid seeming altogether dismissive) by saying that of course women are 'good at intellectual things', maths, science and so on. They would be fine as desk-bound engineers. Now he has to face transformation into one of these suspiciously unmanly creatures himself.

Barry Furlough said:

This is one of things that has been most difficult for me in my particular career, the transition from being very much involved with the nuts and bolts end of the deal. At however high a level of responsibility, you were still primarily dealing with the product and its engineering. Whereas eventually you get to the stage when you decide if you are aspiring to higher things in the organization, then you have to make the break and become an administrator. And I'm more or less at that point now – with some regrets . . . I'm a very practical person.

I'm a dirty hands man. So the transition into management for me is a fairly drastic step. Reconciling yourself to the definite fact that you are gradually moving away from the day-to-day engineering and the realization that rapidly comes upon you that you won't keep pace with the technology any more – you'll never go back there again. Because even after two years you are stale in your technology. And whether you could ever make the leap back is debatable.

This moment, a kind of male menopause, takes away from the engineer his most valued faculty: practical control of material things. 'I wouldn't be getting the hands-on experience, I wouldn't be diving into things with a screw-driver'. 'Man-management, it's more abstract. You don't feel so cost effective. You can't measure your value-added any more. There's not as much job satisfaction,' said the other engineers, speculating on their 'change of life'. What they get in exchange for control of things of course may well be more direct control of people. Nonetheless men need ideological devices for sustaining their masculine identity as they step from the hard world of the workshop to the soft world of the slide rule or computer and console and desk. One such device is to distinguish within the range of intellectual occupations, once more, a hard and a soft. Brian Easlea writes:

For example, within physics, the study of elementary particles is typically regarded as more prestigious than other branches of physics, and within biology the study of gene structure and replication is more prestigious than the study of macroscopic biological systems such as ecology. Futhermore, within each discipline or sub-discipline the more theoretical is the practice, i.e. the more 'mental' and less contaminated with 'female' matter it is, the greater is the prestige accruing to the practitioners. Thus within physics, theoretical physics is widely regarded as more prestigious than experimental, in other words, as 'harder' and more 'penetrating'.[40]

This connects with a second device which is simply to

abandon the hard/soft dichotomy and shift to emphasizing a different pair of unequal values: intellectual versus non-intellectual being a popular set. Sally Hacker in a study of academic engineers found that central to their ideology was a 'mind/body' dualism in which the masculine (and the engineer) are identified with mind, and the feminine with body.[41] For some purposes, then, physique, muscular strength, daring and manual skills are given positive masculine value. In this ideology women are weak and ineffectual creatures. For other purposes intellectuality and analytical power are appropriated for masculinity. Women then become physical creatures, linked to organic processes such as childbirth, feeding, cleaning. This latter dichotomy has a long history: the mediaeval church represented women as carnal, men as intellectual and spiritual.

It is not surprising that men are happy when they can unite both sets of positive values in a single occupation. A field engineer working on CT scanners is one of the lucky ones who can enjoy this unity. I asked one of them, *Is this something you value in your work?* 'Oh yes, definitely. You like to sweat. Is that what you're getting at? You get a big hype out of, for me a *big* hype, out of getting the machine into the room, cabling it up, making the room look neat and tidy and clinically ready for patients. You feel you have achieved something physically. Physically. And then the more *mental* work comes from the commissioning.' *So the fact that there is a range of tasks is what is attractive?* 'Yes. That you have to be a plumber, a mechanic, a teacher.' *It makes you a whole person?* 'Definitely. Yes.' This is for many men the ideal engineer, the man who has talents of both head and hand.

The intellectual engineer who cannot claim physical prowess is, however, obliged to find reasons why women cannot compete with him: he needs to engage in yet more ideological effort. The qualities represented as necessary for professional engineering must again be found to include 10 per cent that women 'just don't have'. Is it logic? 'You have to solve these problems *logically*. You can't just jump from one thing to another. I wouldn't think that a woman could possibly be logical enough in her thinking to do the job we do.' But wait, here is someone else saying that 'women are *too* logical': 'Women don't have the imagination, the flair, to diagnose faults.' Because now we find that the engineer requires – guess what – intuition. 'We often tried to analyse what it is our brains do when we are confronted with a dead CT scanner. And we've come to the conclusion that it is half the time intuitive, suddenly something goes click (happy laugh): "It's *that* bit!" And nine times out of ten, it is.' *Intuition?* I asked, *Isn't that supposed to be a woman's quality?* 'Ah, well,' this engineer responded quickly, 'Probably it isn't intuition. It's probably just that we know the machine. We've seen it all before.' And so on, in circles. Patience is it, you need? Women haven't got patience enough for engineering, but they have patience for the drudgery of data processing. Dexterity? Not what it takes to repair a sewing machine, only what it takes to sew.

By whatever contortion it takes, in masculine ideology women are represented as non-technological, as incompatible with machinery, except in the controlled, supervised, guided role of operator.

7. The kitchen and the tool shed

In comparison with the men, the 71 working women I interviewed had much less in the way of technological skills and careers to talk about. There was one professional engineer, Pamela Franks, and the short-lived maintenance technician, Georgina Hodson, at Northshire Hospital. There was the part-time trainee programmer at Clotec, Denise Brown, and some radiographers whose job, though technically demanding, was nonetheless an operator's job. The majority of the women, however, were doing relatively repetitive, immobile and non-technical jobs. Some of these were of the kind that men described to me in terms of pity, disgust and scorn: 'I don't know how they stick to it.'

Despite this, the women, whatever their occupation, all had plenty to say about their work. All but a handful were committed to working – for the money, for the company and for the self-respect that comes of having a role in the world outside home. For those in unskilled and non-technical jobs, however, the prospects of career development were thin. Where could a warehouse 'picker' be promoted to? Where could an electronic assembly worker hope to get training? Day release or on-the-job training of any kind was rarely available for women in these kinds of jobs. Special training opportunities to enable a transfer into technologically skilled work were unthinkable.

Satisfaction in skill

Skilled technical jobs, in contrast, can change and develop for those who do them. It was noticeable that women who were doing work that afforded and required some technical competence were more enthusiastic than others about their jobs. Pamela Franks, the software engineer at Electronics International, said of her job, 'It involves a lot of very challenging areas of technology. To some extent it's very mathematical. It involves quite sophisticated geometry and statistics. There's a strong physical background isn't there, the idea of actually directing a beam of radiation at someone and knowing what goes on inside as a result. That's a strongly physical thing. It combines a lot of very interesting things.' Pamela had shopped around the corporations looking for a place that would offer her challenging work, somewhere where change was afoot. With her qualifications she was in a favourable job market and had been in a position to be choosy. 'The technology is advancing fairly rapidly here,' she said of EIDS. 'This is not a bad place to be.'

At the other end of the occupational scale I met a woman, Maureen Casey, who had got a job at EIDS that was one step up from the bottom-line assembly work. Previously defined as a men's zone, a few women had recently been let into Area B. The work was just a little less routine than the remainder of the women's jobs in the firm. It involved using four or five different tools to fix cable and sub-assemblies to a three-foot cubic frame. The work was not classified as skilled, but it had the merit of giving Maureen more freedom of movement. She was not at a bench, but could move around the assembly. 'I've got quite interested in it,' she said. 'It's nice to see a thing nearly finished. And you aren't sitting down all day. You are up and down, up and down, walking round. Yeah.' The firm had been defining its women workers as the ones whom nature had equipped best for the boredom and immobility of benchwork. Yet here was Maureen saying that she too values the things that men think they are the only ones to need: a sense of completion in the work, creativeness, mobility and a longer work cycle.

Jackie Stein was a trainer at EIDS. She evaluated her job highly and enjoyed its scope: 'It's getting more complex. You have to have a high standard intellectually. We are having to employ older people because they need maturity to cope with the personalities, with the travelling. You are certainly not spoon-fed in the job. You have to use your own initiative a lot. You have to be a very special person to do the job.'

These trainers in imaging technology were among the few women I met who felt they had some career prospect within the firm, though it was still unclear to them just what steps the upward route would involve. They had already made one step in leaving medical radiography and coming into the business world. They spoke about their careers in terms that might have surprised those of their male colleagues who saw women workers as having no interest beyond an undemanding nine-to-five job. 'I feel very satisfied at the moment,' one of Jackie's colleagues said, 'because it is something I knew I wanted to do. I wanted a challenge. I wanted to do something positive with my life.'

Jackie herself is clearsighted enough to know that trainers are really thought of as button-pushers in the firm, just as radiographers are by the physicists and doctors in hospital. Nonetheless she perceived just a slim possibility of overcoming that stereotype. She was feeling her way into the world of upwardly mobile men in her company: 'You know, you have got to really perform well. I lack confidence in a man's world still. I know, I really *know* I can do it. But it takes you, it's taken me, a while.' She explained how you have to be strategic about a career: take one job in actual preparation for something else you can see beyond it. She had not known this at the outset: 'I've been sort of waiting for *them* to think "She's good, let's move her". Waiting for them to make the advance. It doesn't happen. You've got to make it, say, "I want this". And they'll look at you and if your performance is good enough you'll go. You have to tell them.' She felt that there was no hard-and-fast discrimination against women in the firm. The problem she felt was 'sexist attitudes' and a pervasively masculine environment.

It is helpful to compare the experiences of the very few technological women I encountered with those of similar women elsewhere. Other researchers have shown what this kind of work means for women and what problems they encounter. There is general agreement that, in spite of all the difficulties, the actual work, the acquisition of skills, is greatly valued by women who enter non-traditional fields. Brigid O'Farrell and Sharon Harlan, in their study of women craftworkers and clerical workers, found that the blue collar women were 'significantly more satisfied than their white collar counterparts with pay and work . . . They enjoy the craft work and perceive themselves as capable of performing the job.'[1] Mary Walshok, too, found that in spite of all the problems they faced, the harassment, teasing and loneliness, her sample of women blue collar workers liked the work itself. 'Our findings suggest that women in skilled blue collar jobs are extremely, even surprisingly satisfied . . . Welders, carpenters, mechanics, forklift operators and cable splicers, they expressed the same enthusiasm that I heard men expressing.'[2] It seemed that 'whether domestic or paid, traditional women's work has become increasingly diminished and trivialised in urban-industrial societies and no longer offers these women what they want.'[3] Walshok concluded, 'There is much to suggest that what women workers seek in their work parallels in general terms what men seek in their work. Both men and women seek feelings of competence, of making a contribution, of being necessary, of being productive and of being in control of their time and energy.'[4]

The personal costs they paid for doing the work, however, researchers agree is always a heavy factor on the debit side, and the women who are prepared to take the risk are a somewhat special and untypical group. Walshok found that her women were younger, had fewer children and were better educated than the average. A large proportion came from fatherless homes.[5] She emphasizes that they are the pioneering type, prepared to live the life of the 'outsider', 'a special group of independent, risk-taking individuals with unusual energy, tenacity and focus'.[6] Ironically, as a result, such women may not even be the best possible choice as technical workers because 'the qualities it takes to be a pioneer are different than those it takes to be a good worker or journeyperson.'[7]

Pamela Franks was confident of women's untested abilities: 'I don't think there's anything in the way a woman's brain is put together that makes it [engineering] impossible for her. I don't regard *myself* as some kind of amazing intellectual freak. I think we'll only see what the truth is on that when we have roughly equal numbers of men and women working in a profession like this.' Even among women with no technical training I often found an appetite for understanding machinery, getting behind the casing, making things work. Of course, when it comes to technology some women do, from long conditioning, accept the hegemonic ideas and echo men's low evaluation of women's abilities. Even some women who were in other ways clearly adequate and competent people would take the line 'Who? Me? Can't mend a plug!' But just as many women were clearsighted about the circumstances that had prevented them from gaining more technical competence. Some said it was men who had stood in their way, not just by filling the better jobs but simply by *knowing better*:

I think if you put your mind to something – I think you can do it. You've got to be that way inclined, but, I think it's because it's got to do with machinery that they [women] become flustered and they don't really understand what the machine is all about. I think it's that they've been progr— (laugh) yes, I was going to say programmed. I think it's the way you've been brought up by your parents. The women get the women's roles, like doing the cleaning, things like that, and the men get all the other jobs. A lot of it has to do with, 'Oh, she's a woman, she can't do it.' And I think a lot of men have that feeling about women. Many a time Tim [her husband] will say, 'Well, (scornfully) you're not mechanically minded are you', and you end up thinking, 'Well, I'm not mechanically minded.' But I don't think that is the case. If I change a plug or something he will always check it to see if I've done it right. And I *know* I've done it right. And I think that does infuriate me a bit. He says it might come off. And I know it won't. I've *done* it right.

Men's know-how is seldom passed by men to women as a cost-free gift, taught in a serious, generous and genuine way. Often it is hoarded behind a cachet of professional knowledge or craft skill and handed out sparingly, reluctantly. Sometimes it is dispensed from a great height and purposefully used to put women down.

On masculine ground

Because work is gendered terrain, a lone woman entering a man's world immediately feels out of place, odd and isolated. 'It was as though I was on the outside looking in', one young woman told me of the time she had tried to join in the work of a male work group. 'They could see me but I wasn't really there.' Women have to fight to be taken seriously as workers. They have continually to assert themselves if they are to get the training, the tools and the experience that are available to men.[8]

Behind the cultural intimidation, of course, is the threat of open hostility. Sexual harassment is commonplace wherever men and women work in proximity. It ranges from a general put-down of women's competence, through tactical use of 'tits and arse' conversation, to actual physical molestation.[9] Suzanne Carothers and Peggy Krull found two forms of sexual harassment, one for women in traditionally female jobs and one for women crossing into men's preserve:

> Harassment of women in traditional jobs appears more often as hints and requests for dates which, when rejected, are followed by work retaliation. Harassment of women in male-dominated settings is typically more overtly hostile at the outset. The motive for harassment in the traditional setting appears to be exploitation of role and power differences, whereas in the non-traditional setting the motive seems to be a defense against what male workers take to be an implicit challenge to their gender power and work roles.[10]

Sexual harassment at work is the clearest expression that men wish to maintain rights in technology as men's private property. They are engaged not only in the public project of dominating nature but in the private project of controlling women.

Women, then, as they take up men's work, enter a situation

of 'pressures' and 'dilemmas' so that the key question is always one of finding the right strategies for *coping*.[11] The most common strategy, it seems, is to adapt. 'You have to go with the norms of the dominant group.'[12] I found too that women I met, whether they were venturing into the business world or into the technical workshop, felt obliged to make a continual series of adjustments. Whether trying out her competence as a stand-in forklift truck driver or sitting at a computer terminal in a roomful of male graduate engineers, the lone woman is wary as a cat, adapting continually to avoid trouble.

The strategy chosen by Pamela Franks was 'cool':

When you first arrive, people are sensitive about obvious things, like swear words, naughty pictures, the old *Sun* calendar, whatever. And what happens after that really depends on how you react to it. I think, if I expressed *extreme* distaste for naughty pictures or swear words, probably they would be kept out of my immediate section. As it happens, I'm not terribly bothered. Because I believe it's up to individuals to decide that. I'm not very interested. It's up to them. It's a question of not flying off the handle at any obvious attempts at provocation. There are some people that will try to provoke you and you just have to dismiss it . . . Things settle down after a while. They [the men] score off one another. It's the straight man and the funny man, sort of thing. It's a bundle of monkeys playing in a tree, quite honestly. Sometimes it gets so immature. I think, unfortunately, I do think, men are a bit immature.

Pamela's response was generous and tactically shrewd. It avoided aggravation. For women as a whole, however, such a response, sustained over a lifetime of work, amounts to suppression of spontaneity and sexuality.

'Male sponsorship' is reported by other researchers to be a significant aid to women in trying to work in men's work. Muriel Lembright and Jeffery Riemer, in their study of women truckers (long-distance lorry drivers) in the USA, describe an electrifying environment of danger and harassment for the women in which they are able to avoid trouble only by being co-drivers of men who are assumed to be, and normally are, husbands or boyfriends.[13] When a woman cannot be seen to belong to a man, but appears to be attempting to operate out there in the 'public sphere' autonomously, she is vulnerable.

Jackie Stein and other trainers, travelling the world on their own, staying in hotels, entering strange work enviroments without this kind of 'male sponsorship' found that they had to be continually alert. We saw how Jackie's open and friendly nature, until she became more sparing with the smiles, resulted in doctors supposing 'she came with the machine'. 'We have to get over the idea,' she said, 'that men seem to have, that we are there for them. That we are their plaything.' This is how she described her technique for dealing with travel on the job, alone: 'I just avoid situations where I can get into trouble. If I'm in a hotel, invariably if there is nobody there with me I just sit in my room rather than go out. Because you can't fight it, it *exists*. A woman by herself, you are fair game.' Because of this, the women cannot relax and enjoy the perks of a remarkable job as their male colleagues are able to do. 'It's a shame, because it is a fantastic job. You may be in a beautiful city and you won't be able to get out to see it. I think it can be a much better job for a man, because he can make the best of all the facilities while he's away.'

Another trainer, Lee Dysett, described how she learned to avoid looking directly at people, to keep her eyes lowered, and to wear modest, carefully thought-out clothes. Here is her experience as a single woman among the male business fraternity in a Canadian hotel, when she was at a convention organized by the multinational for which she worked:

First, they brought champagne to the bedroom with two glasses. When I pointed out that I was alone, the waiter withdrew one glass, with overdone apologies. Next I went down to dinner and said, 'A table for one please.' 'Oh you are eating *alone?*' I said, 'Yes, I am eating alone.' And by this time I was getting really fed up with it. So I sat down in the chair and the waiter came over and started clearing the second place setting away. And I said, 'It's okay, you can leave it.' And he said, 'Ah, I see, just in case someone comes along, hey? Wink, wink.' I was *so* angry. That is the sort of thing. If a man had sat there and said what I'd said there'd have been no comment and the waiter would just have walked away. You know.

Small matters – but even the toughest 'sense of humour' grows threadbare after many experiences of this kind.

Is the price worth paying?

The central issue in 'adaptation' is, of course, that of gender identification itself. If occupations are gendered and a person's work is, in the normal run of things, part of their own individual gender identity, the way they see themselves and are seen by others, then to cross into wrongly gendered work presents quite acute problems. As a woman the question arises, for instance, whether one should dress in feminine or in masculine clothing. It is not unknown for employers to take the decision for the worker. Karen Beck Skold describes how in the Second World War women working in the shipyards were subject to strict dress regulations. This was only in part for safety. It was also that, 'like soldiers infiltrating enemy lines, women in the shipyards had to be camouflaged in concealing and sexless clothes lest the difference in sex be too evident.'[14] Male nurses, it will be observed, are not required to wear skirts.

The study of the EITB girl technicians shows how in these male situations the young women have to decide between a strategy of merging with the men, becoming 'one of the lads', and the alternative of maintaining a feminine identity even if this means being singled out for treatment as 'a special case' among the technicians.[15] It was found that many of the girl technicians felt 'that being feminine was incompatible with being an engineer'. The girls who dropped out of the scheme (and the failure rate was higher for females than for male technicians) tended to be the ones who saw themselves as similar to other girls of their own age, while those who succeeded included mainly those who felt they had little in common with other girls.[16]

Mary Walshok also found a link between surviving in non-traditional blue collar work and not identifying oneself as positively heterosexual. 'More than half the women described themselves as not particularly attractive in adolescence, as not dating, as not being boy-conscious and clothes-conscious the way so many girls are.'[17] It did not however follow that the women had the autonomy that would come of being lesbian. Walshok emphasized the contrary. The women were therefore in some way being obliged to negate their sexuality. A personnel manager I spoke with in one of the companies I visited illustrated the prevalent double standard for men and women concerning sexuality. He reported on two women he had experimentally appointed to an otherwise male department. It hadn't worked, in his view, because 'one of them went out with a guy in the section, with a couple of guys actually. And another one got pregnant. I don't know what *she'd* been up to. I'm afraid she didn't do her gender any good.' He seemed to be saying, 'Women who work here must not be sexual people, having relationships with men.' No questions however are asked of the nature of male employees' sex lives.

There is a difficulty, in the gendered world we live in, in establishing a difference between 'being feminine' and 'being a woman'. It is even more difficult to make the latter, the set of practices and beliefs involved in being simply a woman, a female person, acceptable to male colleagues and to other females and compatible with technological competence. In its turn of course technical competence would have to be seen in a different, ungendered light. One person alone can't achieve such miracles, but it is possible to see women trying. Some are trying to do things their own way, holding onto their values and self-identity yet also holding on to 'male' jobs.

'We *are* different. Mentally we have the same powers,' said Jackie Stein. 'But I think probably we approach things from a different way. We can achieve as much, the same standard as a man. And who's to say if it's not a better approach? We are as capable.'[18] Jackie disgreed with what she termed 'women's lib', something she interpreted as meaning competing with men in a masculine style: 'Women's libbers have got the wrong attitude. Because I think you *are* a woman. You can't do everything a man can do. But women are more imaginative than men. You have got to have this compromise whereby you are still a woman but they accept you as a woman *and* for your brain.' It is perhaps worth noting here the contradiction that while it takes a degree of feminist strength in a woman to make a bid for work in a man's field, nonetheless a woman who likes women's company, who has a critique of men, finds the situation intolerable. It is this perhaps more than anything that narrows down the number of women willing to have a try, and still further the numbers who succeed.

Women report finding themselves in a cleft stick with regard to technological work. Either you remain a 'real' woman as defined by men, or you become a competent technologist. If you become quite clearly a competent technologist you will be seen as an 'iron maiden', undesirable to men. ('They do tend to get a bit Thatcherite.') Girls are caught in a similar cleft stick in learning mathematics at school. Rosie Walden and Valerie Walkerdine found, 'Girls appear to be in a "no win" Catch-22 situation. If they fail at mathematics they lack true intellect but are truly female. If they succeed they are only able to do so by following rules, and if they conquer that hurdle they become somehow less then female.'[19] Flouting gender rules can spell death for sexual relationships. A woman engineer (outside the research) told me of the conflict she encountered in her relationship with her man friend. An engineer himself, he found it hard to accept her competence in his technical field. She said in despair that an average, competent woman engineer could hardly marry anyone less brilliant than Leonardo da Vinci. As George Eliot remarked in *Middlemarch*, 'A man is seldom ashamed of feeling that he cannot love a woman so well when he sees a certain greatness in her: nature having intended greatness for men.'[20]

The rift between work and home

A second kind of adaptation made by women taking up technological careers is the sacrifice of a supportive and fulfilling family life. Very few work places provide child-care facilities. Community and state nurseries are hard to come by. The longer-term problems – of covering for sick children, providing adequate care after school and enjoyable company during the holidays – are often impossible to overcome. Overtime, night and weekend working, overstrains such arrangements. This is what holds so many women back in unskilled, part-time jobs. At Newstyle Ltd. most women on the sewing and cutting floors work part-time; to become a supervisor you must work full-time. *So anyone with children is held back from anything beyond the basic job?* I asked. 'Yes. Right. You have to choose. I don't know *why* I can't have both,' said one of the women there. 'In my opinion if you are the best person for the job and they have to put themselves out because you work a little different hours from anyone else, I think they should. And not take the second-best person for the job just because they happen to be there full-time.' That is to say, because they have no child care or other domestic responsibilities holding them back.

The career structure open to women radiographers in the NHS, limited though they themselves may call it, is remarkable in its way. When it is combined with an on-site nursery, as at Southerton Hospital, it is far beyond the possibilities for the average woman worker. Pamela Franks had decided not to have children at all. She said that to have an engineering career *and* children would 'require *enormous* determination and energy'. Two out of the three trainers I met at EIDS had made a similar choice. Jackie Stein said 'You have to choose. By the time I got to a secure position here, in which I could afford to leave [i.e. for a child break] I'd be too old to have children anyway. I've come to terms with it. I've got over it now. But sometimes I think, now it's fine. But when you get to be 50 or 60, what will it be like then?' Her colleague, Lee Dysett, said, 'The way I feel at the moment is I don't really want children.

I'm not maternal in any way. I don't want that responsibility. I may be selfish in a way because I enjoy what I'm doing. I know that John's not going to give up medicine and unless we had enough salary to get a nanny or something, who has to give up their job?'[21] However, family and neighbours can make her feel unnatural. 'Whenever we go out to dinner parties the first question is, "Which school do *your* children go to?" And if you say, "I don't have children. . .", they apologise. "*Terribly* sorry," they say.'

Children apart, the marriage that can sustain a woman working in this kind of career has to be an exceptional one. Lee Dysett is continually asked, 'How does John cope while you are away, poor thing?' She points out that no one asked her how *she* coped while John was living in hospital as an intern. She does feel, however, that without John there as a stable and supportive person to come home to, in a way that many wives are 'there' for their husbands but few husbands for their wives, she would not be able to tolerate the pressures of the job. Ina Wagner, in her study of girl apprentices in metal and building trades, found that most of them wished to have a family:

> They perceive care for a family and commitment to work as separate and incompatible. We found that the harder the young women try to conform to a male work culture, the fewer options they perceive for themselves in the future. They tend to draw a clear line between what is now – the pride and pleasure they draw from their work – and what has to be in a few years' time, to conform to the social image of a good wife and mother built upon renunciation. We found this conflict in many of the young women.[22]

Women are continually conscious of negotiating between hours spent at work and hours needed at home. Men of course make such a negotiation too, but whereas women negotiate under many constraints and compulsions, men do so from a position of relative autonomy, more on their own terms.[23] Many women are doing a complete double shift, an eight-hour day at work and an eight-hour day at home. Maureen Casey, the assembly worker at EIDS, finds her new job so tiring that when she goes home at night, she must cook the family meal before she sits down or she would 'never get up again'. Many women said as much: when you get back from work, never sit down, that's fatal. Keep right on and get the evening's tasks finished. Alice Morrison, a picker at Delta Ltd., is unusual in working at the carousel full-time. I asked her, *Would you wish to have more time at home than you do, to get the housework done?* 'I would, yes, definitely. Being full-time I just go home, do my husband's and myself's meal, wash up and that's it. Soon as I sit down that's it. I don't want to do *nothing*. Sometimes it can get a little bit untidy, but to most people it's spotless compared to them. When I say I'm untidy, they say, "Don't talk rubbish." But to my eyes it is, because I'm never there, you see.' *Work piles up for the weekend?* 'Yes. I work seven days a week really. Shopping on Saturday, that day's gone because it's the only time I see the shops. Then Sunday it's the housework.' Note that this is a woman *without* children.

The effect of the 'exhausted woman' can be put down, of course, to the inequality in which sex does the housework and caring tasks, and the scarcity of community services in support of domestic life. But beyond this, more women than men appear to *want* to give a substantial part of their lives to home, and it is good that they do. Janice Dolman, a pattern cutter at Newstyle, said, musing on why more women don't 'get on' in the firm, 'I understand it when some women, they maybe don't want to give all their lives to it, especially if they're married. They don't want to spend ten hours a day here. Some of the men they want to get on and they'll stay longer hours. It impresses people. The women want to go home, to their families maybe. I think probably [that's why] men do get on better.'

Women often cannot and will not separate home from work in the way that many men are prepared to do. A consultant I met, working late nights and weekends so that he seldom saw his children, recognized that he might be losing something. But what he wanted *most* was those private commissions he did on the side, on top of his already taxing job in the firm. They gave him an added interest, extra earnings. So while he toyed with the contradiction he felt, he went along with the stronger feelings.

Employers of course make conflicting demands concerning child care that are impossible to meet. A characteristic personnel manager will have a wife and children at home. He will have wanted *her* to have time off from work to care for the children while they were young. He condemns women, in general, who do not do this. Yet when a woman he appoints to a career job in his firm leaves to have a child, he feels she has cheated him and the firm. He does not, however, deal with this problem by instituting personnel policies that would enable her to continue work while caring for children, or to return without penalty after a break at home. Work, though it is predicated upon successive generations of workers, does not allow for reproduction. A world in which women have a right to work, an 'equal opportunities' world, is apparently one without children, for the personnel manager does not expect his male employees to have responsibility for children either. Certainly he would not be in *his* job if he had taken such a career-break. This was confirmed by Richard Pellatz, a software engineer who, in contrast to the majority, did not feel any very strong career drive. He would have been quite happy, he said, to consider staying at home to look after his children while his wife continued to work. But:

> If there's a hole in your career, if you haven't been on a steady track since the day you left school, you have to explain that. If you say, "Well, I had a baby and stayed at home to look after her for a year" I think they – (pause). For a man, it is very unconventional to take time off, and I think they'd wonder quite what sort of a person they were getting if you were that unconventional.

Many of the male engineers and managers I met worked phenomenal hours of overtime. It is part of the expectation of the job to be frequently away at night and weekend. Men often like this because it boosts their pay and hence their domestic power: many of them were supporting a wife and children. But the enthusiasm for overtime is also partly an entrancement with the job and with technology. Barny Short, ex-field service engineer, had recently been promoted to a more sedentary, nine-to-five management post. It meant a drastic cut in overtime. He couldn't think what to do with himself, had a real problem adapting to all the empty time he suddenly had at home. He had been involved also in some time-consuming DIY, building an extension to his house, which had simultaneously come to an end. His response was to join a cycling club. At one stroke of the pedal it enabled him to place a spatial distance between himself, house, wife and children *and* gave him back something of the sense of physical initiative and power he had lost when promoted from his hands-on engineering job.

I asked what they did, these men, with their time at home, away from work. Naively perhaps, I expected to be told of domestic tasks and duties: mowing the lawn at least. But many men responded initially with an account of some sport in which they engaged. Sport is a way for men to build or reinforce their masculine identity. As Bob Connell has said, 'To be an adult male is distinctly to occupy space, to have a physical presence in the world.'[24] Besides, sport is a way for men to establish independent links and friendships with men at home, in the community, rather than to get swept entirely into the world of women or married couples. It seemed, among the men in my study, as though sport played a crucial part in linking men's two worlds, the indubitably masculine world of technological work and the perilously feminine world of home and community, by providing a clearly masculine, yet community-based activity. Cars, involvement in car maintenance and rallying, is another important technological linking mechanism. It gives men a social identity to reinforce the frail role of 'husband and father'. It was much less usual to find among the women workers I interviewed, particularly the manual workers, any reference to sport.

For men, the negotiation between work and home is not only a matter of time (as it is for most women), but it is also a matter

of reconciling conflicting cultures. Paul Browning, a technological manager, said:

> By the very nature of the job and the person you become,
> dedicated to the job in hand, it is a dangerous area. For
> instance, if you go home you have to, you need to sometimes,
> to stop at the door and say to yourself, "I'm home now."
> Otherwise you could walk through the front door and take
> your problems indoors with you. We have all been guilty of
> that. There is your front door and you have approached it
> with your mind wound up with your thoughts. The other side
> of the door is another person with another mind, another
> wind-up, different problems. And if you are not careful when
> you open the door, woomph! The only reason being, you are
> both in opposing frames of mind. You can even go home
> elated about something and – as you go through the door you
> can be *down*, down there.'

And a colleague present at the interview added, 'You have to
put it [work] where it is, in a department with a trapdoor, so
that it is get-at-able, but. . .' And Browning re-emphasized, 'It is
so difficult.'[25]

Of course not all men live out the demanding ideology of
difference and inequality that male supremacist society
engenders. Some, even against their inclinations, force themselves to make a little corrective shift in the disparity between
conventional male and female responsibilities. Barry Furlough
said, for instance, that he had felt it was his duty, 'Well, not my
duty but my *part*', to help his wife bear the burden of children.
He had given up some hobbies so as to stay home sometimes
and allow her to go out in his place. Some men do not want to
deny themselves the creative possibilities of life as it is lived in
the home, or community, nor the affection of their children. I
met one or two men who held their technological work light in
this respect. But often a preference for equality and sharing is
defeated by what appears to be economic compulsion. Watch
what happens in the first few years of Derek Pellatz's marriage:

'We did about the same at first. We'd take turns to cook and do the housework . . . We'd do shopping together, go to the launderette together, sit and read a book . . . We used to work on the basis that it would be equally split, and if it wasn't that was mainly choice.' Then, however, three things occurred that are common enough. They acquired a house that needed doing up, had a baby, and Derek was given more responsibility at work. 'Generally, our policy would have been that I would have spent a lot of time with the baby. But wanting to get on with the house quickly, and given the fact that Judy is very tied up in the day time, meant that I've been doing more of it. And also we've been surprised at how the baby has established the sex roles. It is quite horrifying to see ourselves falling into them. Because we need the money I am working a lot of overtime. So Judy cooks for me because if I came home at that time and started cooking we'd never eat. And Judy is looking after the baby all the time. If the baby is particularly bad at night I might get up to look after it – but . . .' *You have to get up to go to your job in the morning?* (Rueful laugh) 'That's it. It's a terrible trap really.'

Both Richard and Judy were distressed by the way the sexual division of labour had clamped down on them. They were saying, 'when we get the house sorted out', 'when the baby is older', 'when I can cut out the overtime', they would spend more time together again, start sharing tasks again. But will they? The experience of many couples is that the tentative step they may take when they first set up home to reverse conventional gender differences, once it is itself reversed by the hard realities of work and children, is all but impossible to re-establish. *Are you both losing equally?* I asked. 'Um. No. I think I've got quite a good deal at the moment. Because looking after the baby is such a never-ending thing, a 24-hour day. It's limited her interests a lot. Whereas I've been doing a job that I enjoy, that interests me, that I'm involved in, and having a lot of interesting jobs to do around the house too. Judy's had a lot of hard work – which she's had thrust on her. She really might prefer doing other things. I get to meet people at work and she doesn't.'

This same effect was noted by a technical consultant at SHC

Ltd. 'You have children. By definition the wife stays home to look after them. Your income is reduced, you can no longer afford those services [window-cleaner, laundry] and they have to be performed by a household member. If the wife is home all day and the husband is out at work, she tends to do them. And also because of that I think the husband expects more when he comes home. "You've been at home all day, where's my tea?" So, no, it would have been impossible to have continued on the old basis.' *Who has gained and who has lost?* '(Firmly) I would have gained. My wife would have lost.'

Black & Decker versus Moulinex

Technology of course features in home life as well as at work. If a woman's work is non-technological, the closest she may come to having to deal with the demands of the physical environment and of machinery and equipment is in the home. I therefore asked both men and women to spell out with some precision the actual practical tasks each carried out at home.

Before I had got beyond the introductory phrase, 'I'm interested to know how responsibilities are divided in the home', it often happened that whoever I was talking with, woman or man, would break in with 'Oh, we share everything.' It seemed something that confirmed a loving relationship, to believe that all work is shared. My first question then was, 'In general, do you feel that you divide things up between you, or do you each do the *same* things?' And again, very often the answer was 'We do the same things.' However, once the individual tasks were mentioned a different story began to emerge. It appeared that both women and men wanted to think that equality and similarity prevailed between partners, but in actual fact a sharp distinction in the tasks done by the sexes in practice defeated this object.

Here are some such sequences. First, a woman's account. Barbara Sheldrick is a keyboard operator on a computer terminal in a warehouse. 'We just share everything,' she started. *Who does the cooking?* I asked. 'I do, because I get in first.' *Who shops for food?* 'I do. Because I go past Tesco's on my way home. But if I needed something when he comes in at night, he'll go out for it. And he washes the pots after we've had our tea. So I do all the cooking and he does the washing up.' *What about the jobs that mean using tools, like hammers and screwdrivers, that kind of thing?* 'He'd have to do it. I'm not – I don't know nothing about those things.'

Secondly, here is a man. We have met him before, Tom Delaware, warehousing consultant. 'Not a sharp division. No. I tend to do as much cooking, if not more, than my wife.' *What about repairs, electrical things say?* 'She wouldn't do any of those things, no.' *Decorating?* 'Painting yes. I have a preference for papering. She doesn't have any skill in papering but she likes to have a paintbrush in her hand.' *Sewing curtains?* 'She would do all those. Up to a point, and then she might decide to get a woman she knows down the road who might do them for her.' *What about the garden?* 'Combined.' *Tell me in detail.* 'I tend to do the hedges, eight hours on Saturday, with a machine. Whereas she would do the flowerbeds. She would tend to do the weeding. Not the heavy vegetable patch, which I would maintain. And she has a total knowledge of flowers. I have a zero knowledge of flowers. It is her background as a farmer's daughter.' *Does she ever use the hedge cutter?* 'No. I've trained her in the lawn mower, but not to a great extent. No, no.' And then he added what might appear to be a *non sequitur*. 'It's quite a nice comfortable life, I suppose.'

Donald Ramsey demonstrates that, though men may do some conventionally feminine tasks and even *vice versa*, a division of labour of some kind, quite humorous in the detail in which it is known and understood, continues to exist. That is the important thing. 'I always cook the meal, during the week. Monday to Friday, because she has other things to do. She has her washing and ironing and cleaning and hoovering. I never do that. Ever. If we are having people round for a meal, I do the cooking [ie., even at weekends]. Or rather my wife does the starter, I do the main course and she does the sweet. Because I can't bake. She is good at some things, I'm good at others.' *She does your washing, your clothes?* 'Yes. She does all the washing, hoovering, ironing and cleaning and I never help on that side because she is a perfectionist. The only thing I clean is the kitchen, after I have cooked. Then after the meal we do the dishes together. I wash, she dries. And then if we are going out we go out. If we are staying in, she will do whatever she wants to do and I'll read, or go and play chess with the neighbour.

Barny Short, ex-field engineer, I pursued through a detailed and specific sexual division of labour in cooking, cleaning, shopping and finally through to decorating ('she paints, but I don't like her hanging wallpaper, that's a man's job') and gardening ('I do the digging, she does the rest') until we arrived finally at a hobby they shared: upholstery. Ah, I thought. Something that *both* of them do? 'I repair the wooden frames, she puts on the fabric.'

Where the reality is a division of labour systematically denied, it is refreshing to encounter someone who says frankly, as Alice Morrison does:

No (firmly), we don't share things equally. I do practically everything. I do cooking, cleaning, shopping. But if I were ill then he completely takes over. He is very capable of doing everything. He's a better cook than what I am and he knows how to wash, clean and sew and everything. But because I'm there he thinks I should do it. On the odd occasion he has given me a hand. He'll say, 'Is there anything you want doing?' Like, for instance, this weekend, because we wanted the weekend free, being nice, he said, 'Is there anything you want doing' and I said, 'Yes, will you just do the front door step' and he says (putting on a peevish tone), 'I don't like doing that'.

Alice explained that he disliked being observable by neighbours when contributing to housework.

It is beginning to be clear that technology is just as significant a factor in the division of labour at home as it is at work. Very few women were saying they did any DIY in the house, beyond painting and decorating. Few used hammer or screwdriver for more than hanging the occasional picture or 'mending' the proverbial plug. Fewer still would use an electric drill, even a lawn mower. Men were proprietorial about these tools and the role that goes with them: 'I've fitted our central heating system, I've re-wired the house. I built a shower, knocked up a bit of a bedroom,' an engineer said to me. 'Oh, it's beautiful.' I asked, *What is your wife's role in this?* 'I keep making the point', he said, 'if you can keep the kids out of the tool kit, out of the paint, that's making a contribution. That's helping as much. Do a bit of painting, wallpapering, of course. Not a job *I* like much. I like hammering up the stud wall, doing a bit of wiring, things like that.'

And another: 'If I'm working on the car, she'll do little bits. Hand me tools and that.' And another: 'She's not averse to picking up a screwdriver but no, generally . . . She wouldn't do anything electrical . . . She wouldn't do things needing a lot of strength.' *Where do you keep your tools?* 'In the garage.' *Does your wife ever use them?* 'Never, ever.'

Of course, as several women pointed out, if men are not doing the cooking, cleaning, shopping, washing and child care, the least they can be expected to contribute is the physical repairs. Jen Gouldner, a packer at Delta, says of DIY, 'I think to myself, "I could have a bash at that". So I do. That's me personally. But a lot of my friends, well, yes some of them do think I'm a bit daft because "That's his job, you should let him do it." '

Nonetheless, it is still surprising and sad that a woman like Maureen Casey, who at work uses pliers, screwdrivers, Allen keys, soldering iron and other tools, sees herself as technologically illiterate at home. *Do you feel a different person when you are at home, to when you are at work?* 'Oh, yes. I think I *am* a different person.' *Would you take a socket set like that to your car for instance?* 'No, I don't know anything about cars. I wouldn't know how to.' *You don't have a set of tools of your own at home?* 'No.' *You don't want to, you're not interested?* 'If I had to I would. But because I have someone there that will do it, well, I suppose I've always had someone there who will do it, so I don't . . . I don't think I could do it efficiently enough, good enough. I think my job is to clean the house.'

Just occasionally, especially but not exclusively in middle-class professional couples, you find a woman reporting that she is the practical one, the husband the intellectual, the dreamer, the incompetent one. In these situations the woman may use tools about the house. But it is noteworthy that this is predicated on the 'freak man' who is inadequate with technology: 'He's one of those, you want it done, you end up doing it yourself.' Such men are in the main gaining their gender identity through intellectual work and achievement.

Being close to a man who is technically competent seems to stop women gaining know-how. An electrician's wife, it was understood, knew *less*, not more, about electrical repairs than other women. A marriage, like Jen Gouldner's, in which the two of them stripped down and rebuilt a car together, knocked down a chimney, cleaned off the bricks and rebuilt it together, is very rare. Where women do do these things they feel better: 'It gives you more self-respect. It does, yes. Especially if you can say, "Look, I've done this." It's great. It's good. Yeah.'

Normally, women use utensils and implements – the dishwasher, vacuum cleaner, car. They don't use tools. The utensils and implements are, in their way, tools, of course, and they are used by women with skills (making food, sewing clothes) certainly equal to the male skills of their husbands. But women cannot fix these utensils and implements when they go wrong. It is men on the whole who are in control of women's domestic machinery and domestic environment. Women depend on men, husbands or tradesmen, for the completion of many necessary physical tasks.

Men gain social status in the community by the skills they learn at work. The mechanic and engineer are known among their friends as 'the one who can fix things'. What boys are taught early at home also helps them gain their status at work. Women are cut out of this process. The women apprentices studied by Ina Wagner realized the asset they would gain from breaking their way in:

They are aware that technological competence acquired through work extends to their role outside the workplace, by giving them a symbolically visible share in what is commonly considered men's domain: participation in discussions on technical issues and in socially highly valued leisure activities. The young women themselves highly value these more general benefits they draw from technological competence. They perceive themselves as more well-rounded personalities who are able to take an active part in what they themselves consider a privileged world.[26]

The secret world from which women are excluded, the world of the man and boy, is symbolized in 'the shed at the bottom of the garden': 'My grandfather was a maker of things. He had a workshop at the bottom of the garden and he was always making things. And going to my grandparents, I can remember it being an Aladdin's cave, all these lovely things. Boats and trains and cars and toys. And I used to have endless fun standing and watching my grandfather make things.' This engineer himself had had a room which he had made into the equivalent of this remembered Aladdin's cave. It had been his own place. And he felt it hard that 'once the children had come along, I lost it and was banished to a shed . . . But all the same it is a place that is mine and I don't get lumber slung in it. It is my work shop.' *Does your son come down and join you there?* I asked. 'Yes. He'll come down there and suck a chisel and play with the electric saw (happy laugh). Yes. I can remember my grandfather being quite an influence in that way.' He was talking energetically, enthusiastically. Three generations of men here, the passing down of knowledge and proprietorial rights over technology. The shutting out of one generation of women after another from Aladdin's cave.

The 'opposite' sex

I want to wind up this account by telling the story of two couples. In each case it was the young man I talked with and he told me about his relationship with the young woman in his life. Each of the young men was proud of his girlfriend, of their closeness, the way their relationship worked. For me what was interesting was the way that technological competence could be observed as a live political issue for the couples. That is to say it was an issue of power, initiative and choice.

Paul Cardew was a fair-haired, fresh-complexioned young man of 22. He was working as a general-purpose maintenance engineer on the new equipment in the warehouse at Delta Ltd. Quite early in the interview he apologised to me for his hands, which he spread out for me to see, cracked and engrained with dirt. But there was a certain pride in the gesture and I asked him, *Is it a badge of some kind, dirty hands?* He agreed that, yes, he thought it was. And went on to tell me how his first job on leaving school had been in a butcher's shop where he had to be continually washing his hands for reasons of hygiene. He had quite quickly left his job and started in engineering, even though the prospects had been good for him at the butcher's. 'The reason I left, it was my hands were so soft and clean all the time. I didn't like it. It didn't feel manly. I'm not a male chauvinist (pause) – at least I don't think. But engineering, it's a boy's job or a man's job.' His present occupation gave him satisfaction for that reason.

Paul's girl friend, Tracy, is a hairdresser. 'She enjoys it. She's very good' he said proudly. 'Very artistic in that sense, very keen on what she does.' Of course, Tracy's hands are always soft and clean, and 'being clean all the time, she gets a bit upset when I come home with a bit of dirt, you know.' Nonetheless, to him the contrast of the two gender-styles produced and made possible by their two occupations is pleasing. 'We was only saying the other day, although we got a lot of different interests, we never argue. I'm not sure if that has a lot to do with it, but I'm sure it has, you know. Because Tracy doesn't know a lot about engineering, she can't tell me anything. I'm a bit stubborn when it comes to my own job.' And he added as an afterthought, 'And I can't tell her anything. Because I don't know anything about her work.'

While Paul respects Tracy's skill, the fact that hairdressing is a clean job meant that he himself would never think of doing it. Nonetheless, he finds that he has become a bit more open-minded about women and women's work since he met her than he once was. At work, for instance, although he had started convinced that he couldn't ever bring himself to work 'under a woman', he was interested to find that he could accept the presence of quite senior women at Delta. They were not engineers, however, but at a comfortable distance in the purchasing and quality control departments.

I asked Paul how he would feel if Tracy started to show an interest in technical things, wanted to take a course in car maintenance for instance. He thought for a moment, then said he was open to the idea of women having more general basic understanding of machinery. He could see it might be good for them, and perhaps also it would help understanding between the sexes. But if she were to do an evening class in some technical subject, he felt he would probably want to go on to study too. 'Or keep up with the technology a lot more than I do now, actually to try and keep one better than her, if you know what I mean.' And he went on, 'I'd like to be the main one – to be a *better* engineer than my girl friend. That's the way I will always be. And that's why I say I may be a little bit more male chauvinist than some people.'

To be the better engineer, of course, would ensure Paul more than just self-respect in the marriage. It would ensure him higher pay than his girl friend, together with a set of skills that would give him greater leverage in the world than hairdressing was going to afford her. Nothing could express more clearly and more poignantly three things about gender relations. First that the politics of bodies and the politics of technology are closely connected. Second, that a concern with masculine identity involves a strong emotional need for complementarity between the sexes. And third, that the complementarity is structured in such a way as to produce inequality.

In the same warehouse where Paul worked I met a forklift truck driver who was refusing this kind of relationship. Like Paul, he was in love. The man is Dan Perry, age 22, whom we met in Chapter 6. I enjoyed his account of his life with his girlfriend Tessa, with whom he lives. They own three motorbikes between them, machines recognized in the motorcycling community as 'class bikes', being 850 or 1000 cc. He and Tessa simply share all household tasks, the quicker to get onto the real business of life: maintaining the bikes and riding them. He was close to Tessa and preferred to spend his time with her rather than drinking with the lads – for which he got a bit of backstabbing. He described with pride her skill as a rider and mechanic, and with anger the way the guys at the bike club treated her. Because their bikes were less powerful than hers, because she was a woman and, as he saw quite clearly, because they resented her access to sheer power, they wouldn't socialize with her. They wouldn't wave when they passed on the road, as was the convention between the men. He was angry too at the way the young lads responded at the RAC motorcycle school where she was an instructor: 'You get this girl of five foot-two standing there telling your macho six-foot 17 year old on his Honda what to do. They don't take kindly to it: "Fancy being taught how to ride my bike by a girl." Now that is all wrong. She has more riding skill in her little finger than they have got in their whole body.'

In his paid work Dan had sensed the fraudulence of today's deskilled and degraded engineering apprenticeship system, the result of capitalism's thrust to cheapen the craftsman's technical labour power. Because he was neither being taught real skills nor earning real money he had opted out, settled for semi-skilled work and invested his liking for technology in his motorbikes. It seems he had somehow managed to buck the system of gender differentiation and inequality in his relationship with Tessa too. In human love there is an ideal of equivalence and companionship. Very often we don't really want to be differentiated, so that one dominates, the other complies. But we are bearers of relations for the rest of society: it is hard to escape becoming different from the 'opposite' sex, complementary and unequal. We may prefer to be a pair but we find ourselves a couple.

8. Beyond pink and blue

What we've seen in clothing, warehousing, radiography and engineering is that technological change doesn't of itself affect the long-lived pattern: men have technical skills and knowledge, women don't. There is every reason to believe that these workplaces are typical of others in Britain and elsewhere. In a recent study of the electronics industry in Ireland for instance, James Wickham found women on the shop floor 'stuffing boards', while 85 per cent of the professional employees, 94 per cent of the technicians, 99 per cent of craft workers and 97 per cent of managers were men.[1] In the electronics industry in Britain in 1984, 95 per cent of scientists and technologists, 96 per cent of technicians, 98 per cent of craft workers and 97 per cent of managers were men.[2]

Economic recession and industrial restructuring have changed many things. A large number of workers of both sexes have lost their jobs. Some male workers have been shaken out by new technology and women recruited by employers to fill the deskilled occupations. This is the fate, characteristically, of the remaining craft workers involved in immediate production of goods and services for consumption, such as cutters in clothing and compositors in printing. Positive new opportunities have opened up in particular for those workers who *deal with* the instruments of labour rather than actually producing by means of them. Within engineering too, however, jobs have been subject to yet another cycle of rationalization and deskilling. Capital has dispensed with some old-style engineers only to become dependent on the next group to emerge with today's brand of know-how.

These transformations of the late 1970s and early 1980s have not brought women technical training and jobs. The age-old relationship between man, machine and woman has barely been touched by the turmoil. Technology remains a 'black box' to women. Their jobs teach them nothing of the internal structure and processes of the equipment on which they work. They are concerned with outputs, not inputs. Women's relationship to technology, as technology itself becomes more 'intelligent', has become less, not more interactive.

Women's characteristic roles continue to be those of unskilled and semi-skilled assembly workers *on* machinery and the operating *of* machinery: dishwasher, word-processor, sewing machine, X-ray equipment. In such roles women are vital to capitalist production and state services. They exercise more knowledge and know-how than are ever openly acknowledged or rewarded by the employer. But the transferable technical skills used in design, manufacture, marketing, installing, servicing and managing technology remain almost universally men's skills. As a result, men as a sex continue to be in a position to dominate and manipulate women's instruments of labour and their labour processes, while women as a sex barely influence those of men. Just as new technology does not fundamentally reshape, but is just one more phase in, the class relations linking capital and worker, so it confirms the relations of sexual domination. What we are experiencing is, in Jan Zimmerman's phrase, 'the encoding of old values in new technologies'.[3] Those values, as we've seen, have a history that stretches back through feudalism to the earliest slave civilizations. It was a false hope to suppose that the short leap from the electro-mechanical to the electronic stage of technology could do for women what two revolutions in the entire mode of production had failed to accomplish.

Worse, however, technology does not stand still: women's situation could well deteriorate further. It may seem an achievement when women acquire or hold on to operating jobs as technologies change, but this doesn't in itself bring women job security. It is in the nature of such jobs that they are vulnerable to further technical change. A progression often occurs over time from male operator to female operator to no operator at all. The aim in the warehouses was clearly to reduce labour to a minimum. Capital does not even need to wait for the robot: the carousel system is now being adapted by its inventors for automatic 'reading' of orders, potentially replacing 150 workers in some firms with a single one. In computer-aided pattern processes, several occupations that can be seen today (digitization for grading by computer, for example, or lay-making by intervention of the scope operator) are transitional jobs, liable to be bypassed as programs are refined and as firms gain the confidence to shift into full automatic mode. There are signs that as manufacturers of X-ray equipment achieve their aim of making its operation more and more 'foolproof', the radiographer's skilled judgement will become less and less necessary. Of electronics factories similar to that of Electronics International, James Wickham says, 'women workers are concentrated in jobs which are extremely vulnerable to being automated out of existence'.[4]

Of course, firms make misjudgements. They often over-estimate the potential of new technology and are over-sold by suppliers. They do not find it as easy to do without the human element as they sometimes hope. All forecasts predict, however, that it will be relatively unskilled work – the work in which women are predominantly found – that will suffer the fastest rate of attrition through the combination of recession and restructuring.[5] The jobs from which women today are absent are those with the least disastrous prospects. The number of technicians employed in the engineering industry fell by a relatively slight 15 per cent between 1978 and 1984; the number of scientists and technologists actually increased by 40 per cent; and meanwhile clerical, operator and other jobs, 'women's work' in the industry, fell by 39 per cent. The net result was a loss to men of 29 per cent of their jobs, to women of 36 per cent of theirs.[6] Technical maintenance jobs in all industries are expected to increase proportionately if not absolutely, and the electronics engineering industry is one of very few growth areas in the British economy.[7] As time passes, therefore, it becomes more urgent that women acquire technical skills and technical jobs if they are even to have access to a wage.

The experience women gain in their current work is not of the kind that will help them to move from declining firms to prosperous firms or from obsolete to growth industries. In the words of a woman trade unionist, 'What you come in as, that you stay'. In her study of women's employment in engineering firms, Pauline Wilkins emphasized that the structural barriers between very minutely defined areas of 'men's work' and 'women's work' meant that even where a woman won promotion to supervisor or junior technician in one company, her abilities would not be marketable in another firm or even in another department of her own.[8] Technologically informed men on the contrary have adaptive, transferable and cumulative skills that can grow over time and serve them in a variety of work situations.

If 'the sub-division of labour is the assassination of a people', as Marx said, then the sexual division of labour is a mutilation of women.[9] Women's confinement to a narrow band of occupations is a form of deprivation. Besides, the technological barrier keeps women out of many creative activities. Lack of access to film and broadcasting technology for instance, impedes women's progress in media and the arts. A grasp of technology is personally empowering. Why should women be deprived of the independence and pleasure that comes of having a measure of control at least over their own environment and the instruments of their own labour? Women who learn to service their own cars, maintain their own homes and help other people to do these practical things get a sense of satisfaction and autonomy. A woman electrical mechanic expressed just this feeling in interview with Terry Wetherby. Sophenia Maxwell is black, skilled, earns well and keeps a child on her wage: 'Death, man', she says, 'you can come any time because I feel that I am really whole. I feel like I can fit into *anything*, that I can *do* anything, that I can go anywhere and *be* anything.'[10] How many women can say their work gives them that kind of confidence and strength?

It is sometimes argued that women's status has been improved by the scientific and technological developments of the last two decades, that labour-saving devices in the home and contraceptive techniques in particular have been responsible for 'liberating' women. There is plentiful evidence, however, that the Pill damages women's health and the hours devoted by women to housework have not become any fewer. If our position has improved it has surely not been a gift from the multinationals and their engineers but a prize of our own struggle to turn economic and social trends to our advantage. If we are to gain technological skills and jobs it seems that that too will have to be by virtue of our own analysis of the situation and our own actions.

Reproducing the sexual division of labour

The sexual division of labour has a curious ability to survive disruption and reproduce itself through time. In the Second World War, for instance, women in the automobile industry entered hard and heavy male jobs. Yet it has been shown that occupational segregation by sex was quickly recreated 'for the duration' within those sectors previously monopolized by men. So, as Ruth Milkman points out, 'Rosie the Riveter did a man's job but more often that not she worked in a predominantly female department or job classification'.[11] In the early days of computers many of the occupations appeared to be accessible to women and men on equal terms. But the situation was not the clean slate it first appeared to be. Soon the jobs were sub-divided; some were routinized and deskilled. The least-skilled and lowest-paid categories of work became female occupations while the more technical and prestigious became male.[12] Whether responding to the disruption of war, crisis or invention, the sexual division of labour has proved markedly resilient. Two questions need to be asked: *in whose interest is it?* and *how is it sustained?*

Clearly, employers gain by operating in a segmented labour market in which they can play off women against men. Women seldom get training and they are often part-time workers, temporary workers, provisional workers. Their difference from men in these respects enables employers to keep everyone's wages down. Employers also gain by a working class weakened by rivalry. Although, as we've seen, in some circumstances capital does not show marked sex preferences, men as a sex invariably gain from sexual divisions.

As individuals men benefit from women devoting time and energy to maintaining the home and rearing their children. They profit, in other words, from precisely the effect that produces the difference between women and men in the labour market. Men also gain as workers both from women staying out of the labour market altogether and from a structuring of the labour market in such a way that those women who enter it do not compete with men for all the available jobs. In addition, men's superior self-identity as a sex is sustained by separatism, because it enables them to avoid direct comparison with women. If men did exactly the same work as women, some of them might be seen to do it less well. Some might in due course even find themselves working *under* women. They would, besides, no longer be able to lean on the mere masculine associations of the job they do to give them prestige.

Male supremacy is a social system in which men as a whole are affected by what happens to individual men, and vice versa. Sex segregation in general ensures that men who are not in any proven sense more competent than women do not 'let the side down' and diminish the status of the sex as a whole. In technology, of course, the exclusion of women secures men as a sex a very tangible form of authority and power. Even though many men personally will never wield it, they do not need to.

It is not surprising, then, that trade unions, which are male dominated, have played an important part in maintaining segmentation in labour markets and demarcation and segregation at work.[13] While a sexual division of labour at home and at work may or may not have advantages for capital, it can *always* be shown to benefit men as a sex.

If the action and interests of men are what lie behind the sexual division of labour, we should be able to detect some of the processes by which this advantage is engineered. Pressure on women to maintain their responsibility for domestic work and child care – the ideology of the male breadwinner and the 'family wage' – is clearly one such process. What the foregoing story has suggested, however, is that the nature of workplaces and the relations of work, too, help to perpetuate sex segregation over time. Underpinning the sexual division of labour are two factors, both of which have been visible in the labour processes we've looked at. The first is that *both people and occupations are gendered*, which makes it costly for the individual to cross into work defined as belonging to the opposite sex. The second is that *workplaces tend to be hierarchically structured*, with many different grades and levels, while *work processes are subject to continual redefinition, sub-division and fragmentation*. This dynamic in capitalist production enables men to respond to the movement of women into male areas by continually placing distance between them, by moving horizontally or vertically. Let's take these two factors in turn.

People are gendered into masculine and feminine beings in a compelling cultural process that begins at birth and does not end till death. Home, school, street life, recreation, the media *and work* – all our experiences tell us repeatedly, from the initial gender ascription made a few seconds after birth, that we are male or female. It is something we never for a moment forget. We are expected always to behave in a way that is recognizably masculine or feminine. Nothing disturbs most people more than being unable to distinguish a person's sex. A great deal therefore depends on our observing gender distinctions. To be valued, even to be acceptable, to our parents, to employers, officialdom and the opposite sex, we normally need to dress, behave and think in ways appropriate to our own. Since there exist only two opposed and complementary genders, and because everyone must *have* a gender, any difference we manifest is likely to be interpreted as being a taint deriving from the opposite sex. We are an 'effeminate' man or a 'butch' woman. As such, if we are lucky or determined, we may find a way of surviving within some sub-culture, but we will have an unremitting struggle with society as a whole.

Add to this, then, that occupations are gendered too. By long association with the sex that is found in them and which has developed them, jobs are, with few exceptions, either masculine or feminine. The job of maintenance engineer is masculine, that of picking in a mail order warehouse is feminine. The maintenance engineering job involves wearing boiler suits, getting dirty, sweating, lying on the floor, using tools, exerting muscle and taking risks. In short, it demands behaviour that is expected of a man, held to be improper for a woman. The job of picker calls for quite different behaviour – staying in one spot, making repetitive movements, handling delicate clothes, being diligent and observant. These are things that 'go against the grain' for a man. Everything about these jobs, from the pay packet to the environment and the human company, reinforces their gender. It rubs off on the men and women who do them. To cross into work that is non-traditional for one's sex is, while not exactly to court disaster, at least to invite discomfort. Nor is the discomfort momentary. The effort of adaptation is needed not just for one day's work but every day through a working lifetime. Work is hard enough without the added struggle of defending oneself, explaining oneself, over and again, both in work and outside. For a man thinking of taking up feminine work there is, of course, the added disincentive of lower pay and status. For a woman, the promise of an interesting and rewarding occupation may be enough to attract the exceptionally determined one, the pioneer. It will not, however, compensate the average woman with the average motivation, and it is ordinary women with whom we should now be concerned. The days of this Frontier have gone on too long already.

We live, then, in a two-tone world. We and many of the things that surround us are either blue or pink. Occupations, with few exceptions, are two-tone also and we match ourselves to them. We partly take our own colouring from the job we do and in turn the colour of the job is affected by our presence in it.

This is one mechanism sustaining the sexual division of labour over time. The second is the never-ending articulation of work into new horizontal and vertical sub-divisions. One industry and one occupation is distinct from the next. Production is shared by hundreds of types of workers each contributing a part. Trade unions, struggling to protect their members' interests, actively reinforce the barriers that separate jobs. When women move into men's occupations, perhaps drawn into them by the preference of the employers, enabled by 'equal opportunity' laws or by women's own determination, men are often able to step sideways into somewhat differently specified jobs, with the effect of re-establishing horizontal space between the sexes.

As women have entered warehousing, for instance, a detailed sub-division of tasks has split up the work of the general-purpose warehouse 'hand' of 10 or 20 years ago. Women have become pickers, packers, replenishers and form-fillers; men have become goods handlers, truck drivers and maintenance engineers. If women move on to the 'picker truck', with its simple controls, on their own or their employers' initiative – as looks increasingly likely to become the practice – it is probable that that job will quickly become female gendered and men will soon cease to be found driving or wanting to drive such trucks. But the driving of the heavier forklifts and the new turret trucks and stacker cranes will – for the moment – be reasserted as masculine jobs.

In the clothing industry we have seen men's grip on production jobs weakened as they lose place to women, first in sewing, then in cutting rooms and finally in pattern-making. As they are driven out of one occupation they for a while maintain their hold on an adjacent one. Even with a new and predominantly female area such as the new computerized pattern room, capital's perennial restless fragmentation of tasks may for a while open up a male slot. One that has become masculine in some firms is operating the plotter that prints out patterns and markers.

It may seem that women are gaining in this process of change simply because some men are losing. There are certainly contradictions here for masculinity – mass unemployment being among the most serious. The curious fact is, however, that sex segregation to the advantage of men, is sustained. In clothing, while men lost some middle-ranking jobs, they kept the higher posts in technology and management. It may be that keeping a distance between men and women is even more important in principle for masculinity than keeping jobs.

Where horizontal segregation fails, a second option remains

for those men who have the abilities to climb. Quite minutely differentiated hierarchies are typical both of industry (whether public or private) and of the professions. Vertically, therefore, work affords a series of ladders with distinct rungs up which men can step out of reach of direct comparison and equality with women. This is a practical instance of the meshing of the processes of class and sex power. Even in the most feminine-gendered field of work, the higher the rank the more masculine becomes the occupation. We saw that in radiography men are represented disproportionately at the top of the profession. A male chef is respected, a male school-dinner cook risks ridicule. In hairdressing, where women are 86 per cent of the workforce, men cluster at the top of the trade and anxiety is expressed about the lack of boys in the lower ranks only because 'they are tomorrow's managers and owners'.[14] Worry is often voiced about how to raise the prestige of a job when men enter it – a worry that doesn't occur so long as it is a woman's job only. Women are, of course, what gave it its low prestige in the first place.[15]

Apart from simply climbing existing ladders, men may respond to pressure from women by actively creating new vertical sub-divisions. This may be happening in technology as women succeed in entering it in greater numbers. Sally Hacker has shown how, in the USA, more and more advanced mathematics has been introduced into the engineering curriculum as a way of stratifying the qualifications. The elite groups are those that have the maths, the rest fall to a lower status. Given their background, women are more often disadvantaged by this than men. As a result, women who get some purchase on technology do not gain as much from it as they might. 'As the ratio of engineers to technicians declines, women and minorities are being actively recruited to become the technicians – that is, engineering *aides* – who form a growing proportion of the new technical workforce.'[16]

By such sideways and upward steps the male sex maintains separation from women. The process is assisted by ideology. We saw how in engineering masculine ideology made use of a hard/soft dichotomy to appropriate tough, physical engineering work for masculinity and thus ran into a problem when it came to evaluating its 'opposite', cerebral, professional engineering. We saw how the ideology coped with this contradiction by calling into play an alternative dichotomy, associating masculinity with rationality and the intellect, femininity with the irrational and with the body – incidentally turning an almost complete conceptual somersault in the process. This kind of ideological work has certainly assisted the step whereby electronic engineering – light, clean, safe work, apparently the very opposite of manly mechanical engineering – has been successfully appropriated for masculinity. An over-arching dichotomy, of course, that men everywhere and always are able to deploy to their advantage is quite simply: masculine equals superior, active and powerful; feminine equals subordinate, submissive and directed. Lowly jobs may be pink or blue, and men manage to establish a compensatory advantage for masculinity even here in the 'heroisms' of heavy manual labour.[17] Top jobs in any field, however, are blue, through and through.

More women every day, however, are stepping out of line. Women are refusing their subordination, becoming active on women's issues and also seeking new forms of self expression. They are looking for more rewarding work and, in spite of the obstacles, are climbing into higher positions in industry, commerce and public services, gaining a presence in politics and cultural life. Men are threatened by this movement. Holding on to the heights of technological advantage is more and more important to them as women chip away at the foundations of other male citadels. Men can ill afford to lose their historic position as the world's engineers just at the point when they can no longer feel themselves secure in the status of family breadwinner and head of household. By making use of the confusion in male hierarchies generated by the recession, restructuring and very rapid technological change, there is scope today for women to press an advantage.

In the USA more and more women have been deciding that the advantages of obtaining technical skills outweigh the considerable social costs. The 1960s saw the first proper skill training in blue collar jobs for women. The number of women in skilled, male trades rose by nearly 80 per cent in the two decades 1960–80, twice as fast as the growth of women in employment and eight times as fast as the growth in the number of men in skilled trades. This still only amounted to a 2-3 per cent increase in women's share of these jobs, and women remain rarities in any given male workplace, but the total number of women has crept up to nearly half a million.[18]

We are seeing a slower, later, but nonetheless steady increase in Britain in the number of women seeking technical training. In 1982 there were over 1,000 degree students in engineering and technology courses where 15 years before there had been 147. The 'training rate' of women technicians (the ratio of those in training to those already qualified) climbed from 8 per cent to 24 per cent between 1975 and 1982 while that for male technicians stood still at around 12 per cent.[19] The important thing, however, is to ensure that this gentle upward slope in the graph of women's participation is the beginning of a steady climb. In the past it has been a plank that women walk, only to drop off the end, actively pushed or simply in despair at the difficulties they encounter. To tilt the graph significantly upward implies intervention that goes far beyond the current notion of 'equal opportunity'.

Women's autonomous access to technology

The first priority is women's own collective action for women's autonomy in technology. Women have made it clear just how men's prior grasp of technical competence, their knowingness and confidence with tools and machinery, make it hard for women to approach technology. At best, when a man is around he is just too helpful, taking the tools into his own hands at the first sign of hesitation. At worst, women can feel put down, told they are incompetent. Especially in technical workplaces, where men have not yet had to accept women as colleagues, they can make women feel literally out of place.

We have to hear what women have been saying: it is men's relationship to technology and to women that makes it difficult for women to learn. Women's confidence flowers when men are removed from the scene. What is needed is space in which training and work can be carried on by women, among women and on women's own terms. As Janet Holland says, there is a 'reality principle' at work here. 'Change the actual situation in which women find themselves and the behaviour of the women will change.'[20]

In the last few years women have begun to take matters into their own hands and to change a few situations. Several support and pressure groups have been formed. One of the earliest was *Women and Manual Trades*, formed in 1975 as a mutual support organization. It developed into an active pressure group and now has four paid workers and an office and has, among other things, produced a video on skilled manual work for use among girls in schools. Another group of this kind is *Women and Computing*, a network formed by women working in the computer field. It organized several annual conferences and gave rise, first, to the *Women's Computer Centre*, which runs courses for women, and later to *Microsyster*, a computer consultancy serving women's groups.

To counteract the isolation of girl apprentices in manual trades, the Young Women's Christian Association have organized an action-research project involving short courses. Eighteen young women from H.M. Dockyards, including apprentice welders, caulker-rivetters, electrical fitters, fitter-turners, coppersmiths and painters, attended one such course. Twelve apprentices in mechanical, electrical and electronic engineering from half a dozen major companies attended a second. The aim was for the young women to share experiences, review the problems they faced and work on possible solutions.

Several women-only technical training initiatives have been set up. *Women in Training (S. London)*, for instance, started with carpentry and has now expanded to offer six months' training in motor mechanics, giving women the basic skills and confidence to go onto Training Opportunities Scheme (TOPS) courses and City and Guilds craft courses. The *Women's Technology Training Workshop* in Sheffield trains women over 25 in micro-electronics and computing skills. In Wolverhampton a woman-only YTS scheme was, until it was closed down, teaching young women practical manual skills in the process of converting a bus for use as a play centre.

One of the most remarkable women-only training initiatives is the *Haringey Women's Training and Education Centre*, in London. Here women teachers run courses for women, particularly aiming to recruit women of ethnic minorities, disabled women and single women with children. The organizers point out that the few women who do manage to get into further education technical courses and into Skill Centres are almost invariably white women, leaving Black, Asian and other minorities doubly disadvantaged. The courses offered by the Haringey centre include carpentry, plumbing, electrical installation and electronics. Child-care costs are recognized as intrinsic and necessary expenses in training women, so the centre has its own nursery but also arranges for women trainees to have the alternative of a child minder near their home. A grant of £60 a week is made available to trainees and in addition £25 a week per child is paid direct to childminders.[21] Hours and holidays usually match those of local schools, and where they do not, they are covered by child-care provision.

Women in these projects say that they are continually oversubscribed. The demand is as yet scarcely tapped, and women often gain the confidence and determination to go on from these to more advanced levels of training which, ideally, would also be women-only. Women are so clear about what they gain by learning in a situation free of men and of masculinity that they often want to form women's working co-operatives so as to be able to put their new skills to use within the same kind of favourable environment. All the women with whom I spoke emphasized the need for a massive extension of funding and support to women-only projects, presently on temporary grants and with uncertain futures.

One of the ironies of the sex equality law is that official dispensation has to be sought under Section 47 of the Sex Discrimination Act 1975 for each and every single-sex training initiative, a slow and cumbersome procedure. It shows how equality policy is based on a fundamental misunderstanding of the processes of women's subordination. The present policy is one of 'what is sauce for the gander is sauce for the goose': measures for women must not exceed or differ from provision for men. Women must simply be integrated into men's world. By this philosophy, positive action for women and separate action by women will always appear to be 'unfair to men'. Men, however, have always been the separatists: what is needed now is the counterweight of separate provision for women. The best proof of the state's genuine commitment to equal opportunity for women would be a high-level change of policy toward support for autonomous women's technology initiatives.

Reshaping training

More is needed, however. We may work towards much more women-only training in technology but it is unlikely that such courses will reach more than a minority of women. To suppose that women's working co-ops could ever substantially encroach on capitalist and male work situations is also more of an ideal than a reality. They will be nurseries of women's skill and catalysts of bigger changes, but they are always likely to be dealing with small-scale applications of technology. This is a direct consequence of the association of technology with economic power: the significant technologies today are developed only in the business world, mainly in large corporations and often with state backing. We need a women's strategy for change in existing vocational training and in workplaces. The trade unions are women's most direct point of leverage. They could, in theory, help achieve the changes that are needed through their characteristic processes of policy formulation, pressure and bargaining.

In a survey of women in Britain in 1968 it was found that the proportion of individual types of work done by women for which any on-the-job training had been received was only 15 per cent. No more than one type of work in 50 done by women involved an apprenticeship, only one in 100 involved a 'learnership', and fewer than one in 20 involved training lasting more than six months.[22] It was hoped that discrimination against women in training would begin to disappear when the effects of the 1964 Industrial Training Act were fully felt. The Trades Union Congress lamely noted in 1972, however, that the Act had failed to bring about 'any improvement in the opportunities for vocational training available to girls and women'.[23] And when the Finniston Committee, 15 years on, reported on *Engineering Our Future*, they still found that 'half a per cent of the current stock of engineers are women' and could find little better to do than 'urge all to work towards the goal' of increasing women's training and qualification.[24]

Meanwhile, efforts have been put into encouraging girls at school to take physics, maths and technology subjects. The results have been disappointing for the very same reasons identified in this study: girls are deterred by boys' appropriation of the subjects.[25] Research into the way young people make their occupational choices shows that young women are well aware of the gender of the occupations spread out before them, and turn away from the masculine ones.[26] Wholehearted support and detailed help and advice from parents, teachers and careers officers is seldom there for the girl who wants to try technical training. (It is even rarer for the boy who wants to do girls' work.) Positive measures in school and in the careers service could be priorities for trade unions such as the National Union of Teachers and The National and Local Government Officers' Association, as well as progressive education authorities.

Meanwhile, of course, the national training system that is so signally failing to give women technological skills is itself in crisis. The government's economic policies are tending to degrade, not improve, training. The majority of industrial training boards have been dismantled by the Thatcher administration. The influence in technical training is being shifted away from the education authorities, whose concern has traditionally been student-centred, to the Manpower Services Commission, which is employer-centred and market-oriented. Market forces have never served women well in the matter of skill. The government's New Training Initiative[27] is dismantling apprenticeship systems. Though women have been excluded from many forms of apprenticeship in the past, it will not mean much of a gain if the system that replaces it, though more accessible to women, involves a lowering of standards as many trade unions fear. In the field of youth training, the MSC's most far-reaching impact is in the Youth Training Scheme for school leavers. A very large initiative, transforming the step from school to work, YTS already involves more than half a million young people and is being doubled in scope. Many doubts have been expressed about the quality of training the scheme offers.[228] A significant opportunity is being missed in YTS to break down sex-typing in training and work, to shake up the field of occupational choice on a scale that has never been possible before. The number of young women entering schemes that offer technical skills is negligible.[29]

Unions involved in the vocational and further education system, the National Association of Teachers in Further and Higher Education (NATFHE), could also have a positive influence on women's chances if this became central to their policies. Further education colleges and universities should be pressed to do much more 'outreach' to schools, careers officers and the community to help girls who have the inclination to get onto technical courses. They could discriminate positively in favour of women when selecting students, and in some cases institute quotas – not only for women as a whole but for women of ethnic minorities who are even worse served by the system as it is. Some colleges already have policies that involve monitoring their intake by sex and ethnic group, but few consider technology courses as deserving of special efforts. Recruiting women in more than token 'ones and twos' is essential. It is hard to be an isolated oddity, easier to deal with the male majority by strength of numbers. Monitoring and support programmes are needed to help women students over the difficult early months. Many more women engineering and technology teachers are needed, so that both women and men can have the experience of learning from women. Regulations governing courses, such as maximum age on entry, may sometimes need altering to help women. The tradition in vocational training is for boys to start at 16. Yet adolescence is a particularly difficult time for a young woman to take the decision to enter non-traditional fields of training. Besides, many women are prepared to make a second start in training after having one or more children. Hours of attendance, then, sometimes need adapting. Skill Centres, for instance, often start classes at 8 a.m. and so rule out women who have children to get up and off to school. Besides, nurseries should be as obligatory a facility in further and higher educational institutions as the library and the canteen are today. These things ought to be central to trade union demands rather than something that is tagged on after the wage round, often to be dropped altogether.

Restructuring work

Supportive measures of this kind in training are of limited use if the conditions of work remain as they are. The workplace needs restructuring in two distinct ways – first, in the way that jobs and career paths are defined; second, in the way men relate to women.

The definition of jobs and the relationship between jobs is, as we've seen, one of the mechanisms that prevents women learning and progressing. The dynamic process of fragmenting and ranking tasks in the interests of productivity and control is characteristic of industrial capitalism. It has an adverse bearing on all least-skilled workers but it affects women worse than men. It produces a series of separations that, in practice, result in the subordination of women as a sex. First, a separation occurs between those who know about machinery and those who nothing about it – between technical personnel and secretaries for instance. Second, it ensures a split between those who know how machinery works and those who only know how to operate it. It effects a parallel separation between those who supervise production and test for quality of products and those whose knowledge is limited to putting bits together in a routine manner. These are the subdivisions of which we've seen men as a sex profit in securing their advantage over women at work. Men have repeatedly proved able to make sideways and upwards moves, re-establishing both horizontal and vertical occupational segregation. The processes of fragmentation and ranking are reflected in pay differentials, and women are in the lower earning groups. Career paths are designed in such a way that the bottom rung is normally above the heads of most women workers. They only start where technical or administrative skills and qualifications have already been achieved. Those who obtain none, predominantly women, are condemmed to immobility.

If women are to accede to technological competence (and better earnings and prospects) once they are *in* their occupation and workplace, first, the pattern of jobs must change and, second, women must be given in-service training opportunities to help them escape from their sex-typed slots.

The aim with jobs should be to re-integrate them wherever possible, levelling hierarchies, adding responsibilities to lower grade jobs, building in more interaction with the technology in the case of routine operator or assembly jobs. The aim would be to provide pathways by which lower-skilled workers could progress and learn during a lifetime of work.

The aim in training should be to encourage women of *any* age and occupation to consider on-the-job or off-the-job training for more technical work. It doesn't cross the mind of the average manager that 'his' secretary, the audio-typists in the pool, the women workers on the production line, are potential technicians. A small current project, supported by the Engineering Industry Training Board and funded by the Manpower Services Commission, is seeking out one or two willing firms and working with them on a programme of training for women operators. Interested women are identified and equipped with the skills for up-graded operator tasks, including setting and first-line maintenance of the machine, for instance. If they show ability at this level they may be offered technician training. Moves of this kind may, it seems, be considered by some equality-minded employers at moments of restructuring within the firm, due to the introduction of new products or new technologies.

The researcher on this project says, 'It's upsetting that so many women are doing work that is way beneath what they are capable of. They have all this pent-up potential. The firms take women on as operators and they don't know anything about them or their real capabilities.' She points out that most men who go into technical work start at age 16. Women at this age have not escaped the conditioning of home and school. They may not yet have thought themselves capable of technical work. 'But by age 20 they are interested and confident. A lot of women really feel they've missed out. Women of 40, who have many years of work still ahead of them, who otherwise will be stuck in a repetitive operator's job, may really welcome training.'[30]

A second way in which the workplace has to change to accommodate women is in men's behaviour. One young woman engineer was told by a male colleague, 'The only things that have changed since you came here are the graffiti on the toilet wall.' He meant: the obscenities are now addressed personally to you.[31] That is true of most male workplaces that recruit a woman. Their masculinity does not diminish, it intensifies to handle the perceived threat. If women are legitimately to be encouraged to look for technical work, there is an obligation to transform the social environment. This doesn't mean just taking down the pin-ups; it means changing many things about working relationships. Many of the men who harass or make life difficult for women in the workplace are, unfortunately, women's fellow trade unionists. In the same way, most of the trade union representatives that devise the union's workplace priorities are men and few have women's interests in the forefront of their minds or any sense of how a workplace would need to adapt to meet women's needs.

Feminizing trade unions

It has to be recognized that the changes women are demanding run directly counter to traditional trade union policies. The unions representing engineers were born in the nineteenth century as craft unions and have always been strongly committed to protecting the rights of certain groups of men to trade knowledge. Their tactics have involved strict job demarcation and the fostering of hierarchies of pay differentials, separating and distinguishing grades of workers. Though the practice has brought men into conflict with capital, both patriarchy and capitalism seem to share the principle. As the unions shifted from a craft to an industrial base in this century, many unskilled and semi-skilled workers, even clerical workers, both women and men, have been swept into membership. The old habits of craft exclusiveness that were intended to strengthen the membership have long since, in reality, divided it. The Equal Pay Act and the Sex Discrimination Act have laid the foundation for ending the undercutting by women of men's rates of pay and have established the right of women to equal access to training and skilled work. A recent amendment to the law enables women to seek equal pay for work that, though it may be different from a man's job, can be shown to be of equal value. The way is open then for unions first, to re-evaluate the work women actually do, recognizing its similar social and economic worth in many cases to that of skilled male members, and second, to ensure women's route out of the ghetto of women's work altogether. It was a scandal in the past that women were kept out of the unions. It will be a scandal in future if the unions don't put their full weight behind the struggle for more training and better jobs (i.e. 'men's jobs') for women.

Women today are 14 per cent of the membership of the Engineering Section of the AUEW. Yet it has no women's officer, no women's committee, no reserved seats for women on other committees, no special training policy – just an annual women's conference. The white collar section of the AUEW, the Technical, Advisory and Supervisory Section (TASS), does a good deal more for its 15 per cent woman membership. It has a national women's sub-committee, a full-time research officer dealing with women's issues, and it actively urges branches to monitor employment policy for women in workplaces. It has piloted some positive action programmes among employing companies. The difference between the policies of the Engineering Section and TASS reflects a class inequality we have seen from the start in this story. Those women who get the better start in life, moving via A-levels to higher education, certainly experience a technological disadvantage relative to men. But it is less severe than the disadvantage felt by the majority of women, who leave school without the appropriate exams. Hard as it may be, it is still easier to be a 'woman engineer' than a 'woman craft worker'.

Women's challenge to unions and their male members today is also a class issue of a somewhat different kind. It amounts to obliging men to accept a redefinition of what constitutes the working class. For skilled men, women have not been full members of the working class but secondary members, wives and daughters. If unions do not respond positively now to the needs being expressed by women, they may well find women increasingly acting outside the framework of the union movement. As in the EITB/MSC re-training project described above, the unions may find themselves merely responding to initiatives by others, including 'progressive' employers.

Just as women's autonomous collective organization is the first priority in providing training and technical work for women, so it is the base line of any improvement for women within the unions. Until women organize independently as women within the shop, branch and national union organizations, if necessary breaking union rules to do so, we will not be able to develop the perspective or mobilize the power to redirect union strategies. The instance of Beta Warehouses PLC, described in Chapter 3 shows what is possible. It was USDAW women, organizing as women, who forced the management and male workers to accept a complete overthrow of occupational sex-typing practices in the firm.

The feminizing of the unions would transform the nature of union demands. Let's imagine a union team negotiating a house agreement, perhaps in an engineering firm with a substantial proportion of women employees. We should suppose the team to be led by a woman shop steward and to embody a fair representation of women members. It would be advised by a house equality officer (a union post) and by a women's committee in the branch. It might lay on the bargaining table a 10-point set of demands which would look very different from anything that management had been presented with in the past.

1. Recruitment and promotion: women to represent an agreed percentage of all apprentice, technician, trainee and graduate engineer recruitment within an agreed number of years. The union's equality officer to be a member of all interview panels with a right of veto.

2. Appointment of a women's training officer by the firm. A programme of on-the-job and off-the-job technical training for an agreed quota of women employees from clerical grades and from unskilled and semi-skilled manual grades (including canteen workers and cleaners) to give them access to skilled work.

3. An end to the informal practice of defining certain occupations as male and others as female. Women and men to have equal chances of filling all vacancies.

4. Re-evaluation of job evaluation procedures to rid them of bias in favour of 'male skills'. Women's status in grades and earnings, relative to that of men in the workforce, to be monitored and brought to agreed levels within an agreed number of years.

5. Criteria for evaluation of the personnel manager's individual performance to include her/his success in achieving points 1–4 above.

6. Subsidized care for children of both female and male employees.

7. Hours and holidays: provision, under union control, for flexible hours of attendance to accommodate employees' individual domestic needs. A right for those with parenting responsibilities to take annual leave entitlement during school holidays. Improved provision for maternity/paternity leave, dependant sick leave, and career continuity after breaks for child rearing – applicable to both sexes.

8. Overtime to be restricted for both men and women of all

grades. Compulsory time-in-lieu in place of overtime payments.

9. Grade structures and pay differentials throughout the firm to be progressively narrowed. Job restructuring to re-integrate fragmented tasks and enrich unskilled ones by the addition of the technical and other responsibilities.

10. A generous flat rate (*not* percentage) pay increase for all grades.

Of course, no such negotiation could even be conceived, let alone launched, without a long and patient process of con-sciousness-raising within the union itself. Members in higher occupations will feel their needs are being subordinated to those in lower. Those without children may grudge being asked to make efforts on behalf of those who have. Above all, male members will feel threatened and angry at a reversal of traditional values. For men to be represented by a woman shop steward is itself experienced as emasculating. A prerequisite, then, within this imaginary firm, would certainly be the existence of a union equality officer and a regular 'equality forum' where women's needs and men's fears can be aired and a process of education begun. Experience shows that some of the most urgent problems raised by women will be instances of sexual harassment. During the process of feminizing the union's processes and policies the harassment may well increase before it diminishes.

The need, then, is for a turn-around in trade union organiza-tion to change what union membership means to women; and a change in trade union strategies to bring about a thorough-going transformation of work itself. Only action of this kind and on this scale can significantly open up technological careers to women.

Dismantling gender

The steps we've discussed above would make it easier for that minority of women who know they are interested in technology to take up training. They would also change the circumstances of many women already in work. But as we've seen, it requires not just a few but tens or even hundreds of thousands of women to obtain significant technological skills if equality in technology is to be achieved for women. What more is needed to make this possible? The question is related, of course, to a second problem. How do we deal with the fact that technology has always been, since patriarchal and class societies existed, a medium of class and sex power, serving profit and domination?

These questions bring us into the mainstream of historical processes and call for long-term perspectives. There is no doubt that for women to acquire 'masculine' skills and work means that men must move in the opposite direction in equally large numbers. We are talking about the dissociation of gender from job and ultimately a breaking of the gender mould that we have clamped on our world. Anything short of this can be converted by men into a new source of power.

Where women enter work that men continue to define as their own a struggle will occur over either the gender of the job or that of the person. In some cases women will be masculinized, made into 'honorary men', and in a similar way the handful of men who cross into traditionally female areas of work will be written off as effeminate, tolerated as eccentrics or failures. Sometimes the gender of the job will swivel round in some way to deal with the problem of assimilating new entrants, or simply to explain them. Joseph Corn reports that after a few determined women had clocked up enough thousands of flying-hours to be considered at last for training as commercial airline pilots, airlines began to see an advantage in using the existence of women pilots to counter the bad publicity from plane crashes. It was supposed that a nervous public would be reassured to see that flying was perfectly safe: any fool could do it.[32] The way radiography is perceived is likely to depend on the proportions of men and women in the profession. The more men, the more it will be seen as a technical job. The more women, the more it will be seen as a routine push-button job or a 'caring profession'. No solution works so long as we have gendered jobs and gendered people.

If one prerequisite of ending technological inequality is a dissociation of gender from occupation, the other is the ending of the broader social division of labour by which masculinity is associated with economic production and femininity with reproduction and domestic life. Sex-specific skills, qualities and inequalities develop within the home as well as in paid work. Women's position in one sphere affects their status in the other. The fact that women are assumed to, and in the main do, carry the responsibility for time-consuming daily tasks and tending other human beings may give women certain marketable skills but it also makes them cheap and super-exploitable labour. Men, being free to work long hours, to strive for training and qualification, build careers and sell their soul to the company, are able to market themselves as more valuable labour power. At present women who want to compete with men for good jobs are obliged to present themselves on the labour market *as men*, domestic persona and cares carefully tucked out of sight. Pamela Franks, Jackie Stein and Lee Dysett, in earlier chapters of this book, had decided to give up children in order to have their 'male' careers. It was, as they saw it, a matter of either/or, and of course they made the choice as they felt best for them. But they should not have to make such sacrifices. Employers must be deprived of this choice between gendered forms of labour and for this to occur the labour market must be unified, women and men seeking work from positions of practical equality, their differences simply individual differences and no longer attributes of gender. For that to happen, men's relationship to domestic life has to change.

Men have purchased freedom from reponsibility at home by 'bringing home the bacon'. (Sometimes of course they have not even contributed that.) Men would have to share the right to earn equally with women and also look after themselves and other people as much as women do now. Bearing a child would not necessarily entail being the person mainly responsible for rearing it. Upbringing would cease to be a gendering process. Boys would not be differentiated from girls. The affective qualities learned in tending and caring, and the practical abilities learned in cooking, sewing, cleaning, and teaching, would be skills learned interchangeably by men and women. The confidence, knack and know-how developed from childhood onward in dealing with houses, gardens, cars, bikes and domestic equipment would be the heritage of females as well as males. If these things happened in the home, trade unions would begin to look different, and so would colleges and workplaces.

Once we talk about un-linking gender and technology, gender and domestic role, we are of course straight away talking about dissolving away the gender dichotomy that puts people as *people*, and not just as workers, into two complementary categories. We are talking about undoing the pervasive gendering of the way we think. The sheer scale of the undertaking becomes visible.

The sexual division of labour in and around technology has existed since the end of the neolithic period at least. Gendering appears to have been, for as long as we can see backwards in time, a major organizing principle, if not *the* organizing principle, in our perception of the world and everything in it. It structures our lives from the level of pure ideas to that of body-building and behaviour. Poetically, gender is ascribed to colours, movements and sounds. But it is utterly concrete too: the conviction some people have of being born the wrong sex and ascribed the wrong gender can drive them relentlessly to mutilating surgery.[33]

In thinking about the subject matter of this book, I started out with the idea that, of the pair of terms 'gender and technology', technology, with its resonance of the hard, the effective, was the more powerful term. Gender seemed the abstract one, the ephemeral factor. Now I am sure that, of the two, gender is the more implacable and tyrannical. It affects our lives more deeply and more damagingly than technology, for it is gender that is behind technology. It is there, in partnership with class, behind fast cars and fast breeders, behind nuclear warheads and their phallic delivery systems. Gender, besides, has fewer compensating features.

People often find the idea of dismantling the gender structure alarming and threatening. So closely has gender become linked with sex, for instance, that un-gendering is felt, quite wrongly, to be un-sexing. Sexual difference is necessary for the continuation of human society. Gender distinctions are not – difficult though it may be to recognise the fact. All the true diversity that people are capable of experiencing and expressing, of needing in their sexual, domestic and working lives and of contributing to society, is repressed by gender. It is crammed into two narrow formulae. Men and women as individuals are trapped into relating to each other in specialized and unequal ways. We are all pushed in the direction of Paul and Tracy – a life of 'his' and 'hers'. The odds are stacked against Dan and Tessa, hoping to go on sharing motorbikes, skills and tasks. Gender difference is not true difference at all. The relationship between the genders is that between the mould and the object that is moulded. The surfaces follow each other and touch at every point, but where one is convex the other is concave. They are fundamentally opposite and complementary. The social processes of differentiation and separation serve power, whether that of a class, a race or a sex. They are universal devices of oppression. The specifying of complementary qualities in the oppressor and the oppressed makes inequalities appear less unequal ('We're good at different things'). By avoiding direct comparison between ruler and ruled, rule itself is perpetuated.

Although – indeed because – masculinity loses as we escape from gender complementarity, individual women and men have a lot to gain from doing so. The good qualities deemed masculine – courage, strength and skill, for instance – and the good qualities seen as feminine – tenderness, the ability to feel and express feelings – should be the qualities available to all and recognized and acclaimed wherever they occur, regardless of the sex of the person. Perhaps even more importantly, the lack of some human quality should not be condoned in a person just because of her or his sex. An inability to sympathize or respond should be felt to be just as undesirable in a man as in a woman. Lack of initiative or rationality should be equally missed in a woman as in a man. Any society we set out to organize anew would surely be a celebration of multiplicity and individual difference. As Genevieve Lloyd wrote, 'understanding the contribution of past thought to "male" and "female" consciousness, as we now have them, can help make available a diversity of intellectual styles and characters to men and women alike. It need not involve a denial of all difference.'[34] Lloyd's concern was philosophy. If what she says is true of styles of thinking, how much more true is it of ways of working, playing and loving.

Making technology human

This whole discussion of gender and technology has been built on a fundamental contradiction that still remains to be explored. It is the contradiction between women's need for technical competence and the destructive, exploitative and inhuman nature of current technologies.

Military spending has a shaping influence on technology, determining research priorities and the designs that are selected for development and production. More than half the British government's research and development budget and presumably therefore the efforts of more that half of the government-funded engineers, is devoted to 'defence'. As Dot Griffiths says, 'girls and women opt out of technology because they reject its goals and values: the development . . . of weapons of destruction, of boring and dehumanizing work processes and products designed with artificial obsolescence in mind.'[35]

We've seen that technologists are more often than not employed in putting other people out of work or making their work less tolerable. An engineer said to me, defiantly: 'We are in a situation where we can *see* that as a direct result of our labour people are being made redundant. It is something you have to come to terms with, otherwise you would be fighting shy all the time.' There is a particular danger that women may be caught up in capital's purposes, because the historical circumstance in which women have been enabled to steal a march over men in production has invariably been when capital has been attacking sectors of the male working class with new technology. It is not surprising that some women think technology is irredeemably masculine and that women will do better to keep their hands clean of it. Boel Berner concluded from her research on women and technology that women's role should be 'not to become engineers or technicians but to struggle for a democratisation and de-professionalisation of technical work and for the development of a more humane technology based on women's visions of a better world.'[36]

Such arguments are too forceful to brush aside. Can we avoid women taking on the class mantle of the male engineer, becoming the employers' white-coated 'yes men', the brains behind exploitation at work? The possibilities of resisting sometimes seem slight. In *America By Design*, David Noble describes the defeated efforts of a minority of engineers in the early decades of the twentieth century to redirect technology. Progressive-minded engineers realized that anti-business political activity grounded on engineering expertise led to technical impotence. 'Radical engineers, they understood, had to choose between being radical and being engineers.'[37] Women have somehow to avoid becoming accessories to exploitation as they become technologists. Yet without technological knowledge, women's scope for changing the relations of technology and the direction taken by an already technological society is limited to rhetoric. It is only by getting inside it that women have a chance of succeeding. Besides, we have to listen to women's own demands for training.

We've seen how the access of women, not individually but *as a sex*, to technology depends ultimately on the dismantling of gender. It is in other words inescapably part of a feminist movement. Equally, it has to be part of a socialist movement. As women become technologists they have a choice between escaping *into* power, the power to dominate people, or using their own new individual power alongside the less-skilled and weaker sections of the workforce. The latter course means joining and changing trade unions. It means teaching other women. It means selecting the workplaces to work in, the processes and products that are designed and produced with as much discrimination as the labour market and the strength of the labour movement allow. And it also involves organizing politically in Left movements with a critique of technology.

These include the environmental, anti-nuclear and 'appropriate technology' movements.

Women entering technology can, after all, present it with a challenge that has never been posed before: a challenge to its masculinity. In the hands of men, technology has been wrenched apart from the fundamental human concerns of life. In Mary Shelley's *Frankenstein* the young scientist conceives of a Faustian project.[38] He makes a creature in human form and succeeds in giving it life. The experiment goes disastrously wrong and the monster turns against its maker and the world. The reason this short novel, written in a light-hearted moment, has echoed on for so long is that its theme is very close to our own tragedy. To achieve his aims Frankenstein shut himself away, out of reach of the woman he loved, far from the real world, answerable to no one. He had no clear purpose in his invention beyond the manifestation of his own power, and he could not predict its effect on the world. He was incapable of loving the creature he made and would not respond to its plea for a mate of its own to love.

It is often proposed that technology today, like Frankenstein's monster, is 'out of control'.[39] It is not technology that is out of control, but capitalism *and men*. As we have seen, masculinity has often been associated with the idea of transcendence, femininity with its opposite, immanence. Simone de Beauvoir saw technological invention itself as an inspired act of transcendence by men: 'It is because man is a being of transcendence and ambition that he projects new urgencies through every new tool: when he had invented bronze implements, he was no longer content with gardens – he wanted to clear and cultivate vast fields.'[40] 'The male,' she wrote, 'is called upon for action, his vocation is to produce, fight, create, progress, to transcend himself towards the totality of the universe and the infinity of the future.'[41]

Transcendence is a wrong-headed concept. It means escape from the earth-bound and the repetitive, climbing above the everyday. It means putting men on the moon before feeding and housing the world's poor. It is essentially treading down the feminine and diminishing as feminine all that women have

...ife. Women, says de Beauvoir, 'wallow in immanence'. ...rankenstein was involved in, like the scientists who ...the atom bomb in the 1940s,[42] and the technologists of the space programme today, is transcendence. There is a Dr Frankenstein in every work-obsessed engineer clocking up overtime while his wife puts the children to bed. Entranced by his masculine project he knows no greater dread than being stuck at the kitchen sink up to his elbows in immanence. Remember the distaste of the male physicist for women, especially married women with children, coming to work in his department. It was as though they would contaminate it with odours of kitchen and nursery.

The way forward proposed for women often implies that we ought to seek transcendence in our turn. This is Simone de Beauvoir's view. It is also, in a sense, the logic of 'equal opportunity' and 'WISE year'. It is the wrong route, not only for women but also for the world. The very dichotomy of transcendence/immanence is a masculine concept. We will move beyond gendered ways of thinking. Instead of seeking our own transcendence in technological exploits, women will redefine the terms and the relationships.

There is, after all, an entirely different way of seeing things and of saying them. These so-called triumphs of the male technologists have, it is true, sometimes taken the form of useful work. But they have often been non-productive – at best gratuitous display, at worst military or economic rape. The work women have traditionally done has by contrast always been the primary, necessary work of human communities. Men need more urgently to learn women's skills than women need to learn men's.

Women, however, could use more possibilities for self-expression. We could use more opportunities for questioning, inventiveness, imagination, creativeness and adventure. We could also do with more choice over our place in production and reproduction, and with better earnings. We would gain from a knowledge of the properties of energy and matter, and of practical tools that could help us to apply them to governing our own environment and labour. Women need these things not instead of but *as well as* the attributes and concerns we already have. We will find ways of using them without depriving someone else of them and without converting them into power over others.

The right decisions about technology will only be made by people who, like radiographers, have to deal not only with machines but, at first hand, with human life and pain. It would not change things greatly for the better were women simply to step into the male world of technology, leaving our own concerns and values behind. It would change things for the worse to have masculine ideas and behaviour take over child care and home life. The revolutionary step will be to bring men down to earth, to domesticate technology and reforge the link between making and nurturing.

Such things may seem a far cry from the innocent concerns of 'women in manual trades' and 'women into engineering'. But we are led to face the fundamental issues of human society from the moment we embark on the project of enabling women to saw a straight cut or tighten a nut. Women getting a grip on technological competence is not the end of a struggle but the beginning of one.

Notes and references

Chapter 1

1 Department of Employment, *New Earnings Survey*,1983, Part E, Table 135. Figures relate to Great Britain and show women as a percentage of the occupational and industrial labour forces.
2 *ibid.*
3 *ibid.*
4 Catherine Hakim, *Occupational Segregation*, Report No.9, Department of Employment, 1979.
5 See, for instance, Angela Coyle, 'Sex and skill in the clothing industry' in Jackie West (ed), *Work, Women and the Labour Market*, Routledge & Kegan Paul, 1982; Ruth Cavendish, *Women on the Line*, Routledge & Kegan Paul, 1982; Anna Pollert, *Girls, Wives, Factory Lives*, Macmillan, 1981; and Sallie Westwood, *All Day Every Day*, Pluto Press, 1984.
6 Jean Martin and Ceridwen Roberts, *Women and Employment: A Lifetime Perspective*, Department of Employment and Office of Population Censuses and Surveys, HMSO, 1984, pp.27–8.
7 Catherine Hakim, *op.cit.*, p.43.
8 Edward Gross, 'Plus ça change? . . . The sexual structure of occupations over time', *Social Problems*, 16, Fall, 1968.
9 Organization for Economic Co-operation and Development, *Women and Employment: Policies for Equal Opportunities*, Paris, 1980.
10 Esther Boserup, *Women's Role in Economic Development*, George Allen & Unwin, 1971.
11 G.W. Lapidus, 'Occupational segregation and public policy: a comparative analysis of American and Soviet patterns', in M. Blaxall and B. Reagan (eds), *Women and the Workplace: The Implications of Occupational Segregation*, University of Chicago Press, 1976. See also Michael Paul Sacks, *Women's Work in Soviet Russia: Continuity in the Midst of Change*, Praeger, USA, 1976.

12 Department of Employment, *op.cit.*,1983 and 1975.

13 Department of Education and Science, *Statistics of Education* and *Statistics of School Leavers*, 1970–83, cited in Equal Opportunities Commission, *9th Annual Report*, 1984. Figures relate to England and Wales, summer examinations.

14 Figures obtained from City and Guilds of London Institute during 1984.

15 Figures obtained from the Business and Technical Education Council during 1984.

16 Department of Education and Science, *Statistics of Education: Further Education*, November 1981, table 22, and the Welsh Office. Figures relate to England and Wales and are cited in Equal Opportunities Commission, *op.cit.*

17 Statistics published by the Department of Education and Science (*Statistics of Education: Universities*) and the University Grants Committee (*University Statistics*) and cited in Equal Opportunities Commission, *op.cit.*

18 Department of Employment, *New Earnings Survey*, 1970–84, Part A, Tables 10 and 11.

19 *ibid.*

20 M.W. Snell, P. Glucklich and M. Povall, *Equal Pay and Opportunities*, Department of Employment, Research Paper No.20, 1981.

21 Engineering Industry Training Board, *Women in Engineering*, Occasional Paper No.11, 1984, tables 2.1 and 2.2.

22 The stereotype cave-man reflects scientific theories as they were developed, almost entirely by men, in the patriarchal and ethno-centric societies of western Europe in the nineteenth and early twentieth century. It has been pointed out that it would not be surprising if these men had looked for and found a replica of themselves in pre-history. Nancy Makepeace Tanner suggests that these scientists in effect produced a modern 'origin myth' (*On Becoming Human*, Cambridge University Press, USA 1981, p.3). The effect of male bias among anthropologists on the study of societies in early stages of development is demonstrated by Ruby Rohrlich-Leavitt, Barbara Sykes and Elizabeth Weatherford in 'Aboriginal women: male and female anthropological perspectives', in Rayna R. Reiter (ed), *Toward an Anthropology of Women*, Monthly Review Press, 1975.

23 See, for instance, Sally Slocum, 'Woman the gatherer', in Rayna R. Reiter (ed), *op.cit.*

24 Nancy Makepeace Tanner and Adrienne Zihlman, 'Woman in

evolution: innovation and selection in human origins', *Signs*, Vol.1, No.3, Spring 1976; and Nancy M.Tanner, *op.cit.*.

25 M. Kay Martin and Barbara Voorhies, *Female of the Species*, Cambridge University Press, USA, 1975.

26 Autumn Stanley, 'Daughters of Isis, daughters of Demeter: when women reaped and sowed', *Women's Studies International Quarterly*, Vol.4, No.3, 1981.

27 Eleanor Burke Leacock illustrates this point by reference to the sex-egalitarian gathering and hunting community of the Montagnais-Naskapi of Canada in the period immediately preceding their conversion to Christianity by Jesuit missionaries (*Myths of Male Dominance*, Monthly Review Press, 1981).

28 Çatal Huyuk, a settlement of *c*.6000 BC, represents the transition from neolithic village to bronze-age town. James Mellaart's excavations revealed a society based on cattle breeding and irrigation agriculture, supplemented by gathering, hunting and fishing. (James Mellaart, *Çatal Huyuk: A Neolithic Town in Anatolia*, McGraw-Hill, USA, 1967.) House design and burial arrangements, evidence of female deities and female priests, lead to the conclusion that women were socially pre-eminent at Çatal Huyuk (Ruby Rohrlich-Leavitt, 'State formation in Sumer and the subjugation of women', *Feminist Studies*, 6, No.1, Spring 1980).

29 A well-authenticated instance of this, explicit in epic poetry, laws and codes, occurred in the Middle East between the fourth and second millennia BC (Ruby Rohrlich-Leavitt *op.cit.*). The process was theorized by Frederick Engels in the nineteenth century in *Origin of the Family, Private Property and the State*, Pathfinder Press, 1972. A material Factor that may have enabled men to subjugate women is proposed by Autumn Stanley. Drawing on evidence from foraging societies that have adopted a sedentary agricultural existence and a grain-based diet, she suggests that this change precipitates an increase in body-fat, earlier puberty in women and regular ovulation, all tending to a dramatic increase in fertility. It could have been excessive childbearing that, in neolithic agricultural communities, first put women at a physical and economic disadvantage relative to men (Autumn Stanley, *op.cit.*).

30 Whether fully matriarchal societies ever existed is doubtful. There is, however, evidence of matrilineal and matrilocal societies which would certainly have ensured a centrality for women, and also of societies existing in the more recent past in which the sexes were very much more equal than our own (see Eleanor Burke Leacock, *op.cit.*) In place of 'patriarchy', therefore, as a time-less trans-

historical expression, it is helpful to use the concept of a 'sex/gender system', as proposed by Gayle Rubin ('The traffic in women', in Rayna R. Reiter (ed), *op.cit.* p.159). This enables us to conceptualize changes over historical periods in the relative power of men and women as sexes, variations in the 'set of arrangements by which a society transforms biological sexuality into products of human activity and in which these transformed sexual needs are satisfied'.

31 See Lynn White Jr, *Medieval Technology and Social Change*, Oxford University Press, 1962, who suggests that the iron age proper began for Europe in the ninth century AD, p.40.

32 Suzanne Fonay Wemple, *Women in Frankish Society: Marriage and the Cloister 500–900 AD*, University of Pennsylvania Press, USA, 1981, p.70.

33 Dorothy Whitelock, *The Beginnings of English Society*, Penguin Books, 1952, p.106.

34 Miranda Chaytor and Jane Lewis, 'Introduction' to Alice Clark, *Working Life of Women in the Seventeenth Century*, Routledge & Kegan Paul, 1982, p.xxxiv. Originally published 1919. Chaytor and Lewis are referring to rural life in the pre-capitalist period.

35 Lynn White Jr, *op.cit.*, p.41.

36 B. Wilkinson, *The Later Middle Ages in England 1216–1485 AD*, Longman, 1969; M.M. Postan, *The Medieval Economy and Society*, Penguin Books, 1975.

37 This and other information in this and the succeeding paragraph is drawn from Alice Clark, *op.cit.* In Chapter V she traces the position of women in craft and trade in the fourteenth to sixteenth centuries, pp.150–70.

38 Quoted by B.L. Hutchins, *Women in Modern Industry*, E.P. Publishing Ltd., 1978, p.38. First published 1915.

39 Lynn White Jr, *op.cit.*, p. 128

40 Sigvard Strandh, *A History of the Machine*, A.&.W. Publishers Inc., USA, 1979.

41 Autumn Stanley, 'Women hold up two-thirds of the sky: notes for a revised history of technology', in Joan Rothschild (ed), *Machina Ex Dea: Feminist Perspectives on Technology*, Pergamon Press, USA, 1983. Autumn Stanley's research on women inventors will be published in 1986 under the title, *Mothers of Invention*.

42 Autumn Stanley, 'Daughters of Isis, daughters of Demeter: when women reaped and sowed', *op.cit.*

43 Lynn White Jr, *op.cit.*, p.119.

44 Lewis Mumford, *Technics and Civilisation*, Routledge & Kegan

Paul, 1934, p.144. The electrification of kitchen equipment, which began in the last decade of the nineteenth century, was the work of electrical engineers not housewives.

45 Nathan Rosenberg, *Inside the Black Box: Technology and Economics*, Cambridge University Press, 1982, p.35.

46 Karl Marx, *Capital*, Vol.1, Lawrence & Wishart, 1954, p.339. First published 1887. Much of the account of the development of industrial capitalism in this chapter is drawn from Chapters XIII–XV of this volume of *Capital*.

47 *ibid.* p.323

48 *ibid.* p.396

49 *ibid.* p.331

50 *ibid.* p.361

51 *ibid.* p.362–3

52 *ibid.* p.399. 'The total production of society may be divided into two major departments . . .
I Means of Production – commodities having a form in which they must, or at least may, pass into productive consumption.
II Articles of Consumption – commodities having a form in which they pass into . . . individual consumption.'

53 Henry Pelling, *A History of British Trade Unionism*, Macmillan, 1976. See also, for a history of the Amalgamated Society of Engineers, James Barrington Jefferys, *The Story of the Engineers 1800–1945*, Lawrence & Wishart, 1946.

54 Jonathan Zeitlin, 'Craft control and the division of labour: engineers and compositors in Britain 1890–1930', *Cambridge Journal of Economics*, No.3, 1979.

55 H.A. Clegg, Alan Fox and A.F. Thompson, *A History of British Trade Unions since 1869*, Vol.1, Oxford, 1964, p.138.

56 David Noble, *America by Design: Science, Technology and the Rise of Corporate Capitalism*, Oxford University Press, 1979, p.5. First published by Knopf, USA, 1977.

57 *ibid.*

58 André Gorz, 'Technology, technicians and class struggle' in André Gorz (ed), *The Division of Labour*, Harvester Press, 1976, p.169.

59 Karl Marx, *op.cit.*, p.411.

60 David Noble, *op.cit.*, p.41.

61 Painstaking accounts of women's work in the industrial revolution can be found in Ivy Pinchbeck, *Women Workers and the Industrial Revolution 1750–1850*, Virago Press, 1981, first published 1930; B.L. Hutchins, *Women in Modern Industry*, E.P. Publishing Ltd., 1978, first published 1915; Wanda F. Neff, *Victorian Working*

Women, Frank Cass, 1966, first published 1929; Alice Kessler-Harris, *Out to Work: A History of Wage-earning Women in the United States*, Oxford University Press, USA, 1982; and Elizabeth F. Baker, *Technology and Women's Work*, Columbia University Press, USA, 1964.

62 Sarah Eisenstein, *Give Us Bread but Give Us Roses*, Routledge & Kegan Paul, 1983, p.55–7.

63 *ibid.*

64 B.L. Hutchins, *op.cit.*, p.75.

65 *ibid.*, p.90.

66 *ibid.*, p.xviii.

67 Daniel Defoe, *Tour*, 1796, cited in Ivy Pinchbeck, *op.cit.*, p.272.

68 B.L. Hutchins, *op.cit.*, p.62–3.

69 *ibid.*, p.66–7.

70 A book by Miss Virginia Penny entitled *Think and Act*, 1869, cited in Annie Nathan Meyer, *Woman's Work in America*, Arno Press, USA, 1972, p.286. First published 1891.

71 B.L. Hutchins, *op.cit.*, p.201.

72 Gayle Braybon, *Women Workers in the First World War*, Croom Helm, 1981, p.46.

73 Norbert C. Solden, *Women in British Trade Unions 1874–1976*, Gill and Macmillan, 1978, p.102.

74 James Hinton, *The First Shop Stewards Movement*, George Allen & Unwin, 1981; and Edmund and Ruth Frow, *Engineering Struggles*, Working Class Movement Library, 1982.

75 Miriam Gluckman, 'Women and the "new industries": changes in class relations in the 1930s', paper to the Economic and Social Research Council seminar on Gender and Stratification, University of Norwich, July 1984.

76 Norbert C. Solden, *op.cit.*, p.152–3.

77 *Employment Gazette* figures, published in Equal Opportunities Commission *Annual Report* 1983, table 3.3.

78 *ibid.*

79 *ibid.*, fig.3.3.

Chapter 2

1 *Census of Production 1981*, published 1983, PA 453, 'Clothing, hats and gloves'.

2 *Bulletin of Textile and Clothing Statistics*, Department of Trade and Industry, May 1984.

3 For an exploration of the international scope of the textile industry

and its impact on women, see Wendy Chapkis and Cynthia Enloe (eds), *Of Common Cloth: Women in the Global Textile Industry*, Transnational Institute, Netherlands, 1983.

4 *Census of Production, op.cit.*

5 Low Pay Unit, *Below the Minimum: Low Wages in the Clothing Industry*, West Midlands Low Pay Unit, Birmingham.

6 Annie Phizacklea, *Jobs for the Girls: The Production of Women's Outerwear in the UK* (forthcoming publication), University of Aston, Birmingham.

7 *Clothing '80: Fighting for Success*, Clothing Economic Development Council, 1980.

8 For the history of the development of the technologies described in this chapter, their application in clothing and the hopes and fears of both suppliers and manufacturers, it is useful to refer to the trade journals. See, for instance: *Readywear*, No.4 and No.9, 1978; *Manufacturing Clothier*, November and December 1982; *British Clothing Manufacturer*, November and December 1978, April and August 1979, July and October 1980; *Bobbin*, January, May and October 1980, August 1981 and January 1982.

9 Angela Coyle, 'Sex and skill in the organisation of the clothing industry', in Jackie West (ed), *Work, Women and the Labour Market*, Routledge & Kegan Paul, 1982.

10 *Keynote Report: Clothing Manufacturers*, third edition, an industry sector overview, Keynote Publications Ltd., 1984.

11 K. Hoffman and H. Rush, *Microelectronics and Clothing: The Impact of Technical Change on a Global Industry*, draft report, Science Policy Research Unit, Sussex University, 1983.

12 Angela Coyle, *op.cit.*

13 I have discussed skill and its class and gender implications at greater length in *Brothers: Male Dominance and Technological Change*, Pluto Press, 1983. pp.112 f.

14 Angela Coyle, *op.cit.*

15 *Bobbin*, January 1980.

16 As note 8 above.

17 Angela Coyle, *op.cit.*

18 Barbara Taylor, 'The men are as bad as their masters', *Feminist Studies*, Vol.5, No.1, 1979.

19 The manager, on reading a draft of this chapter, wished to correct the impression given by this remark. He wrote that what was in fact said was 'that one of the attributes of a manager working with women was the ability to know how to get the best result from a woman – to pinch her bottom, or kick her bottom, and, in fact, this

technique could be referred to as a pat on the head, and a lump of sugar can sometimes produce a good result for a man and sometimes a good kick up the arse would produce a good result as well. This is the point that I think you rather missed and certainly [it] should not be referred to in the manner in which you have quoted it.'

20 Viz. the unsuccessful efforts of the 'Women in Clothing Network' organized by Barbara Shelborn Associates. Personal communication by Kay Smith.
21 Marian Reyes, 'New technology and the clothing industry', *Newscheck*, Vol.2, No.8, March 1985, p.11.

Chapter 3

1 Mintel survey cited in D. Churchill, 'Aggressive sales promotion exploits new markets', *Financial Times*, August 27, 1980.
2 I explored the relationship of capital in the mail order business to women's paid and unpaid labour and to the family in *The Local State*, Pluto Press, 1977, pp.180 f.
3 *The Mechanical Handling Equipment Industry in Europe*, ICC Market Studies International, 1981.
4 Developments in this technology in the period just prior to the research are reported in the trade journals. See for instance, *Materials Handling News*, June and July 1982; *Storage Handling Distribution*, March and April 1982.
5 Warehouse investments were important to the engineering firms in the early 1980s. 'One of the few bright spots in a dull handling industry is the perceptible swing towards fully-automated warehouses', wrote *Materials Handling News* in February 1982. It spearheaded a period of activity. The worldwide materials handling market was estimated to be $20 billion and growth rates of 16–20 per cent per annum for the coming ten years were forecast in *Storage Handling Distribution* in June 1982.
6 This account is based on Keynote Business Information, *Mail Order*, second edition, 1984; Economist Intelligence Unit, *Retail Trade Review*, Retail Business No.282, August 1981; Phillips and Drew Industry Review, *Retailing*, November 1981.
7 J. Stone, 'The mail order question mark', *Financial Times*, November 5, 1980.
8 Ann Game and Rosemary Pringle, *Gender at Work*, Pluto Press, 1984, p.32.
9 'Britain at last seems to have grasped the message about industrial

robots. Last year industry invested £20 million in robot systems.'
The total robot population in Britain by 1983 was anticipated to be
2,000. *Materials Handling News*, April 1982.

Chapter 4

1 I. Moodie, *Fifty Years of History*, The Society of Radiographers,
1970.
2 Technical information on diagnostic imaging can best be obtained
from medical journals during the period 1975–85. See, for
instance, the journal *RNM Images*, published in Illinois, USA.
Other references on which I have drawn are technical literature
published by manufacturers; *CT Scanners – A Technical Report*,
American Hospital Association, Chicago, 1977; D.R. Hegstrom,
'Computerized axial tomography – an important health care
phenomenon', *World Hospitals*, Vol. XV, No.2, May 1979; M.S.
White, 'Altered images', *The Health Services*, No.24, May 28 1982;
F.W. Smith, 'Whole body nuclear magnetic resonance scanning',
Radiography, Vol.XLVII, No.564, December 1981.
3 B. Stocking and S.L. Morrison, *The Image and the Reality: A Case
Study of the Impacts of Medical Technology*, Oxford University
Press, 1978, p.66.
4 D.R. Hegstrom, *op.cit.*, p.136
5 J. Mitchell, *What is to be done about illness and health?*, Penguin,
1984, pp.155 and 183. On technology in the health service, see also
S.J. Reiser, *Medicine and the Reign of Technology*, Cambridge
University Press, 1978; and L. Doyal, *The Political Economy of
Health*, Pluto Press, 1979.
6 For an exploration of sex and hierarchy in medicine, see Eva
Gamarnikow, 'Sexual division of labour: the case of nursing', in A.
Kuhn and A.M. Wolpe (eds), *Feminism and Materialism*, Routledge
& Kegan Paul, 1978; and Ann Game and Rosemary Pringle,
Gender at Work, Pluto Press, 1984, chapter titled 'Sex and power in
hospitals: the division of labour in the "health" industry.'
7 The head of a medical physics department commented on this
when reading the chapter in draft. He wrote, 'I do not think this is
true. What I and many of my colleagues say is that we disagree
with the relative merit radiographers are trying to put on their
qualifications in comparison with our degrees. If we disagreed
with their needing their training we would not be there training
them. [Some physicists teach technical aspects of the subject to
radiographers in the teaching hospitals.] But by virtue of our

knowing what we train them in we know its relative merit to own training.'

8 Department of Health and Social Security, *Report of the Committee of Inquiry into the Pay and Related Conditions of Service of the Professions Supplementary to Medicine and Speech Therapists* (The Halsbury Report), H.M. Stationery Office, 1975.

9 Department of Health and Social Security, *op.cit.*

10 It is interesting, though, that the head of medical physics cited in note 7 above found these welcoming statements by women to be 'condescending'. Simple praise from a woman, implying simple equality, is unacceptable to a man.

11 Information provided by the Hospital Physicists Association, 1983.

Chapter 5

1 An informant at SHC Ltd., who read this chapter in draft, wished me to add that the firm have since taken on a woman trainee who could eventually become a consultant. Owing to her personality – 'she's strong' – she was 'holding her own in the warehouse environment'.

2 Steelwork Ltd. report that during 1984, subsequent to my contact with the firm, they have appointed a female draughter. Sometimes I wonder whether – and hope that – the discussions provoked by the research had a bearing on managers' later recruitment practices.

3 The world market in CT Scanners took a tumble in 1984, dropping 50 per cent below 1983. EIDS, which till mid-year had been 'hiring anything on two legs with a scientific background' did a quick turnaround, withdrew the remaining bits of CT manufacture from its British factory and began laying off up to 100 workers of all grades from the plant. It simultaneously placed its bet on NMR.

4 An EIDS representative, on reading this chapter, asked for it to be stressed that the views ascribed to this personnel manager throughout are his own and do not reflect those of the company.

5 In 1984 EIDS advertised for test engineers. Five hundred applied. Only one of these was a woman. In confirmation of the firm's commitment to women, however, it was pointed out that this woman was taken on.

Chapter 6

1 Suzanne J. Kessler and Wendy McKenna, *Gender: an Ethnomethodological Approach*, John Wiley and Sons, USA, 1978, p.39.

2 Kessler and McKenna, *op.cit.*, say 'all the scientific evidence indicates that chromosomes have little or no direct effect on whether persons feel that they are female or male', p.24.

3 A useful discussion of the social construction of gender is to be found in Michelle Stanworth, *Gender and Schooling: A Study of Sexual Divisions in the Classroom*, Hutchinson, 1983. 'Girls may follow the same curriculum as boys, may sit side by side with boys in classes taught by the same teachers and yet emerge from school with the implicit understanding that the world is a man's world, in which women can and should take second place.' p.58. See also R.W. Connell, *et.al.*, *Making the Difference: Schools, Families and Social Division*, George Allen & Unwin, Australia, 1982.

4 Margaret Mead, *Sex and Temperament in Three Primitive Societies*, William Morrow, USA, 1935.

5 Ann Oakley, *Sex, Gender and Society*, Temple Smith, 1972, p. 189.

6 A useful treatment of sex differences and gender is that of Dorothy Griffiths and Esther Saraga ('Sex differences and cognitive abilities: a sterile field of enquiry?' in Oonagh Hartnett *et.al.* (eds), *Sex-role Stereotyping*, Tavistock 1979). They point out (p.36) that researchers everywhere tend to look for sex differences and overlook similarities. 'We do not deny the existence, at the present time in our society, of sex differences in performance of certain cognitive tasks. We do however reject biological determinist explanations of them . . . Questions concerning the origin and nature of sex differences cannot properly be answered by and in a a society that is predicated on their existence. And in a society not premised on their existence we feel it is unlikely that these issues would be a major concern.'

7 Many sociologists, e.g. L. Davidson and L.K. Gordon (*The Sociology of Gender*, Rand McNally, 1979), use the concept of 'gender role' or 'sex role'. But as Griffiths and Saraga (*op.cit.*) say, it is unhelpful to treat the gendered upbringing of girls and boys as the product of arbitrary social stereotypes. It leads to a neglect of questions concerning the origins of the stereotypes themselves. Role theory cannot help us to ask the question: how do contrasted and unequal genders arise? only: how do we get to model ourselves on them? On this theme see also R.W. Connell, *Which way is up? Essays on Class, Sex and Culture*, George Allen & Unwin,

Australia, 1983.

8 Genevieve Lloyd, *The Man of Reason: 'Male' and 'Female' in Western Philosophy*, Methuen, 1984.

9 *ibid.*, pp.37 and 104.

10 Adam Smith, *An Inquiry Into the Nature and Cause of The Wealth of Nations*, Vol.1, London, 1930, p.17, cited in Cynthia B. Lloyd (ed), *Sex Discrimination and the Division of Labor*, Columbia University Press, 1975.

11 For a fuller discussion of the handling of contradiction in qualitative research, see Cynthia Cockburn, *Brothers: Male Dominance and Technological Change*, Pluto Press, 1983, pp.11-12.

12. Samuel Smiles, *Lives of the Engineers*, Vol.1, David and Charles Reprints 1968. p.v. First published 1862.

13 *ibid.*, p.311,

14 Tracy Kidder, *The Soul of a New Machine*, Penguin, 1981.

15 *ibid.*, p.177.

16 *ibid.*, p.158.

17 *ibid.*, p.66.

18 *ibid.*, p.65.

19 *ibid.*, p.245.

20 *ibid.*, p.118.

21 *ibid.*, p.58.

22 *ibid.*, p.99.

23 See, for instance, the analysis of Bacon's philosophy in Brian Easlea, *Science and Sexual Oppression: Patriarchy's Confrontation with Woman and Nature*, Weidenfeld & Nicolson, 1981; and Carolyn Merchant, *The Death of Nature: Women, Ecology and the Scientific Revolution*, Wildwood House, 1982.

24 Francis Bacon, 'The Masculine Birth of Time or the Great Instauration of the Dominion of Man over the Universe', cited in the above works.

25 Genevieve Lloyd, *op.cit.*, p.17.

26 Carolyn Merchant, *op.cit.* There was, however, to develop a subtle change in the way the natural world was portrayed. If the scientists, the miners and the engineers were to be at liberty to forage in the world and exploit its resources, the idea of the earth as an organism and a spirit – the nurturing earth image that had prevailed from ancient times – must be replaced by a sense of the world as inorganic, as a machine. In a sense 'the female' lost yet further through this, no longer respected as an enigma, reduced to an object.

27 Engineering Industry Training Board, *Women in Engineering*,

Occasional Paper No.11, 1984, tables C.2 and C.4.

28 Heidi Hartmann, 'Capitalism, patriarchy and job segregation by sex', in Zillah R. Eisenstein (ed), *Capitalist Patriarchy and the Case for Socialist Feminism*, Monthly Review Press, 1979, p.232.

29 Andrew Tolson, *The Limits of Masculinity*, Tavistock, 1977, p.87.

30 Phyllis Chesler, *About Men*, The Women's Press, 1978, p.143.

31 Andrew Tolson, *op.cit.*, p.88.

32 Simone de Beauvoir, *The Second Sex*, Penguin, 1972, p.28. First published 1949.

33 *ibid.*, p.97.

34 Ruth Schwarz-Cowan, 'From Virginia Dare to Virginia Slims: woman and technology in American life', *Technology and Culture*, No.20, January 1979, p.62.

35 Cited in Angela M. Lucas, *Women in the Middle Ages*, Harvester Press, 1983, p.5.

36 Sarah Eisenstein, *Give Us Bread but Give Us Roses*, Routledge & Kegan Paul, 1983, p.56.

37 Michael Hiley, *Victorian Working Women: Portraits from Life*, Gordon Fraser, 1979.

38 Angela John, *By the Sweat of their Brow*, Croom Helm, 1980.

39 Boel Berner, 'Women, power and ideology in technical education and work', paper to the International Conference on the Role of Women in the History of Science, Technology and Medicine in the 19th and 20th Centuries, Hungary, August 1983, p.4.

40 Brian Easlea, *Fathering the Unthinkable: Masculinity, Scientists and the Nuclear Arms Race*, Pluto Press, 1983, p.172.

41 Sally Hacker, 'The culture of engineering: woman, workplace and machine', *Women's Studies International Quarterly*, Vol.4, No.3, 1981.

Chapter 7

1 Brigid O'Farrell and Sharon Harlan, 'Craftworkers and clerks: the effect of male co-worker hostility on women's satisfaction with non-traditional jobs', *Social Problems*, Vol.29, No.3, February 1982, p.257.

2 Mary Lindenstein Walshok, *Blue Collar Women: Pioneers on the Male Frontier*, Anchor Books, 1981, p.153.

3 *ibid.*, p.153.

4 *ibid.*, p.xviii–xix.

5 In a British study of undergraduate women engineers, Helen Weinreich-Haste and Peggy Newton found these young women to

be disproportionately well qualified, better educated, tending to come from more middle-class backgrounds than the equivalent male students, and to have fathers predominantly in engineering or education. ('Profile of the intending woman engineer', *Research Bulletin* No.7, Equal Opportunities Commission, Summer 1983.) Ina Wagner reports of women blue collar apprentices in Austria, again that the girls are 'exceptional' and that for many of them fathers and brothers exerted a strong influence. The girls were frequently included in the male domain of doing repair work in the family home. ('New work experiences for women: the case of women apprentices in Austria's metal and construction industries', draft report, University of Vienna, 1983.)

6 Mary L. Walshok, *op.cit.*, p.42.

7 *ibid.*, p.284.

8 *ibid.*, p.237.

9 Mary L. Walshok, *op.cit.*, found that 'all the women faced some form of negative reaction or initial harassment when they moved into a man's job in a blue collar environment', p.236. Brigid O'Farrell and Sharon Harlan, *op.cit.*, found that a sizeable minority of women craftworkers experienced harassment. Many of the women who speak of their experience in Terry Wetherby's *Conversations: Working Women Talk about Doing a 'Man's Job'*, Les Femmes, USA, 1977, tell the same story. A young woman heavy truck driver tells how men test a woman by giving her the hardest tasks and misleading information. Men may choose to help, but it is they who have the power to decide whether the woman is to survive in the job.

10 Suzanne C. Carothers and Peggy Krull, 'Contrasting sexual harassment in female- and male-dominated occupations', in Karen Brodkin Sacks and Dorothy Remy (eds), *My Troubles are Going to have Trouble with Me: Everyday Trials and Triumphs of Women Workers*, Rutgers University Press, USA, 1984, p.224.

11 The Engineering Industry Training Board has for some years run a 'girl technicians scheme', paying a premium grant (currently £6,000) to any employer willing to take on a supernumary girl among its engineering technicians. These girls have been the subject of research, reported in Glynis M. Breakwell and Barbara Weinberger, *The Right Woman for the Job: Recruiting Women Engineering Technician Trainees*, Manpower Services Commission, 1983; and Peggy Newton and Janette Brocklesby, *Getting On in Engineering: Becoming a Woman Technician*, report to the Engineering Industry Training Board, The Equal Opportunities Commission

and the Social Science Research Council, Huddersfield Polytechnic, 1983. The researchers emphasize the strategic choices the girls have to make to survive in this male environment. Often the situation they describe appears a 'no-win' one for the young women.

12 Mary L. Walshok, *op.cit.*, , p.232.

13 Muriel Lembright and Jeffery Riemer, 'Women truckers' problems and the impact of sponsorship', *Work and Occupations*, Vol.9, No.4, November 1982.

14 Karen Beck Skold, 'The job he left behind: American women in the shipyards during World War II', in Carol R. Berkin and Clara M. Lovett (eds), *Women, War and Revolution*, Holmes & Meier Publishers, USA, 1980, p.60.

15 Peggy Newton and Janette Brocklesby, *op.cit.*

16 Glynis M. Breakwell and Barbara Weinberger, *op.cit.*

17 Mary L. Walshok, *op.cit.*, p.111.

18 Elin Kvande considers the chance of women engineers changing the dominant values and behaviour in the engineering profession slight. A woman showing evidence of women's values is quickly excluded. The values she finds herself up against, Kvande points out, are represented to her as 'professional' not 'male' values. ('Deviants or conformists? On female engineering students and work related values and attitudes', paper to the Second International GASAT Conference, Norway, September 1983.)

19 Rosie Walden and Valerie Walkerdine, *Girls and Mathematics: The Early Years*, Bedford Way Papers 8, Institute of Education, University of London, 1981, p.64.

20 George Eliot, *Middlemarch*, Penguin, 1965, p.424. First published 1871.

21 Lyn Bryant in her study of student engineers found that seven out of 20 women said they did not intend to have children, while the remainder saw the question of how to cope with both children and an engineering career as an unresolved problem. ('Women in engineering: images and identifications', paper to the British Sociological Association Conference, April 1984, Plymouth Polytechnic.

22 Ina Wagner, *op.cit.*

23 It seems that in general men are not rapidly increasing their association with housework and child care. In a recent survey of women, 73 per cent of married women, working and non-working, said that they did all or most of the housework. Even among women working full-time, 13 per cent said they did all and 41 per cent most of it. The authors suggest that this is an understatement

of the proportion of housework most women are undertaking. Jean Martin and Ceridwen Roberts, *Women and Employment: A Lifetime Perspective*, Department of Employment and Office of Population Censuses and Surveys, 1983, p.114.

24 R.W. Connell, 'Men's bodies', in *Which Way is Up?*, George Allen & Unwin, Australia, 1983. p.19.

25 Boel Berner in her study of the engineering community in Sweden in the periods pre- and post-World War II writes: 'male engineers still keep a very strict division between work and home ... women engineers, for many reasons, are not able to keep this demarcation line between work and public life.' ('Women, power and ideology in technical education and work', paper to the international Conference on the Role of Women in the History of Science, Technology and Medicine in the 19th and 20th centuries, Hungary, August 1983.)

26 Ina Wagner, *op.cit.*

Chapter 8

1 James Wickham, 'Women workers in Irish electronic factories', paper to the Irish Congress of Trade Unions Annual Women's Committee Joint Seminar, Dundalk, November 1984. Trinity College, Dublin.

2 Figures supplied by the Engineering Industry Training Board.

3 Jan Zimmerman, 'Technology and the future of women: haven't we met somewhere before?', *Women's Studies International Quarterly*, Vol.4, No.3, 1981, p.355.

4 James Wickham, *op.cit.*

5 See, for instance, E. Braun and P. Senker, *New Technology and Employment*, Manpower Services Commission, 1982.

6 Figures supplied by the Engineering Industry Training Board.

7 Tim Brady and Sonia Liff, *Monitoring New Technology and Employment*, Manpower Services Commission, 1983.

8 Pauline Wilkins, 'Women and engineering in the Plymouth area: job segregation and training at company level', *Research Bulletin*, No.7, Equal Opportunities Commission, Summer 1983.

9 Karl Marx, *Capital*, Vol.1, Lawrence & Wishart, 1954, p.343. First published 1887.

10 Terry Wetherby, *Conversations: Working Women Talk About Doing a 'Man's Job'*, Les Femmes, USA, 1977, p.156.

11 Ruth Milkman, 'Redefining "women's work": the sexual division of labour in the auto industry during World War II', *Feminist*

Studies, 8, No.2, Summer 1982, p.338. Karen Beck Skold also found that in shipbuilding during the war years women gained access to high wages, equal pay and jobs from which they had formerly been excluded. But the employers achieved war production, working with an inexperienced labour force, by introducing new techniques and fragmenting tasks. As a result, 'although women's entry into shipbuilding challenged the sexual division of labour, the basic distribution between men's work and women's work was not altered . . . women were over-represented as unskilled workers and in some of these jobs nearly all of the workers were women.' ('The job he left behind: American women in the shipyards during world war II', in Carol R. Berkin and Clara M. Lovett (eds), *Women, War and Revolution*, Holmes & Meier Publishers Inc., USA, 1980.)

12 Joan Greenbaum, 'Division of labor in the computer field', *Monthly Review*, Vol.28, No.3, July-August 1976; Philip Kraft, 'Industrialisation of computer programming: from programming to "software production" ', in Andrew Zimbalist (ed), *Case Studies on the Labor Process*, Monthly Review Press, 1979; Margaret Lowe Benston, 'For women the chips are down', in Jan Zimmerman (ed), *The Technological Woman*, Praeger, USA, 1983; Philip Kraft and Steve Dubnoff, 'Software for women means a lower status', *Computing*, February 1984.

13 Jill Rubery, 'Structured labour markets, worker organisation and low pay', in A.H. Amsden (ed), *The Economics of Women and Work*, Penguin, 1980; and see also Cynthia Cockburn, *Brothers: Male Dominance and Technological Change*, Pluto Press, 1983.

14 Margaret Attwood and Frances Hatton, 'Getting on: gender differences in career development, a case study in the hairdressing industry', in Eva Gamarnikow *et al* (eds), *Gender, Class and Work*, Heinemann, 1983.

15 For instance, A. Kadushin, 'Men in a woman's profession', *Social Work*, No.21, 1976, recommends males to move toward administrative posts in nursing to counteract their discomfort in being male in a female profession. This is discussed by Carol Tropp Schreiber, *Changing Places: Men and Women in Transitional Occupations*, MIT Press, USA, 1979, who also cites B. Segal, 'Male nurses: a case study in status contradiction and prestige loss', *Social Forces*, 41, 1962. Segal concluded that 'men would not be considered successful in women's occupations until they had moved into positions of authority over females in these fields', p.23 of Schreiber. *op.cit.*

16 Sally Hacker, 'Mathematization of engineering: limits on women and on the field', in Joan Rothschild (ed), *Machina Ex Dea: Feminist Perspectives on Technology*, Pergamon Press, USA, 1983, p.39. Hacker points out that the 55 per cent pay differential between engineer and engineering technician or aide approximates the distance between men's and women's average earnings generally. p.49.

17 Paul Willis, *Learning to Labour*, Saxon House, 1978.

18 Alice Kessler-Harris, *Out to Work: A History of Wage-earning Women in the United States*, Oxford University Press, 1982, p.312.

19 Engineering Industry Training Board, *Women in Engineering*, Occasional Paper No.11, 1984, p.31.

20 Janet Holland, *Work and Women*, Bedford Way Papers No.6, Institute of Education, London University, 1981, p.35.

21 1984 figures.

22 Audrey Hunt, *A Survey of Women's Employment*, Vol.1, Report, Government Social Survey, HMSO, 1968, p.158.

23 Trades Union Congress, *Women Workers 1972*, Report of the 42nd Annual Conference of Representatives of Trade Unions Catering for Women Workers, 1972, p.37.

24 Committee of Enquiry into the Engineering Profession (The Finniston Report), *Engineering Our Future*, Cmnd.7794, HMSO, 1980, p.71.

25 See, for instance, A. Kelly, J. Whyte and B. Smail, *Girls into Science and Technology*, Final Report on an Action Research Project, University of Manchester, 1984.

26 Gloria Morris Nemerowicz, *Children's Perceptions of Gender and Work Roles*, Praeger, 1979; Irene Rauta and Audrey Hunt, *Fifth Form Girls: Their Hopes for the Future*, Office of Population Censuses and Surveys, HMSO, 1975; Janet Holland and Gella Varnava-Skouras, 'Investigation of adolescents' conceptions of features of the social division of labour', Institute of Education, Sociology Research Unit, London University, 1979; and Lynne Chisholm, Institute of Education, London University, current work.

27 *The New Training Initiative*, Cmnd.8455, HMSO, 1981.

28 National Association of Teachers in Further and Higher Education, *The Great Training Robbery*, 1983; Cliff Allum and Joe Quigley, 'Bricks in the wall: the Youth Training Scheme', *Capital & Class*, No.21, 1983; and Equal Opportunities Commission, 'Positive discrimination in the Youth Training Scheme', 1983.

29 This observation is based on my current research, *YTS: Making or*

Breaking Sex Segregation, funded by the Equal Opportunities Commission and the Economic and Social Research Council 1985–6.

30 There is evidence that white collar workers both welcome and succeed in training for technical work in Mary L. Walshok, *Blue Collar Women: Pioneers on the Male Frontier*, Anchor Books, USA, 1981, p.278; and Brigid O'Farrell and Sharon Harlan, 'Craftworkers and clerks: the effect of male co-worker hostility on women's satisfaction with non-traditional jobs', *Social Problems*, Vol.29, No.3, February 1982. A report emanating from the British Cabinet Office, which can hardly be suspected of extremism, urges employers to 'recognize the key role of employers in training for changing skills: people are educated for about twelve years, employed for about forty. We want employers to see themselves in the vanguard of a national effort to realize the potentially massive contribution of ten and a half million women workers to the economy'. In particular, employers should 'recognize that many women workers, including part-time workers who do not at present have opportunities for formal training/promotion, would like these and would reward investment by performing well in new skills. Consider developing women as supervisors and managers and also consider *horizontal moves into technical work*'. (my italics) (Women's National Commission, *The Other Half of Our Future*, The Cabinet Office, London SW1, 1984, p.20–21.)

31 I am indebted to Lyn Bryant, Department of Social and Political Studies, Plymouth Polytechnic, for this observation. It is drawn from an article in the *New Civil Engineer*, 12 January, 1984.

32 Joseph Corn, 'Making flying "thinkable": women pilots and the selling of aviation 1927–1940', *American Quarterly*, 31, Fall, 1979, p.556, cited in Judith A. McGaw, 'Women and the history of American technology', *Signs*, Summer 1982, p.805.

33 The lonely and painful struggle one individual can have with the so-called 'merely' social phenomenon of gender is apparent in the autobiography of Jan Morris, *Conundrum*, Faber & Faber, 1974.

34 Genevieve Lloyd, *The Man of Reason: 'Male' and 'Female' in Western Philosophy*, Methuen, 1984, p.107.

35 Dot Griffiths, 'The exclusion of women from technology', in Wendy Faulkner and Erik Arnold (eds), *Smothered by Invention: Technology in Women's Lives*, Pluto Press, 1985, p.60.

36 Boel Berner, 'Women, power and ideology in technical education and work', paper to the International Conference on the Role of Women in the History of Science, Technology and Medicine in the

19th and 20th Centuries, Hungary, August 1983, p.11.

37 David Noble, *America By Design: Science, Technology and the Rise of Corporate Capitalism*, Oxford University Press, 1979, p.63. First published 1977. Consider also the frustrated efforts of the shop stewards combine at Lucas Aerospace to redirect technology to the production of socially useful equipment (Hilary Wainwright and Dave Elliott, *The Lucas Plan: A New Trade Unionism in the Making?*, Allison & Busby, 1982.)

38 Mary Shelley, *Frankenstein: or the Modern Prometheus*, Signet Classics, The New English Library, 1965. First published 1831.

39 See, for instance, Langdon Winner, *Autonomous Technology: Technics-out-of-Control as a Theme in Political Thought*, MIT Press, USA, 1977.

40 Simone de Beauvoir, *The Second Sex*, Penguin, 1972, p.88. First published 1949.

41 *ibid.*, p.467.

42 For an analysis of the masculinity of this project see Brian Easlea, *Fathering the Unthinkable: Masculinity, Scientists and the Nuclear Arms Race*, Pluto Press, 1983.

Index